William F. Ogburn
ON CULTURE AND SOCIAL CHANGE

THE HERITAGE OF SOCIOLOGY

A Series Edited by Morris Janowitz

William F. Ogburn

ON CULTURE

AND SOCIAL CHANGE

Selected Papers

Edited and with an Introduction by

OTIS DUDLEY DUNCAN

THE UNIVERSITY OF CHICAGO PRESS

CHICAGO AND LONDON

Library of Congress Catalog Card Number: 64-23418

THE UNIVERSITY OF CHICAGO PRESS, CHICAGO & LONDON
The University of Toronto Press, Toronto 5, Canada

Published 1964. Composed and printed by
THE UNIVERSITY OF CHICAGO PRESS
Chicago, Illinois, U.S.A.

Designed by Andor Braun

Contents

301.2
Og1 a
cop. 2

Introduction

THE IDEA that his writings would have a secure place in the history of sociology must have occurred to William Fielding Ogburn, for he was not given to false modesty. Yet he would not have wanted us to study his work if the only motivation were a sense of its historical importance. He thought that recapitulation of the history of sociological doctrines bulked entirely too large in sociological training and contributed to an overemphasis on "intellectualism," the hypertrophy of which constituted a positive obstacle to the development of a science of sociology. The curriculum in chemistry, he liked to point out, does not include a sequence of courses in the theories of the great alchemists.

In offering the contemporary student a selection from Ogburn's writings, then, one is under some obligation to respect the criterion that he would have avowed: the work must stand on its merits as a contribution to living science. Such contributions might consist of general explanations of phenomena that are consistent with the data at hand and not superseded by more cogent explanations; of bodies of verified data that support or call into question a hypothesis; or even of unsystematic observations that open up a topic for study and await further verification. Ogburn saw science primarily as an accumulation of knowledge, but an accumulation whose structure is subject to continual change as new relationships among its parts are perceived or as discoveries shed new light on supposed relationships.

The writings exhibited here represent all the foregoing sorts

of contributions. It is thought, moreover, that they reveal a structure, the development of which was the central task of the author's
life work: the achievement of an understanding of the problem of
social change. It would be quite incorrect to suppose, however,
that this task accounted for the entirety of Ogburn's efforts as a
scientist, for his interest and competence encompassed a wide
range of topics, not all of them connected in any obvious way with
the main concern, social change. Some notice, however abbreviated, must be taken of his work as a whole, for two reasons. First,
an appreciation of the variety of problems on which he worked
will help to explain his sensitivity to the point that changes in
one part of culture or society have ramifying effects upon many
other parts. Second, an assurance that Ogburn had at his command a wealth of information based on firsthand investigation
may be worth something to a reader who misses the familiar
apparatus of citation and documentation in some of Ogburn's
papers. When in the course of an argument he appeals to a fact or
proposition without giving data, the presumption is that the matter is one that he "once looked into" (one of his favorite locu-
tions), for he had, indeed, "looked into" many things, many more
than even his lengthy list of publications, reproduced at the end
of this volume, can reveal.

During his varied career, Ogburn taught courses in several of
the social sciences—economics, history, political science, statistics, and sociology—and made effective use, as well, of his broad
knowledge of anthropology and psychoanalysis. Of the major social institutions, only religion, though he was fascinated by the
phenomenon (as is shown by an unpublished essay of 1935, "Nationalism as a Religion"), failed to claim his sustained attention
in a series of empirical investigations. His articles include numerous studies of topics in economics, government and politics, and
the family. He returned again and again to the problem of variation in the characteristics of cities and to the analysis of population change as cause and effect of social trends. An admiring student, A. J. Jaffe, has called him "the last of the great social scientists who wished to know it all." The published record, extensive
as it is, fails to document the curiosity that led him through near-

ly completed projects on such subjects as the effects of birth order on personality, or the income of baseball players. In many such ventures he was content to satisfy only himself, and he had concluded to his own satisfaction, for example, that the player with the highest batting average is rewarded out of proportion to his contribution to the success of the team.

Ogburn's earliest publications, including his doctoral dissertation (1912), were in the field of social legislation and the politics of democracy. There can be little question that interest in these topics issued from political sympathies, for the small amount of available autobiographical information clearly indicates that Ogburn began his career as a social scientist with a strong interest in social action and reform. In his early days on the West Coast, just before the involvement of the United States in World War I, he worked extensively with labor and civic groups in the cause of good government and toward the goal of reform in the distribution of power and wealth. "I was much interested in socialism," he explained to an audience honoring him upon the occasion of his retirement from the University of Chicago in 1951, "and spent a good deal of time in radical circles. One of my prized possessions is a three-volume edition of Karl Marx's works, inscribed to me by the Portland unit of the Industrial Workers of the World, who as you recall differed from the socialists in that they wanted the workers to own industry directly and not through government." Despite his admission that at this time "my teaching was a mild indoctrination of a liberal or radical social philosophy," the publications of this period attest to an attempt to bring objective scientific techniques to bear on problems of social import. Franklin H. Giddings, Ogburn's "old master" at the Columbia Graduate School, had given him an understanding of science, and his professor of statistics, Henry L. Moore, a founder of the discipline of econometrics, had likewise inspired him to dedicate his efforts to science.

Thus an article like "Initiative and Referendum Tested in Hard Times" (1915) is a solicitous review of current experience, which suggested that there are unexpected difficulties in achieving reform through direct legislation. The paper, though brief

and simplified for popular consumption, evidently embodies the
conclusions of some extensive statistical analysis directed to the
hypothesis that acceptance of measures in referendums is re-
tarded by depression conditions. Other studies investigated the
effect on voting of the introduction of women's suffrage and the
economic differentiation of the electorate. The later was a topic,
like a number of others, that was "looked into" early in Ogburn's
career and was followed by several subsequent studies a number
of years later.

The war years brought a period of service in the cost-of-living
section of the National War Labor Board and in the Bureau of
Labor Statistics. Only a small part of the work of this period was
published, but enough to establish Ogburn as a pioneer in methods of analyzing family budgets and constructing price indexes.
There was still, in all likelihood, an element of sympathy for social reform in the drive behind this work, for Ogburn continued,
for example, to contribute to a socialist publication, *American
Labor Year Book,* through this period. The research, however,
was rigidly scientific by his standards and is, indeed, not to be
recommended as inspirational reading.

Ogburn, by his own testimony, was becoming more skeptical
of the possibility of moving the world by the force of idealism
alone. He found, moreover, that it was impossible to exercise
leadership in social movements while engaging in a full day's
work as a scientist. The decision to forego the role of reformer did
not, of course, remove Ogburn from the scene of public service, as
is evident from the impressive list of assignments as consultant to
such government agencies as the National Recovery Administration, the National Resources Committee, and the Bureau of the
Census.

The resolution of the conflict between the man of action and
the man of science was accompanied, as internal conflict sometimes is, by reflection and intellectual reorientation. The conviction grew that the ideological component of reform movements
was largely rationalization of wishes, a phenomenon akin to the
fantasy or daydream. Seeking an understanding of this phenomenon, Ogburn read widely in psychoanalysis and himself under-

went analysis. He came to appreciate the pervasiveness of bias in the absence of facts and developed the idea that social scientists should seek a knowledge of their own prejudices and rationalizations to the end of reducing the output of theories shaped primarily by emotion and desire. Yet, such self-knowledge would not, of itself, lead to a social science, "for we cannot have a science without measurement. And science will grow in the social studies in direct ratio to the use of measurement" ("Bias, Psychoanalysis, and the Subjective in Relation to the Social Sciences," 1922).

The psychoanalytic concept of rationalization was employed in another way, as Ogburn reflected on the moving forces of history. The "economic interpretation of history" had to reckon with the fact that men give all sorts of reasons for their actions, many of them suggesting socially altruistic rather than selfishly economic motives. But psychoanalysis had discovered that motives often are disguised to avoid social disapproval. Wars nominally fought over religious issues may actually have been motivated by economic factors of which the participants were unconscious. The introduction of profit-sharing and employee-welfare schemes, to the actual advantage of the employer, is rationalized as an altruistic concern for the workers. The emphasis on the slavery issue in the Civil War is an acceptable disguise of the conflict between two economic systems ("The Psychological Basis for the Economic Interpretation of History," 1919).

As soon as this position was reached, however, it began to be modified, as Ogburn gave increasing attention to another body of ideas and data, those of the cultural anthropologists. On the one hand, he began to see the economic problem of a low standard of living not as basic, but as symptomatic. Marx had stopped too soon, for he failed to go behind the economic factor to search out the mechanisms accounting for the growth of culture and thereby for the transformation of economic systems. On the other hand, while the penetration of disguises made possible a more realistic analysis of motives, often giving a greater weight to economic ones than was at first apparent, any investigation of motives is likely to be superficial without the recognition of cultural factors, which can be discerned only through historical investigation. "As

I thought more about it," said Ogburn in his 1957 restatement of the cultural-lag hypothesis, "the disguise factor in social causation seemed less important than the time factor."

Within a decade or less of the completion of his formal education, therefore, Ogburn had completed a considerable amount of research exemplifying his initial conviction that science can grow only with the accumulation of descriptions and measurements. He had, as well, thought through—doubtlessly with no little mental travail—several basic issues regarding his orientation to the world of social phenomena and had significantly shifted his position on several of them. From a concern with action and reform he had moved toward an emphasis on fundamental science. Beginning with a conviction that the social problem of first rank was the one for which eugenics was proposed as an answer (we depend on autobiographic testimony for this point, since it is nowhere evidenced in publications), he had come to see that the biological nature of man cannot change fast enough to make eugenics a realistic program of social action. From an appreciation of the economic factor he had moved toward an emphasis on invention as the more basic determinant of welfare and the level of civilization. While not giving up an interest in discerning more truly the motives of human action, he came to emphasize more and more strongly the cultural and historical changes that give rise to alterations of motives and their acceptable disguises. The continuity behind these reformulations is clear: a faith in scientific method and a drive to identify the "basic" or "underlying" forces that generate social problems and social progress. The emphasis on Ogburn's intellectual flexibility is salutary in indicating that his subsequent position on the importance of invention and the ubiquity of cultural lag was not a preconceived doctrine but a hypothesis won through hard work.

The emphasis on continuity is likewise well taken, for Ogburn never really relinquished his interest in social problems. A favorite course for many years was "Modern Social Problems." Ogburn enjoyed teaching this course, in which he outlined his views on what he called "the big questions." He regarded the course as his major contribution to the liberal education of students, as contrasted with their training in science. An outline dating from the late 1940's includes the following headings:

1. What to do about big business?
2. What should the functions of government be?
3. How to raise our standard of living?
4. How can nations get along with each other?
5. The education of children and the character of a people.
6. The elusiveness of happiness.
7. Our shifting beliefs and ideals.
8. Morals in a changing world.
9. Machines: Masters or slaves?
10. The cave man in the modern city.

Ogburn realized that the immediate motivation of many students initiating the study of sociology is their concern with social problems. As he and Nimkoff wrote in the Introduction to the first edition of their *Sociology* (1940):

> Sociology may be a great aid to an understanding of social problems because of its interest in the broad basic aspects of social life. The way sociology sheds light on the whole matter of social maladjustment is suggested, for example, by the observation that nearly all our social problems result from either (*a*) difficulties of adjustment between the superorganic and inherited nature as, for instance, in many problems of sex and of crime, or (*b*) maladjustment between the different parts of culture, due to the fact that one part changes faster than another, as, for instance, in unemployment and business depressions [p. 14].

Many of the questions that had concerned Ogburn in the period up to 1920, as well as the direction in which he had come to believe their answers must be sought, found definitive expression in the small volume published in 1922 that was to become a widely read sociological classic, reprinted some eleven times, *Social Change with Respect to Culture and Original Nature*. Here he argued that to explain social change we must focus attention on culture and its development or evolution. The biological nature of man, though a significant condition for the emergence of human society, is not appreciably variable over the relatively brief period in which vast transformations of society have occurred. It is, moreover, fruitless to seek an explanation of social change in terms of the presumable psychological mechanisms manifest in social interaction, for either these are themselves biologically inherited, and hence relatively constant, or else culturally induced, in which case their change must be traced back to cultural change:

> If social evolution means changes in the mechanisms of association then such changes may be quite truly cultural, for there are cultural mechanisms of association just as there are biological mechanisms of association. Social evolution, in such case, consists largely in the evolution of social organizations and social ways of behavior, as seen in religion, art, law, custom, etc. Social evolution thus includes a large part of the evolution of culture, virtually all but material culture. And if the objects of material culture are the products of social influence and behavior then the evolution of the whole of culture is a part of social evolution [*Social Change*, pp. 59–60].

Ogburn wisely never undertook a revision of *Social Change*, perhaps sensing that any slight gains in conceptual precision or factual timeliness would be outweighed by disturbances of its stylistic unity and coherence. In the 1950 reissue of the volume, he contented himself with appending a supplementary restatement of the thesis of cultural accumulation (reproduced as the second paper in the present collection). Yet the great bulk of his subsequent writing may readily be interpreted as an expansion of the themes of that book. What we hope is a judicious selection from these writings is then virtually tantamount to a second systematic treatment of the subject.

There is no question that Ogburn considered his explication of the problem of social evolution to be his major contribution to sociological theory. In response to Howard W. Odum's request for a self-evaluation, he wrote:

> I shall be bold. I claim that the problem of social evolution is solved and that I have played a considerable part in solving it. By solving I mean solving in the sense that Darwin solved the problem of biological evolution. Darwin did it by pointing out three factors, variation, natural selection, and heredity. Darwin added the factor

of natural selection. The problem of social evolution is solved by four factors, invention, exponential accumulation, diffusion, and adjustment. My contribution has been largely in the factor of exponential accumulation and also in the development of the factor of invention. I also think that my role has been significant in the adjustment of one part of culture to another (cultural lag).

Ogburn was parsimonious in his use of a term that has become the watchword, if not the shibboleth, of today's social scientist, to wit, "theory." Oftentimes, too, his application of the term was faintly pejorative, as when he sensed that a "theory" consisted of an exposition of ideas for their own sake or for their moral or aesthetic appeal. Yet the claim to have "solved" the problem of social evolution evidently implies that his account provides a general *explanation* of the process, one which identifies "the essentials of the problem" and which, above all, stimulates and guides "further researches on social change." Note his insistence (in the final paper of this volume) that "Organization of knowledge [read 'theory'] aids method. Its great value consists in the relationship of one part to another, which thereby facilitates its use particularly in constructing hypotheses." It was no part of Ogburn's program to engage in or encourage what, in current jargon, is called something like "the elaboration of the most abstract implications of a conceptual scheme." For Ogburn the important thing was not the conceptual scheme, but the discoveries to which its application might lead.

While no systematic exegesis of Ogburn's theory is here required—unlike that of some "theorists," his writing is clearer than any secondary exposition could make it—a few comments on one topic may be in order. This is the famous and controversial concept of cultural lag. Interestingly enough, as the vehemence of critics has increased, the concept, or at least the terminology, has won widespread use, and "cultural lag" may now be found in the dictionary, written with initial lower-case letters and without Ogburn's name attached.

It is erroneous to characterize Ogburn's theory of social change as "the cultural-lag theory." He did not regard cultural lag as "a fundamental part of the theory of social evolution." This is because, while rapid change induces many lags in a closely integrated society, "in the long perspective of history . . . lags are not visible because they have been caught up." The high incidence of cultural lags may explain the current intensity of social problems but does not particularly bear on the great question of "how our society evolved" or "how our civilization came to be."

Equally misleading are some of the objections that have been offered to the idea of cultural lag itself. As Ogburn makes quite clear, it is not supposed that all lags are initiated by mechanical inventions to which social forms must, sooner or later, adapt. This proposition is suggested as an empirical generalization for a specific historical period and is not assumed to be without exception, even for that period. In other settings, the sequence of change may run in the other direction. It is not, therefore, a counter-example to the cultural-lag hypothesis to suggest that Greek drama represented a higher order of achievement than did Greek plumbing, on the assumption that the hypothesis implies the contrary. The lag relationship comes into play when it can be *demonstrated* that, of two hitherto closely related and mutually compatible parts of culture, one changes in such a way as to disrupt the relationship and impair the compatibility. Each of the steps in the analysis of an episode of cultural lag—and they were explicit enough in the original presentation, if even more so in the 1957 restatement—requires careful assessment of evidence and is not something to be judged either way in an offhand manner.

Whatever the importance attributed to cultural lag as an incidental product of social evolution, the study of the details of social evolution was certainly not limited to the diagnosis of lags. The lag concept, indeed, recedes into the background of a great deal of the empirical study of social change that Ogburn undertook and stimulated, a collection of work for which the label "social trends" is more descriptive. Ogburn's first research, the study of changes in child-labor laws, betrayed an interest in discerning the long-run tendency of change that the statisticians term the "secular trend." The term "social trend" does not appear with great frequency in Ogburn's early writings, however, although use was made of "trend lines" in investigating "The Influence of the Business Cycle on Certain Social Conditions" (1922).

The characteristic attitude toward "social trends" is perhaps given its earliest clear expression in the short essay that opens Part II of the present collection and was originally the Introduction to the first of the annual series of volumes on *Recent Social Changes*, edited by Ogburn (1928–35; 1942). Here Ogburn states his conviction that in a rapidly changing society the social sciences must "render aid" by uncovering the tendencies of change and estimating their probable persistence into the future. To bring the full power of science to bear on the problem of change, the problem must be broken down into parts each susceptible individually of analysis and interpretation. Hence the outline of each of the collaborative change volumes, carried over into the monumental *Recent Social Trends* (1933), was a list of topics like population, foreign policy, labor, inventions, the family, and so on. Empiricism came to the fore. What was wanted were reliable measures of the changes that had taken place, actual quantitative descriptions in the form of statistical time series, where possible, or, in lieu of statistics, objective descriptions validated by the agreement of numerous careful observers. Interpretation came at the end of this exacting work, as in the "Statement of Committee Findings" that appears in *Recent Social Trends*.

The explication of the trend concept itself comes quite late in Ogburn's writings, although adumbrations are now easy to pick out in statements like the Introduction to the 1929 volume. Curiously, Ogburn gave little attention to the formal relationship between the general theory of social evolution and the conception of social trends that evidently lay behind the vast amount of empirical research. A statement in an unpublished manuscript, dating apparently from the early 1940's, is perhaps most explicit:

Social evolution is a fact. The evolution of society has been going on since man evolved. Its speed at the present time is quite impressive. The pertinence of this evolution of society for present-day problems ought not to be ignored. In other words we would do well to see contemporary issues as they are related to the great process of social evolution. Unfortunately its study has often centered around primitive peoples and history long past, so that its relevance to what is going on at the present time is not often appreciated and the connection not made.

First, we need a paragraph on what social evolution is. We consider social evolution as not including, at least in the past several thousand years, any biological evolution. What is evolving then is society or the various social groupings such as government, and industry, and the state. Expressed in other language, what is evolving is "culture," that is to say, the environment which men have, but which the wild animals do not have. This culture, or our social heritage, is a composite of many different parts, such as cities, families, farms, philosophies, art, science, etc. Social evolution or, in other terms, cultural evolution may be broken down into the evolution of its parts.

The evolution of the parts is designated as "social trends." Social trends are social movements over a considerable period of time in the same direction or one only slightly changing. This relative absence of violence of change in social trends gives a certain assurance of social stability.

Not to be excluded from the spectrum of human activities in which trends occur were the very sciences to which Ogburn assigned the responsibility for monitoring trends. Throughout his career Ogburn maintained a lively interest in following the progress and noting the changing folkways of the social sciences. He was, moreover, not unwilling to venture an extrapolation of the tendencies observed, and his 1929 presidential address to the American Sociological Society, "The Folkways of a Scientific Sociology," is largely a forecast of the future appearance of a discipline increasingly conforming to the norms of science rather than those of philosophy or the humanities. This phase of Ogburn's interests entitles him to no little recognition as a student of the "sociology of knowledge," especially when it is set alongside his great emphasis on growth in "The Volume of Knowledge" (the title of a paper published in 1932) as a major social process. The last two articles in Part II are representative of

Ogburn's attention to trends in social science, a preoccupation that was revived toward the end of his career, when he found himself in Asia attempting to explain the ways of American sociology to Indian scholars.

If, in a "changing society" whose parts are closely interrelated, hardly any aspect of life remains constant, the study of social trends can accept few limitations on its substantive scope. By the same token, an approach to social life that takes change as its major premise will find applications at every hand. It is, therefore, difficult to separate sharply the work on social trends from the studies Ogburn undertook on such subjects as the family, population, and urban life. Most of the numerous articles and monographs on the family and marriage, for example, develop the theme of change with greater or lesser specificity. Although the present collection gives meager representation to some of the subjects claiming a significant share of Ogburn's attention after 1920, it is not unrepresentative in regard to the preoccupation with change that is exhibited in most of them.

For the most part, the tendency was to stress those sorts of changes that could be explained as aspects or consequences of long-term alterations of society. Ogburn was impressed more by continuity than by novelty. Even his theory of invention stressed the old as a precondition for the new and postulated the dependence of innovations on past developments rather than their break with the past. Consistent with this emphasis was the caution exercised in identifying new trends or modifications of the direction of trends. Thus in the midst of the excitement of F. D. Roosevelt's first year in office, Ogburn wrote: "The dramatic events of the year 1933 usually characterized as the New Deal are not to be viewed as something apart. They have their setting in the culture of the time. Their roots run back into the preceding years. . . . The New Deal may be a revolution in organized effort and basic ideology, but the indicators so far show no revolution in the trends they measure" ("The Background of the New Deal," 1934). A look at time series including prewar, wartime, and postwar years convinced Ogburn that even a major war may not alter the direction of trends in any fundamental way and may, indeed,

produce no more drastic short-run fluctuations than are commonly observed to accompany economic prosperity (see the twenty-
second paper in this volume).

If, on the whole, Ogburn was not greatly interested in short-
run fluctuating changes, he acknowledged their reality and their
nuisance value, so to speak, as false harbingers of new trends. He
was, moreover, greatly impressed by one class of fluctuations,
those known to economists as the business cycle. A thorough empirical study of social correlates of economic fluctuations was
published in 1922 with Dorothy S. Thomas, who later expanded
the inquiry into a well-known monograph. The difficulties of
measurement may partially explain a reluctance to investigate
cyclical changes whose time period appreciably exceeds that of
the business cycle. Yet Ogburn was hardly oblivious of them, and
in the final paper in this volume he offers a hypothesis that would
merit careful examination: "When fact-gathering has been prodigious and many researchers turn out a large body of not very
important researches, as is often the case in later stages of the
maturing of a science, a great need is felt for big ideas. Perhaps
the shift in emphasis from ideas to data and vice versa is cyclical. . . ."

It may be misleading to separate out from the whole body of
Ogburn's work and thought a section to be designated as "methodology." It is true that his tireless advocacy of measurement
gained him a reputation as a methodological zealot, and it is
true that he served for six years as editor of the *Journal of the
American Statistical Association* and was elected president of that
organization. Yet it is not possible to find in the corpus of Ogburn's writing a study carried out as a strictly methodological
exercise. Many of the researches employing techniques relatively
advanced for their time are reported with very little emphasis on
method. In the discussions addressed to methods specifically, the
reader will find no attempt to establish a methodological ortho-
doxy or to engage in methodological controversy with others.
Ogburn prized knowledge, and knowledge to him was verified
information. Verification required examination of large bodies of
data, which could be accomplished most readily by powerful

techniques of data reduction. From this there followed the emphasis on measurement and statistics. Yet it was recognized that not all topics lend themselves to quantification and, therefore, that exclusive reliance on statistical material can give only a one-sided account of a social institution. Statistics, moreover, do not automatically reveal their own meaning, but require interpretation.

A special type of interpretation is often demanded, namely, a statement of the significance of the implications of the statistics. But a reliable statement of the implications . . . cannot be made without evidence, and hence often without further research. Some implications are more or less obvious; others may be suggested as possible or probable. But interpretations, if reliable, require evidence and research as did the original statement. As a form of language, statistics has its limitations ["Limitations of Statistics," 1934].

With reference to the subject of social change, in particular, Ogburn was loath to become bogged down in details of method or methodological controversy. Such methodological injunctions as one will find in a discussion of forecasts (the twenty-fourth paper of this volume) are addressed more to ways of framing the problem than to the specifics of manipulating data. Tolerant in all things, he was tolerant of those who enjoy the exploration of a subject via an analysis of the methods appropriate to its study; but in a personal letter of July 14, 1958, he wrote, "My interest in social change, looking at the matter personally and remembering the adage *de gustibus non disputandum est,* has been largely on significance and meaning rather than on methodology. I have a tendency to try to see what I call 'big ideas' or develop a sense of the significant."

It is probably too soon to attempt a comprehensive assessment of Ogburn's impact on the development of sociology. In any event, it is problematical whether he, no partisan of the "greatman" theory of change, would have approved of expending any great effort on such an intellectual exercise. Identified by A. A. Brill as "the first sociologist to recognize the value of the Freudian concepts in the teaching of sociology" and by A. L. Kroeber and Clyde Kluckhohn as the author of "the first major work by an American sociologist in which the anthropological concept of culture was prominently employed," Ogburn would have been compelled by his own theory of the multiple origins of innovation to acknowledge the contribution of many others to these shifts in social thought. "As a user of partial correlation techniques" (a self-description), he would surely have pointed out the difficulty in holding constant all influences other than his own on the course of a scientific movement. Having observed that "success is more likely to come to those who work for and with a social trend than to those who work against it," he would doubtlessly note that his efforts gained impact insofar as they were in harmony with the forces producing the rise of a true science of society. His work is now part of our social heritage, or culture base, and is hence material to be further elaborated by the continuing process of scientific change.

Otis Dudley Duncan

I. Social Evolution

1

CULTURE *1937*

THE DEFINITION of culture most often quoted is that of
Tyler: "Culture is that complex whole which includes knowledge,
belief, art, morals, law, custom, and any other capabilities and
habits acquired by man as a member of society." A particular
culture has been defined by Redfield as "an organized body of
conventional understandings, manifest in act and artifact, which,
persisting through tradition, characterizes a human group." Excellent definitions both, yet culture is one of those large concepts,
like democracy or science, a definition of which seems very bare
and inadequate to convey its rich meanings. Different students
will emphasize different aspects of culture as most significant, and
in the future important new ideas about culture may be discovered. At the present time the aspects of culture of most interest
to sociologists may be grouped around four ideas.

I

The study of culture developed out of the soil of biological
sociology. The impact of the discoveries of Darwin (particularly
the evolution of man from the anthropoids) on social thought was
tremendous. Nothing like it had so shocked mankind since it was

A lecture given before the Division of Social Sciences, the University of
Chicago, June 3, 1937. Published, with Section I considerably abbreviated, as "Culture and Sociology," *Social Forces*, XVI (December, 1937),
161–69.

discovered that the earth was round and whirling through space, held there by balancing forces. The ramifications of the latter discovery, for instance, reached as far as the theory of the state and supported the doctrine of checks and balances, so evident in our own governmental structure. Likewise the ramifications of the idea of evolution extended quite generally, especially to societies. Out of it were developed the organismic theories of the state. A great impetus was given to biological interpretations of society by such men as Spencer and Huxley. The achievements of man were seen as the direct outgrowth of his inherited capacities. The wasps build one type of house, the ants another, because their biological structures are different. It followed, by inference, that the Aztecs have one type of culture and the Egyptians another because their biological natures are different. Function was seen as following structure very closely. The European was further along in the scale of biological evolution than the Australian blackfellow, since his culture was more advanced. Social evolution was dependent upon biological evolution. The monkeys had no civilization because they had not evolved far enough. Man, however, with his larger brain case, had gone further in biological progress and was capable of developing civilization.

It is interesting that the idea of culture, which later was so often opposed to biology, was developed by one of the most biologically minded men of the age, Herbert Spencer. He remarked that there was a time when there was no life on the earth. Everything was inorganic. In the course of time, inorganic matter evolved to a point when life appeared. Then the evolution of the organic matter began. When it reached the level of man, there appeared culture, or, as Spencer called it, the "superorganic," which in turn began its evolution.

Though Spencer helped to give birth to the idea of culture, he never really saw its nature clearly. For instance, to him the superorganic was dependent in a most intimate and direct way upon the organic. The concept of the superorganic was then only the beginning of the unfolding of the concept of culture. If the variations in the organic determined the nature of the superorganic in detail, as Spencer thought, then sociology not only rested on biology but was really a biological science.

Out of the tide of enthusiasm for biology, there appeared those twin absurdities—the recapitulation theory and the successive stages theory. According to the former, the individual recapitulated the history of the race, so that the supposedly less-evolved primitive peoples were seen only as children. According to the latter theory, since social stages were determined by biological stages of evolution, they must follow in succession, as monogamy followed polygamy. Supposedly Russia could not go from the household agricultural economy to socialism without passing through capitalism. The power of education and of the diffusion of culture traits in breaking up such a succession of stages was not appreciated.

Such was the background of sociological thought when the concept of culture appeared. But as the phenomena of cultural growth were studied, it was observed that social institutions evolved into new forms in periods of history too short for any biological evolution. Hence doubt was cast on any correlation of cultural evolution and biological evolution, at least during the historical period, if not since the Ice Ages. Peoples of the same race were noted to have greatly different levels of civilization, and peoples of different racial types were observed to have the same social institutions. The growth of a particular culture, ethnologists were showing, was not so much from inventions produced within that culture as from traits imported from other cultures. Thus any inevitable succession of stages was negated.

The close correlation of function and structure may exist when such widely different species as rats and guinea pigs are compared, but among peoples the functions as measured by customs and institutions were not found to be correlated with any discernible structure. When an Eskimo adult who could not count above ten and was thus supposed to be no further advanced than a child was taught to solve problems in calculus, the recapitulation theory lost its appeal.

That tremendous cultural variations were possible even if there were no races and that rapid social evolution could take

place if men evolved biologically not at all but were quite stationary were ideas revolutionary to the biological sociology of the
time. Culture cut the chains that tied sociology to biology. This
freedom meant an actual stimulus in proposing new hypotheses
and in generating new ideas about civilization and explanations
therefor on other grounds than biology.

However, it should not be understood from the foregoing account that all fields of sociology were affected in this manner
by biology. There were, for instance, many aspects of institutional
relationships which were studied without any particular relationship to race, inheritance, or instinct. However, many more
phases of sociology were related to biological theories than was,
for instance, the case with economics or political science.

One angle from which these relationships may be viewed was
the controversy over the very nature of sociology itself. It was
being variously described as the study of society, of the group,
or of group behavior. Certainly back of these various conceptions
was the idea of the group and group relations. The individual was
the object of study of psychology or biology, but the group was
the particular province of sociology. Sociology is derived from
the Latin word *"socius,"* meaning a companion.

With the wider acceptance of the meaning of culture, group
behavior as a mere type of inherited activity became of less
importance. Discoveries regarding group processes such as social
control, collective behavior, social pressure, mob action, social
contagion, ostracism, leadership, and the social instincts, remained of importance to sociology, but interest tended to shift to
the cultural forms and patterns carried by the group and to the
various habits and personalities favored by these cultural influences. The field of group action, viewed as a psychological and
biological phenomenon, had been pretty well cultivated and,
though still yielding discoveries, had perhaps reached the point
of diminishing returns, at least at that time. Interest shifted to
the cultural forms and their influence on the individual. Meanwhile, descriptive work on the various cultures of the world was
being carried out by ethnologists in the field. The literature on
different types of culture among different peoples was greatly

enriched, and much was learned about the organization of culture and the variations among the social institutions. This type of phenomenon was inherently interesting aside from race and tended to overshadow the description of biological behavior of groups. The question then may be raised as to whether the definition of sociology as the study of the group gave the proper emphasis. It may be argued that there was a large group of sociologists, never much interested in psychological or biological behavior of the group, who were rather more interested in social organization or in the culture carried by the group. Nevertheless, if interest is primarily in the culture carried by the group, why say that the interest is in the group? To do this, there must be a special definition of the group. It must mean that the group and the culture carried by the group were very closely related, if not synonymous.

Under the influence of biology, group activity and behavior were seen as biological products. It was the nature of man to behave this way in groups. It was instinct. The objective of sociology was to define more elaborately the nature of this group behavior. If this fuller description carried the investigation into social institutions, these became still the elaboration of instinctive social nature. Since function was seen as so closely related to structure, the different group functions, the different social institutions were the product of different group capacities. With this view, sociology as a study of the group was, *ipso facto*, a study of the group products, that is, its culture.

But with the recognition that cultural variations could occur without biological variations, the group and the group's culture were no longer the same. The group might remain biologically the same yet have a succession of different cultures. Hence, the definition of sociology as the study of the group implied no longer that it was the study of the culture of that group. It was customary to say at this earlier period that man created his culture. This was true if men of all time are considered and if man is being contrasted with another species. But one cannot say that the Greeks or the Mayans created their culture, much less the inhabitants of any one village or the peoples of any one century.

The culture is rather an environment in which they live, which, if conditions are favorable, they may modify somewhat in a given time by invention. The term "social heritage," often used interchangeably with "culture," suggests the futility of saying that a particular group creates a culture.

Concluding this part of the discussion, we see that the idea of culture is least as significant for sociology as is biology. As Darwinism and biology tended to define sociology as the study of the group, culture, being in a way the antithesis of biology, has necessarily changed the definition of sociology and added to the tasks of sociology the study of cultural processes. This change in concept of sociology itself suggests questions of new relations of sociology to ethnology and to the special social sciences, such as economics and political science, which are, however, not appropriate for the present discussion.

II

One aspect of this new relationship of sociology to ethnology and the special social sciences is the consideration of culture as a whole consisting of interrelated parts. The ethnologists have always so considered it for the primitive cultures and have brought forward such indicative terms as "culture pattern" and "configuration." An ethnologist goes to a primitive people and writes for the record an account of the whole culture of the people he visits, but he does not generally confine himself to any particular part, as, for instance, their economic institutions, as a social scientist often does in a modern culture, such as those of Europe or North America. The mere writeup of the whole culture of a people necessarily brings out the integration of the different parts into the whole, especially when comparisons are made with other cultures.

No scientific body seems to do for modern civilization quite what the ethnologist does for a simpler culture. Perhaps the task is too large. The historian doesn't do it. He is describing events usually, rather than institutions, and the events he describes are often selected, as for instance, political occurrences, military records, or economic achievements.

In actual practice, the field of labor in studying modern civilization is subdivided. The economist concerns himself with the institutions used in the production and consumption of wealth. The political scientist deals with the governments and their operation. And so on. Perhaps there is no great demand for a description of the whole of Western civilization. What the future may produce in integrated studies of the whole of a culture is not known.

This demand for an integrated picture of the whole of a culture in modern times has come nearer to fruition in the description of communities. It has long been the tradition of the sociologist to do for a particular village or city what the ethnologist does for a primitive culture. The primitive culture, though, is more nearly a closed system than is a single modern community. Hence these modern community studies do not describe with completeness the political, social, and economic institutions of a community. They omit what the readers will in general know, for instance, about the religious or educational system, only noting the variations supposed to be peculiar to the village being described or else facts not available for the country as a whole.

While it is then true that the rise of the study of culture has forced upon the specialists studying modern society the idea that the parts make up a whole, the demand is not so much for a description of the whole as it is for the interrelationships of the parts. The culture pattern is of interest as a whole but also because of the interrelationships of the parts.

Thus, in some cultures, religious practices are closely related to recreational activities in ceremonies, rituals, and religious festivals. The economic system may be closely related to customs of hospitality. For instance, the interchange of gifts associated with ceremonies may be a substitute for money and serve as a medium for the exchange of goods. Or, again, wealth and economic values may be subordinated to prestige as found in rank. Religious ideas may be connected with medical practice, art forms, or even economic activities, and yet have little to do with moral questions.

There are interrelationships between the parts of modern society as truly as in the cultures of preliterate peoples. But these interrelationships tend to be neglected by modern social scientists because of their specialization in particular fields. They are, though, the concern of practical men who have to deal with them. For instance, the points of contact between government and business are very numerous, and some study of their interrelations is forced upon government officials and businessmen more than it is upon economists or political scientists. Government today, as it expands its functions, is making contacts with many more social institutions, such as the family, clubs, recreational organizations, schools, and churches. But the political scientists seldom study these interrelationships as social scientists.

How these interrelationships of different parts of society may be studied in the future is a question. But the concept of culture precipitates the issue. It is true the issue has been injected also by the pressure of practical problems, but here the demand is for a practical solution rather than a scientific study. The ethnologist objects to the treatment of any part of culture apart from the culture pattern. Thus he may say that a treatment of marriage alone, for illustration, throughout a region or a period of time should not be done, since the full meaning of marriage cannot be appreciated except as a part of the culture. Marriage should always be studied in connection with the culture of which it is a part. The interrelationships of the parts of culture seem to be given relatively more attention in the study of primitive cultures than in modern civilization.

It hardly seems practicable that sociologists should be the ones to study these interrelations, though theoretically it might be argued that it is their task. They would have difficulty in covering the necessary ground to give the detailed study necessary for dealing with the practical questions that arise. But, it is possible that they might do much to study the interrelationships of the functions of the different social institutions from the point of view of social science.

III

A third significance of the concept of culture lies in its contribution to the study of social change. The evolution of culture, once free of biology, came to be seen in terms of cultural factors such as inventions, the diffusion of culture traits, culture contacts and isolation, the relation of the stock of knowledge existing at any one time to the rate of new inventions, social attitudes toward change, resistance to the adoption of inventions, and other such factors of a social nature.

The idea of change is not central to the ethnologist's study of culture. It is true he sees the culture of primitive peoples undergoing profound changes due to contacts with the culture of the white peoples, but usually his search is to reconstruct the ancient culture as it was before the changes due to contacts with the whites. The study of the effect of the white man's culture on the native cultures is, of course, a very special type of social change.

The historian records happenings and events but makes no systematic record of institutional changes and the causes therefor. The specialists in the various social sciences do make analyses of the changes in the particular institutions concerned, political, economic, educational, or whatever they may be. But, again, it may be observed that no institution exists alone and unrelated to any other; hence the specialist is handicapped if he restricts his attention to the causes of change lying within the institution concerned. True, he does not always so restrict himself for the reason that often causes of great change in any organization come from outside. The specialist though is likely to see only the more obvious external factors, since they lie without his special field. The growth or change of the superorganic is not best approached by a study of the changes in the different parts of the whole. It is better to view the whole culture pattern as undergoing change, for the very term "pattern" indicates that the parts of culture are fitted together in a configuration rather than the aggregation of so many unrelated units. The parts of culture are not related so simply as the links of a chain but are integrated more like the parts of a machine, so that when one part is changed the various other parts are likely to be affected also, even though in some cases only slightly.

The correlation between the different parts of culture is in unequal degrees. The church and art may be more closely related than government and art. Literature is more closely related to education than to economic processes. Medicine was at one time in closer connection with religion than with science; while in another culture it may be closer to science than to religion. A change, therefore, beginning in any one part of culture will affect the other parts in unequal degrees. Similarly, impinging forces in any part of culture come with unequal forces from other parts of culture.

The evolution of the superorganic then is the change of a whole where various parts are more or less integrated. But the various parts are not propelled forward with equal force. Some are changing rapidly; some, slowly. Some parts change because of inventions occurring in that part. So, for instance, technology or science changes today. Other parts are changing more from inventions occurring outside. Such was largely the case with the family in Europe and the United States in the nineteenth century. These unequal rates of change in the different correlated parts of culture cause stresses and strains in the relationship of the parts of culture.

There thus occurs in a changing society maladjustment between its parts, adjustments which are either less satisfactory than either previous or possible future relationships. As an illustration, the relationship that exists between science and religion has been disturbed at various times by virtue of discoveries in science relating to the nature of the world and of man. These acute tensions become eventually smoothed out, but for the time there is a serious maladjustment, usually for the part of culture which receives the force of invention, social or mechanical. These strains are in many cases caused by the fact that there is a delay or lag in keeping up with the precipitating changes. In modern society mechanical invention and scientific discovery are, in fact, the precipitators of many changes in other parts of culture. The various social organizations, philosophies, and habits are forced to adjust, after a delay, to new situations brought about by these mechanical and scientific innovations.

Thus the study of cultural evolution gives rise to important hypotheses of a purely cultural nature.

IV

A last influence of culture to be considered here is on social psychology. It seemed, from the so-called instinct psychology, that one could start with a blueprint of man's original nature and read off his social institutions. One started with motives and found there the explanation of customs and other human behavior. But inquiries into the explanation of cultural phenomena have reversed the process. It is better to start with the cultural phenomena and by history and description to arrive at motives as the end result. Similarly, the social institutions must first be accounted for on cultural grounds before one can be sure what parts of original nature are involved. A psychological inventory of original nature cannot be used as a blueprint for predicting social organization.

This approach radically revised the explanation of personality. It was once thought that personality was largely the gift of inheritance. But the personality of the young is now held to be more the outgrowth of group experience and of the culture pattern in which the child is reared. Group relationships, as in the family, church, school, club, and playground, are of great importance in shaping the personalities; but so also are the culture patterns carried by the group, be they those of warlike Sparta or the peaceful Greenland Eskimo.

This study of cultural and group influences on the personality of children is not as amenable to study by the ethnologist as is the description of culture patterns. The ethnologist is not in a good position nor well equipped to watch the growth of young children in a primitive culture, though comparisons may be made in the personalities of adults in different cultures. The early Icelanders were so murderous that it was thought they could never settle the island because they killed each other off so fast. But the culture pattern has changed, and it is said there were only two murders in Iceland in the nineteenth century. Comparative studies show the influences of different cultures on producing different personality traits. The development of personality ceases then to be wholly in the province of psychology. The psychologist who works in the laboratory is concerned with the account of general inventories, habits, and the processes of the conditioned reflex, rather than the influence of particular culture patterns on young people. The laboratory psychologist is not well trained for studying the various cultural stimuli, as appear in custom and institution, which shape personality. Likewise it is a study not to be undertaken by special social scientists, such as economists or political scientists. The study of personality would seem to fall within the sphere of activity of the special science of education or of the general science of sociology as well as psychology. If sociologists acquire the task of studying personality as influenced by culture, they cannot be concerned with only one institution. The family may be the most important. But schools, churches, communities, clubs, occupations, etc., must all be studied. The sociologist really must look at culture as a whole. Trained in psychology, he is also in a very good position to make such studies because of his interest in the group and group processes, which are particularly important in stamping the culture pattern on the individual, in making him conform to the pattern or become a variant. Also, in studying the influence of culture on the individual, it is necessary to view culture as a whole.

With regard to the old question of the psychological adjustment of man, the primitive hunter, to modern culture, the question is not now expressed in the earlier biological language of adaptation and environment. It is rather phrased in such terms as the interrelationship between personality and culture. Though personality may be the product of culture, the individual may deviate from the pattern and hence not be adjusted. If the deviation is rather far, he may be called a neurotic personality. In a modern society there are patterns within patterns. Society is heterogeneous and consists of many groups, with different folkways, so the effect of culture on the personality is far from simple. The new approach to culture and personality is not wholly due to the growing appreciation of culture. Psychology also makes its contribution. Researches there have shown many marvelous new habits that can be set up on the principle of the conditioned reflex. Thus the modifiability of original nature, rather than a relatively rigid set of instincts, is a lesson from psychology that offers a basis for describing the different effects of culture on personality.

Not even the different personalities of the sexes are now admitted to be wholly determined by the obviously different sexual constitutions of male and female. But traits which are considered masculine in our culture are found to be feminine in other cultures and vice versa. Furthermore, as cultural change is now taking place in modern culture, the feminine personality is quite different today from what it was fifty years ago in, say, the Victorian era. No doubt there are limits to which biological nature can be bent; and, what is more important, there is probably some kind of biological norm of behavior to which, as culture molds personality, there is a more harmonious relationship established. But for the moment, the culture enthusiasts are forgetting the biological limits to cultural influence, even though there be an alarming number of psychotics.

With a fixed biological nature and a rapidly changing culture, optimistic man with notions of progress is even looking forward to possibilities of bending culture to make a better relationship. But the question, on the other hand, is being raised whether a rapidly changing culture, with all its lags and inequalities of rates of change and uncertain futures, is not a more difficult one to make an adjustment to than a stationary culture.

Personality and culture is more often viewed as a one-way relationship. But, of course, a personality may influence culture. The question of the impact of the great man on culture has no special new emphasis since the intrusion of the culture concept, except perhaps to strengthen the case of social forces influencing the great man rather than the great man influencing social forces.

The personality influences the superorganic through inventions—mechanical, social, or ideational. Hence the importance of how inventions originate. Little evidence seems to be forthcoming that the inventor is a biological mutation or even in the upper extreme of some distribution curve of inherited traits or combination of traits.

In conclusion, it has been shown that the biological influences on sociology of a generation or so ago acted as a springboard for hurling the new idea of culture into sociological thought. The magnitude of the idea is quite comparable with the magnitude of social biology. Indeed, the importance of culture has forced a reorientation of many of the most important concepts of sociology and even the consideration of a redefining of sociology.

2

SOCIAL EVOLUTION

RECONSIDERED   *1950*

I

WHEN *Social Change* was first published, fifty years of writing and discussion of "social evolution" was coming to a close. The interest in social evolution was stimulated greatly by the discoveries in biological evolution, and it was hoped that the theory of social evolution would explain the origin and development of civilization as the theory of biological evolution had explained the origin and development of man. Darwin had reduced the evolution of species to three causal factors: variation, natural selection, and heredity. Of the variations of a species, say, in color, in muscular tissue, or in temperature, nature selects for survival those variations which fit it better for adaptation and allows the less-well-adapted, the weaker, to perish. When heredity passes on any new variation valuable for survival, we see how apes could evolve into *Homo sapiens,* provided new hereditary variations occurred. This discovery was an explanation of a process—a change from one species to another—and not a description. The species had been previously described by a long succession of naturalists such as Linnaeus.

Reprinted from *Social Change*, sup. chap. (Viking Press, 1950 edition), pp. 369–93.

The broad outline of how one species evolves into another, as drawn by Darwin, is remarkably simple, easily grasped by a person of average education; but its significance was tremendous in a religious age to a people who believed literally in the Bible and believed that man, the noblest work of God, was created by God himself in the Garden of Eden.

It was natural then that the anthropologists and the sociologists would want an equally satisfactory and significant explanation of how our society evolved. There had been descriptions in world histories of society since the origin of writing and also descriptions of preliterate societies. What was wanted was explanation rather than description.

Why these attempts were not early successful need not be discussed here except to say that many investigators were too slavish in copying the biological account in terms of selection, adaptation, survival of the fittest, variation, survival, recapitulation, and successive stages of development. Then, too, some of the writers confused evolution with progress, without quite realizing that progress was merely the moral evaluation of evolution. Also, some writers sought to see in both biological and social evolution the guiding force of some supreme being, charting and carrying out the great orderly process of evolution for good, and thus demonstrating that there was a God behind the process of evolution, both social and biological.

The point of diminishing returns seemed to have been reached by these writers, and the reaction was to abandon the term "social evolution." It was about this time that this book was written, not under the title *Social Evolution*, but under *Social Change*. Even though the term "social evolution" has come to be used less, the problem still remains, namely, How does society evolve and how did our civilization[1] come to be? As our progenitors came down

---

1   The word "civilization" has many different uses, such as any set of higher moral qualities of society, varying from author to author; any of the superior virtues of any large, orderly state; the social organization based upon civil status rather than kinship status; synonymous with cul-

out of the trees, their society was simple and crude as compared to our own. They had little society; we have a truly magnificent one. How did it come to be?

The common assumption seems to have been that the reason society evolved was because man, who made society, evolved. In other words, men who had not evolved very far would have a crude culture, while men who were fully evolved, such as the people of western Europe, would have an advanced society. Society was seen as social behavior, and behavior was a function of biological structure. A duck had webbed feet and swam. A chicken did not have webbed feet and could not swim. The animals of the farm—horses, pigs, sheep, and dogs—behaved differently because they had different structures. As we behave differently from the apes, so we have, of course, a different structure, particularly in our ability to speak a language. A European behaves differently from a Melanesian—hence he is supposed to have a different structure. The outstanding characteristic of man is his large brain, more than twice as large as that of the largest living anthropoids. Hence it was readily assumed that superior civilizations were the result of superior brains.

But since the size of the heads of some races with less capable cultures was not greatly different from that of western Europeans, it was assumed that brains differed not only in size but somehow in quality of organic matter. Though writers of the late nineteenth century said they were seeking the cause of the evolution of society, they spoke and wrote as if men created civilization rather than as if it evolved. Since society was created by man, the men with the more complex and elaborate civilizations were, *ipso facto,* men with greater mental abilities and hence with superior brains.

So axiomatic did this seem that a superior culture was considered as genuine evidence of superior hereditary brains. Higher

---

ture, whether preliterature or modern; and the tail end of cultural development which began many hundred thousand years ago. It is in this latter sense that the word is here used.

cultures occurred, therefore, because men with better brains occurred. This assumption of how we got our civilization was considered about as obvious as that God created man. The Garden of Eden story, though, was more widely held, for not so many were concerned with the origins of civilizations as with the Book of Genesis. The identification of civilization with behavior and the correlation of behavior with organic structure were great stumbling blocks in the scientific inquiry of the causes of social evolution, for civilization was seen as society and society as social behavior dependent upon organic structure. This was the obstacle which led to the point of diminishing returns in the early writings. Civilization was not seen as an accumulation of culture or as a conditioning environment in which inadequately organized infants were born.

A mighty blow was delivered against this explanation by anthropologists, particularly Franz Boas in his work on the mind of primitive man and on the mental ability of races. He made an excellent demonstration that peoples with primitive cultures could have just as much inherited mental ability as modern man with his advanced civilizations and that levels of culture of different peoples were not indexes of their inherited abilities.

Then, too, telling was the challenge, stated in this book, that there was no evidence that the genetic capacity for brain function of the whole population of Europe had changed any at all during the past twenty-five thousand years, for the brain cases of men were as large then as now. That the texture of the brains of modern man is superior now to what it was then was charged but really was merely a claim without any data at all to support it.

This demonstration was a purely negative one. It was like showing that the Garden of Eden story of the creation of man was false without telling how man was created. So destruction of the belief that culture evolved only as biological man evolved did not provide an explanation of how culture did evolve.

However, on rereading the section on social evolution in *Social Change* it is thought that the essential factors that explain social evolution are there to be found. They are there set forth quite modestly, with apologies for the scarcity of evidence. Nor are they drawn sharply and with emphasis. Since the first printing of this book, there have been additional researches which strengthen and confirm those there stated. Also, there has been little criticism of these theories of social evolution in the years since their first publication.[2]

This reconsideration of the problem of social evolution is to appraise it in the light of the experience since *Social Change* was published, to outline the problem and the theory more sharply, and to integrate the factors more tightly. The presentation is made brief and with little reference to evidence, purposely, to make the factors stand out without being obscured by detail. It is desired to see the forests without attention to particular trees.

To argue that the problem of social evolution has been solved refers only to the essentials of the problem, that is, essentials that are demanded by a general curiosity concerned with the larger aspects of the problem. For instance, those who want to know the general processes whereby modern civilization became what it is are not for this reason concerned in the details of why the Mohammedan civilization arose or differed from that of the Hindus. Nor are those who are interested in the general processes whereby the apes evolved into men concerned for that reason in the evolution of the wasps. The evolution of wasps and of Mohammedan culture should of course follow these general processes. But the general processes do not explain the details of any particular culture or species.[3]

Nor does the argument that the problem of social evolution has been solved mean that no further researches are needed. Quite the contrary. Science grows by refining and by accretion. For instance, in biology, the factors of variation, selection, and heredity

2   The only part of the theory that has been criticized is the concept of cultural lag—criticisms based, I think, upon distortions and misunderstandings. However, the concept of cultural lag is not a fundamental part of the theory of social evolution.

3   Anthropologists, who have done such excellent work on social evolution, have, I think, not defined the problem properly. In general they have abandoned the explanation of culture for the attempt to explain cultures.

were set forth as one explanation of the origin of species. But we have since learned much about heredity, and there is much we want to know about reproductive isolation and the causes of variation. Indeed, research on the explanatory factors of biological evolution has been accelerated. So, even though we should know the main factors that have developed our civilization, further researches on social change are expected to be accelerated rather than to be stopped.

Before we consider the factors that explain social evolution we may ask the question, "What is it that is evolving?"[4] The answer is usually, "Society." But insofar as society is inherited biological behavior, then we have no evidence that the biological element in society has been evolving during the past twenty-five thousand years.[5] That part of society that has evolved is some other element than the biological.

To the anthropologists, particularly to Robert H. Lowie and to Alfred Kroeber, in 1917, we are indebted for the clearest conception of what this other element is. It is culture. Social evolution becomes then cultural evolution, and the evolution of groups since glacial times is part of the evolution of culture.

[4] There is considerable variation in what the different writers in this field are discussing. Toynbee seems to be discussing culture areas whose boundaries are largely determined by the spread of a particular religion or moral system. Sorokin is concerned with the variation in an attitude across history. Spengler deals with a creative spirit that is tied in with an effective and expanding state. Brooks Adams, when he uses the term "civilization," is talking about an effective and large politically and economically organized state. None of these writers is discussing "culture," as the anthropologists and sociologists use the term.

[5] Up until the brain case of the anthropoid that was to become man had reached its present size and until the ability to use a language was developed, there was a correlation between social evolution and biological evolution.

A species may remain for a long time without any evolutionary change. Such is the case with modern Europeans over the past thousand years (and perhaps over seventy-five thousand years or longer). Since a change cannot be explained by a constant, the change over the last thousand years or longer in western Europe cannot be explained biologically.

II

What then are the factors that explain cultural evolution? They are four: invention, accumulation, diffusion, and adjustment.[6]

1. Invention as here used is not confined to mechanical invention but includes social inventions, such as the League of Nations, and innovations in other parts of culture, as for instance the invention of a religious ritual or of an alphabet. It also comprises scientific discoveries. Invention is defined as a combination of existing and known elements of culture, material and/or nonmaterial, or a modification of one to form a new one. The modification of an invention is often little more than an improvement. The vast number of patents granted to inventors are for quite minor improvements on some basic invention. By inventions we do not mean only the basic or important inventions but the minor ones and the improvements. Inventions, then, are the evidence on which we base our observations of social evolution.

The crucial position of inventions in cultural evolution precipitates the question as to how they are made. They result from the operation of three factors: mental ability, demand, and the existence of other cultural elements out of which inventions are fashioned, sometimes called the "cultural base."

A current theory of inventions is an heroic one. Inventors are geniuses. Inventors, it is true, may have superior mental ability as compared with others in the same group at the same time. But over time the proportion of superior inherited mental ability in a group would be the same if there had been no biological evolution. There would be more inherited mental ability in modern Europe than there was when it was peopled by the Cro-Magnon man only because there are more people in Europe now than then. Insofar as mental ability is learned, then there would be a much

6   Of these four factors, the central one is invention, as the central factor in biological evolution is mutation, viz., a new variation that is inherited. Accumulation, diffusion, and adjustment all lead to further invention, but they do more. Each is a significant and special process, irrespective of its stimulation of new inventions.

larger proportion of men of such ability in Europe than in Cro-Magnon times, owing to the fact that there is more to learn.

The demand for invention, the second factor in the inventional process, does not always meet with success; but extreme demand, sometimes called necessity, is said to be the mother of invention. Many inventions and discoveries are made accidentally while working on something else; for these, demand did not direct the invention. Such are many discoveries in pure science. The use of an invention, however, implies a demand. This demand may vary over time and is a cultural variable rather than a biological one. Thus there may have been much more demand for inventions during the past hundred years than formerly. At any one time it is selective: some are demanded, and some are not. In prehistoric times there may not have been much variation in demand. Social demand now directs the learning process and may be much greater in one sector of culture than in another.

The third factor in the inventing process, which is the number of existing elements, takes us to the second factor in the explanation of social evolution, namely, accumulation.

2. Accumulation occurs when more new elements are added to the cultural base than are lost. In general, the smaller the area, the greater the loss. For the earth as a whole the accumulation of inventions[7] is inconceivably vast at the present time. Presumably inventions accumulate for the same reason they are made: they have utility. But there is replacement of the more efficient by the less efficient, so there may be much loss, particularly in a small area. The loss may also be great in a non-material culture, such as religion, where the subtractions might be greater than the additions. In science, culture is very accumulative. The accumulation process was speeded first by the development of speech and then by writing.

Societies in action are an accumulation of learned ways of behaving. To say that societies are an accumulation has advantages, in studying change, over the customary statement that society is behavior. Society is both behavior and an accumula-

[7]   Counting one invention only once, no matter what the extent of duplication.

tion. But the emphasis on behavior is often associated with biological behavior, which is for man a constant over the time under consideration for a population. It is the learned behavior that has varied with time and is accumulative.

The advantage in studying social evolution or emphasizing accumulation is that it destroys the ethnocentric myth and egotistical fantasy that man created his civilization. Much truer is the idea that he inherited it.

Different peoples are born into different accumulations of culture. Though they have the same inherited mental abilities, their operating mental abilities may vary enormously, according to the pile of culture into which they are born. A baby born of a woman but reared in the meager culture of wolves will probably create not a single element of culture that is different from the culture of wolves, and the child can do only what the wolves do, even though the child were the offspring of an Isaac Newton. So also a child picked at random from the public schools of Greece today can do operations in mathematics that Aristotle could not do. The accumulation of mathematics is much greater today than it was in 350 B.C.

This accumulation tends to be exponential because an invention is a combination of existing elements, and these elements are accumulative. As the amount of interest paid an investor is a function of the size of the capital he has invested, so the number of inventions is a function of the size of the cultural base, that is, the number of existing elements in the culture. In compound interest the principal accumulates, as does the "principal" of culture. There are more inventions in the United States today (per unit of population and per unit of time) than among the Eskimos, not because the people of the United States have any more inherent mental ability, but for the reason that we have a larger cultural base, that is, more with which to invent.

Put in figures, this argument would mean that if a cultural base of a hundred thousand elements yielded one invention, then a cultural base of a million elements would yield a thousand inventions, even if the inherent mental ability of the peoples of the two cultural bases were the same. But in reality the yield of the second cultural base would be more than a thousand inventions. The reason lies in the definition of an invention as a combination of existing elements; and, as the existing elements increase, the number of combinations increases faster than by a fixed ratio. Thus three elements can be combined by two's in three different ways; four elements, in six different ways; and five elements, in ten different ways. Even though only a microscopic fraction of combinations will result in a useful invention, the principle of an increasing rate holds.

So exponential accumulation means acceleration, a phenomenon borne out by the curves of Hornell Hart and Harvey C. Lehman of recent years and by the data of Darmstadter.

Exponential growth seldom exists for long in reality, for the increments quickly become too large for reality, as is obviously the case with compound interest and with population growth. The accumulation of culture has then only a tendency to grow exponentially. Reality lessens the slope or flattens it out eventually, perhaps to begin growing exponentially again for a time. Exponential growth may work out to be irregular—now popularly called cyclical.

This numerical analysis has been proceeding as if all elements were the same, much as the statistics of population are all of the same units, viz., human beings. Actually there is the greatest variety in inventions even in the same part of a culture. A steam engine or a dynamo can be fitted into many more combinations than a windmill or a sailing ship. Some inventions are prolific in their stimulation of other inventions; others, hardly at all; hence more irregularities in growth. When we say that the British and the Americans are very inventive, what should be said is that the inventions of the steam engine, of steel-making processes, and of the discoveries in electricity have led to an unprecedented number of other inventions. A burst of creativeness may be explained in terms of a fortuitous combination of a few inventions, significant in proliferating others.

There can also be declines in the rate of inventiveness without an actual loss in number of inventions. Those who deal with the qualities of culture, as in philosophy and art, often report a decline, a decline which is analogous to a decrease in patents on a particular invention. Immediately after a big invention is made —a plow, a locomotive, or some other—the improvements, as shown in patents, are very numerous, but they are fewer as the years go by until some other fundamental change is made.

If a people happens to be the carrier of a culture that is evolving rapidly, it is given approbation as a creative people. On the other hand, if a people with the same inherent abilities is the possessor of a culture that is changing very slowly, as in isolated islands or mountains, it is spoken of as a backward people. Whereas the difference would be better described by saying that with one people the culture is changing rapidly, with the other it is changing slowly. A people is the carrier of a culture that is growing either rapidly or slowly.

In prehistoric times cultural evolution was very slow, perhaps so slow as to be invisible over four or five generations. Such societies are referred to as stationary. Even so the change could be exponential, but the rate would be very low over a large unit of time. A people in such a slowly changing culture would be far outdistanced by a people in a culture that was accelerating rapidly.

The functional relationship between the size of the cultural base and the number of new inventions, plus the tendency for cultural elements to accumulate, helps to explain how our civilization came from simple beginnings to what it is today. The view of culture as a growing accumulation is more realistic than the conception of it as behavior or as the creation of peoples.

3. Diffusion, the third factor in the process of social evolution, is an expression used by anthropologists in referring to the spread of inventions from one area to others, usually from the area of their origin. The spread of inventions is promoted by the various communication and transportation inventions. We have been speaking in preceding paragraphs as if the only way a culture of a people grew was through an invention made by the people out of existing culture elements. But the people of a culture area may acquire inventions without making them by importing them from elsewhere. In fact most of the inventions of a limited area

are acquired by diffusion, as has been shown in the long literature on independent origin versus diffusion. Diffusion may then be viewed as simply one source of invention in a particular area in contrast to another source, namely, that dependent upon the three factors of mental ability, demand, and the existing elements. But diffusion is also more than the source of invention. It is a process of bringing many different inventions from various sources together in a common cultural base. It becomes then a very important factor in explaining some particular culture, as well as an explanatory factor in the growth of culture as a whole. By diffusion a people profits by the inventional contributions from many different parts of the world. The evolution of culture is more rapid because of diffusion. Thus the growth of culture in any one area arises not so much from the functional relationship between the number of inventions and the cultural base, as from importation. But, of course, the faster acquisition of inventions from elsewhere adds to the cultural base and hence increases the rate of inventiveness.

Bursts of creativeness of a people sometimes occur because of the diffusion of significant inventions or of large numbers of them. Thus the creativeness of the Renaissance period in Italy seems to have been due in part to infiltration of inventions (ideational) from the heritage of antiquity long buried.

One of the puzzling questions about social evolution has been the unequal levels of culture among different peoples and in different areas. Formerly it was attributed to racial abilities, but since this is highly improbable, then the question of why a culture is complex and efficient among one people and simple and crude among another still remains. The answer is to be sought in the rate of accumulation. Still, we want to know why the accumulation has gone further in one place than another. Unequal rates of acceleration partly explain the phenomenon. But location plus diffusion appears to be the better explanation for most comparisons. For inventions to be diffused they must travel. Hence isolated spots benefit less by diffusion than do locations at crossroads. What is a barrier to travel at one time, high mountains and oceans, for instance, may not be at another time, when travel inventions exist to surmount the barriers, as, for instance, the airplane and the steamboat.

As an illustration, at one time the culture of the eastern Mediterranean was at the crossroads, a focus for diffusion. Just at this time there was an unusual number of significant inventions to be diffused into this favored spot: the domesticated horse, the improved sea-going boat, metal-working, the wheel, cattle, the alphabet, writing, ceramics, and a variety of customs and ideas. It is not surprising, therefore, that the cultural advance at this time and in this place received such a great push forward. The advance is usually credited to the genius of the Greek people, as was claimed by Francis Galton, whereas, according to the theory here advanced, there is no reason to think that the great push to culture at this time in this region favorable for the diffusion of new inventions might not have occurred if the Greeks had been Negroes.

With all these important inventions diffused, the culture accumulation accelerated more than it did behind the barriers of the deserts and the jungles and took a commanding lead over other cultures.

Diffusion is therefore a factor in the growth of world culture as a whole, especially in very early times, and particularly is it an important explanation of cultural growth in a smaller area.

4. Adjustment of one part of society to another is important in understanding the evolution of culture, for the parts of culture are intertwined in varying degrees. For instance, government is related to economic institutions; the economic institutions are related to the family; the family is related to education; education is related to science; science is related to religion, and so on. In some cases the connection may be very close, as, for instance, between highway and automobile. In others, the connection is more remote, as between poetry and the steam engine. This interrelationship is the organization of culture.

Because of this interrelationship an invention occurring in one part and producing a change therein will also occasion a change in a part closely correlated. Thus the invention of the factory with machinery driven by steam produced a change in the family by taking occupations out of the home, especially those of women, and putting them in factories. Hence an invention in one part of a culture may produce many changes in other differing parts of a culture.

These changes are often inventions in the non-material part of culture, as for instance the factory, which led to the invention of workmen's compensation. We may speak of this new social invention as an adjustment to a change in the material culture, namely, the factory.

Inventions in one part of culture may occur then as an adjustment to an invention in a related part of culture, as well as by diffusion from another culture area and by independent origin.

The adjustment of one part of culture to a change in another part is then a source of invention, but we treat it as a new factor in social evolution, along with invention, accumulation, and diffusion, because of its very great potentiality in producing changes in culture.

These adjustments do not take place instantaneously but are made after a delay and are called "cultural lags." Over the long course of social evolution, measured in thousands of years, cultural lags are invisible. At any particular moment, however, they may be numerous and acute.

A society long stationary without any social changes is in equilibrium. The various parts, through trial and error, have become adjusted to one another. There is a harmonious relationship of the various culture traits. There is no social evolution. But when a significant invention occurs in one part of culture, the balance is disturbed; change is set up in the other related parts as a process of adjustment to the new invention. Thus social evolution goes forward by inventions which produce a disequilibrium in society, which in turn sets up forces which seek a new equilibrium.

Some parts of culture have been observed to be particularly influential in favoring invention in other parts, at least in modern historical times. A stable and efficient governmental organization appears to be one such condition. Government is intertwined with many other parts of a culture. A disorganized government torn by civil strife and inadequately supported by taxes does not seem favorable to invention in the arts. Again, a densely populated area such as a city seems to be one in which change takes place more readily than in small communities of one hundred or more persons. Certainly the number and variety of social inventions in a community of twenty families is more limited than in a metropolis of five million inhabitants. Perhaps back of the advantages of such social organization lies an economic factor. Economic institutions are also correlated with many other social institutions. Thus it takes wealth to support a large, capable government, and a big city rests upon high productivity at least. Indeed, in modern times variations in economic conditions produce changes that are widely spread over the different parts of a culture. One more of these empirical observations of significant interrelationships may be noted. It is the potentiality of technological and scientific changes to produce changes elsewhere in the culture. The multiplier factor for a mechanical invention or a discovery in applied science is exceptionally large in our modern civilization.

The difficulty of adjustment, as here defined, may be quite great, involving as it may the creation of new social inventions. For a simple and crude culture with an influx of new inventions by diffusion, the problem of adjustment may be too difficult and may be accompanied by great disorganization, as has been the case with some groups of American Indians.

The adjustment of the respective parts of a culture to one another in the inventional process is evidently an important factor in explaining social evolution.

III

The problem of social evolution, in conclusion, is seen as the problem of explaining how society changes and of answering our curiosity as to how our modern civilization came to be. The traditional explanation has been in terms of the evolution of inherited mental ability. This explanation may be largely valid for that long period before the brain of the animal that was to be man had attained its present size and before he attained the free command over language which he now has. For a period of many thousands of years, however, this explanation is not valid, for there is no evidence that the inherited mental ability of man has changed and there is much evidence to indicate that it has not. Inherited mental ability is a factor in our civilization, of course, but over time it cannot be a factor in the changing of civilization unless inherited mental ability has changed. A change cannot be explained by a constant.

With the traditional explanation of inherited mental ability inadequate, what are the factors that have caused the great evolution of our culture from crude and simple beginnings to the magnificence it has now attained? The explanation lies in four factors: invention, accumulation, diffusion, and adjustment. An understanding of these four factors makes it clear how our civilization has come to be what it is. These four factors offer also a general explanation of any one culture, such as that of China or India or Greece. This understanding is one of broad perspective, much as is Darwin's explanation of biological evolution in terms of variation, natural selection, and heredity.

3

THE GREAT MAN VERSUS SOCIAL

FORCES   *1926*

A QUESTION of long standing in sociology is the relative influence of the individual in social change. How important is the great man in history; how important is genius in science and invention; how important the outstanding personality in religion and art and leadership in social movements? The traditional point of view has been to attribute much importance to the great individual in all those achievements and social processes. However with the rise of the idea of determinism as against the freedom of the will, of economic history in contrast to the exploits of kings and military chieftains, and of the studies of the relation of the group to the individual, the importance of factors in history other than the individual has been more and more appreciated. The purpose of the following paper is to add to the analysis of this ever-interesting question some ideas coming from recent researches in sociology, psychology, and statistics.

The analysis of this problem is often confused by the mixing of two different conceptions of greatness, the greatness that is attributable to heredity and the greatness of the developed personality, which is the product of both environment and heredity. For instance, if one wishes to inquire as to, say, Abraham Lin-

Reprinted from *Social Forces*, V, No. 2 (December, 1926).

coln's influence as a great man on the course of history, one may not be particularly interested in dissecting Lincoln into two parts, heredity and environment. But if one wishes to contrast Lincoln as a great man with the social forces of his times, one must remember that Lincoln, the adult man, represents a part of the social forces (since they helped to produce him) with which it is desired to contrast him. And the fact that Lincoln differed from other men of his times cannot wholly be attributed to heredity, since the forces of the environment do not play upon all in the same degree and manner. Our need then, in order to make the analysis of the general problem sharp, is to consider the greatness which is attributable to heredity. And the first task is to learn something of the frequency of the hereditary elements of greatness.

A most interesting fact about living organisms is that when a particular trait of a random number of living organisms of the same species is measured, it is found to be distributed according to the normal probability curve. Measurement in psychology also indicates that mental traits, like such physical traits as height and stature, fall into frequency distributions of the same general shape as the normal probability curve. This distribution seems to be true not only for simple mental traits but also for combinations and complexes of traits, such as logical reasoning and even general mental ability. It seems probable therefore that such traits as inventive ability or any particular combination of traits of greatness would also be similarly distributed. We therefore think that the biological bases of the different kinds of greatness occur in the normal probability curve of frequencies.

The significance of such a distribution is that we are enabled to form an idea of how frequently a particular degree of mental ability, such as greatness, may be expected to occur. For, in a normal probability frequency area, three times the standard deviation on each side of the point of the arithmetic mean on the base line is considered as practically the limit of the distribution. And, such being the case, if a biological trait of greatness were measured on a line from the least to the greatest, then the greatness represented by the upper tenth of the line would be possessed by about 1.5 per cent of the population, that is, about fifteen hundred out of one hundred thousand, on the average. And the greatness represented by the upper quarter of the line would be possessed by about thirteen thousand out of one hundred thousand.

It would appear from the foregoing that high orders of greatness, in so far as they are biologically determined, are fairly plentiful. That is, the potentialities of greatness are common. One may, however, guess that greatness is a biological mutation, in which case, it is without the range of normal variations and hence rare. But mutations are probably so rare indeed, judging from the extensive observations for mutations on *Drosophila*, that the great in human society could in general hardly be biological mutations.

Furthermore, the biological elements of greatness are probably not only plentiful but fairly constant over time. For race is notably stable, and in large civilized groups selection probably operates on large numbers of persons. We should therefore certainly expect constancy within the short space of a few centuries. It is important to consider the point of variation, for our understanding of cause, such as we work with practically in science, is that it is only the phenomena that vary that we term causes. Then if inherited abilities of a high order are probably fairly constant and plentiful in very large groups of civilized peoples, it seems questionable whether one is right in attributing so much weight to inherited greatness as a cause of progress and also in explaining the absence of achievement to the scarcity of inherited abilities.

Yet all of us who have studied history or observed social movements have felt the scarcity and need of great men, of great leaders. Does not this observed rarity of great men invalidate the somewhat theoretical arguments of the preceding statements? This apparent discrepancy is partly due to confusing the two conceptions of greatness, commented on previously, the inherited bases of greatness and the great man as a developed personality. The latter, great men of history with developed personalities, are, it will be claimed later, more likely to vary and hence be scarce than men with the inherited elements of greatness which, alone, have just been under consideration.

There are various ways by which social conditions make greatness rare or frequent. The original material of heredity is subjected to what the psychologists call the learning process, that is, the original impulses are conditioned into habits, so that they operate through a somewhat complex organization of habits. Personalities are thus formed and become fairly fixed by the time adult life is reached. These personalities become varied one from another, for the social conditions setting habits are greatly varied.

The specific forms and directions which these impulses organized into habits take depend upon the particular cultural conditions of the time and of the group. Men become engineers, monks, shepherds, or military men according to the different cultural conditions, which vary from time to time and from group to group. These cultural conditions vary over a very wide range indeed, as compared with the range of variation of the hereditary material of racial stocks.

What great achievements these organized personalities of adults may make depends upon two cultural situations. First are the opportunities arising from the existence of cultural elements or materials favorable for making great achievements. At one time the materials exist for inventing the automobile, at another time not. Among one people the situation is ripe for military conquests. A new country is settled, providing exceptional opportunities for social organization. Under such cultural opportunities great achievement is probable. The second cultural situation which affects the achievement of great men is the social valuation of the group. One group may greatly value artistic achievement and stimulate effort along those lines. Another group values religious leadership; while another encourages commercial enterprise. So social valuations have much to do with great achievement.

These different social conditions that affect the production of greatness include the social forces, which usually mean the dynamic elements arising from the impulses of a plural number of human beings, impulses organized into particular habit mechanisms in different cultural media. Social valuations represent these social forces probably very well, for men do what the group values. These group valuations are quite integrally related to and dependent upon the accumulation of cultural elements at any one time; for instance, the status of the industrial arts has much to do with determining the social valuation of commercial enterprise. The social conditions are therefore very closely related to the social forces.

But however the term "social forces" may be defined, it is clear that our social heritage varies greatly according to time and place and would make great men rare or frequent, even when the distribution of the inherited elements of greatness is constant. Social forces therefore make great men, but before speaking of how great men affect the social forces, it is desirable to try to clarify this somewhat abstract argument with an illustration.

Professor Kroeber[1] has observed and discussed the very interesting fact that there are a number of inventions that have been invented by two or more inventors working independently and without knowledge of the other's work. The significance of this phenomenon, he thinks, is that it indicates the relative unimportance of the great man in cultural development. Dr. Thomas and I[2] have collected the accounts of more than one hundred such major inventions occurring in recent years that have been made by more than one inventor at the same time and without knowledge of each other's work. Such a list is quite remarkable when it is recalled how quickly news is disseminated in recent times. I think that every important invention in electricity has been claimed by at least two inventors.

The inference to be drawn from such data is, for instance, that the discovery of the calculus was not dependent upon Newton; for if Newton had died, it would have been discovered by Leibnitz. And we think that if neither Leibnitz nor Newton had lived, it would still have been discovered by some other mathematician. So also the theory of evolution by variation and natural selection

1   A. L. Kroeber, "The Superorganic," *American Anthropologist*, May–June, 1917.

2   W. F. Ogburn, *Social Change in Relation to Culture and Original Nature* (New York, 1923).

would have been developed even if Wallace and Darwin had never lived.

The reason we think this relatively great role of culture is over-looked in popular thought regarding inventions is because the essential dependence of a particular invention on the existence of other inventions is not appreciated. Our devotion to hero-worship obscures the fact. But an airplane is just as dependent for its origin on the light engine as it is upon a great inventor. The steamboat is similarly dependent upon the steam engine; calculus, on analytical geometry; and each special invention in electricity, on a number of other subsidiary inventions. The existence of such necessary subsidiary inventions for the achievement of a particular invention is extremely variable, so specialized is the relationship, and is much more variable than the existence of inherited mental ability of a high order.

The analysis of invention furthermore shows that the new element in the invention is relatively small, as in the telegraph or the radio, tremendously important though it may be. From this point of view an invention will be seen as a step in a process rather than the entire creation of something new, and the role of the great inventor is correspondingly less.

We have now spoken of two factors in invention—mental ability and the subsidiary cultural material. There is a third factor, which directs the mental ability to the cultural materials out of which the invention is made. This factor is the necessity or the desire, and we shall refer to it as the social valuation. A society may encourage inventions or it may not. The steam engine was greatly desired during the eighteenth century, and much effort was employed by a series of men in making this achievement. In the United States, research in commerce is socially valued, and development is occurring more rapidly there than in other fields where there is less social valuation. Oriental peoples do not have the same social values as the Occidental peoples, nor do the primitive peoples have the same valuations as modern peoples.

These social valuations are essentially of the nature of social forces, for they are the dynamic desires of the group. They are the forces that impinge upon the native impulses, and especially are they the forces that play upon the developed personality, the great man. And in so far as man is a medium, a responding mechanism, these are the forces to which he responds in making great achievements.

These three factors—mental ability, cultural material, and social valuations—which have been deduced from a study of invention, are also factors in various kinds of great achievement as well as in mechanical invention. Sometimes some one of these factors plays a more important role than the others.

For instance, the formation of an empire at a particular period will depend on such cultural elements as priority and differential in economic processes as well as upon great men; and to the degree that these elements are present, to that degree will an empire be developed.

In the field of medicine, another illustration, great achievement is dependent also on the variation of the cultural material, that is, the existence of scientific accomplishment at the time, and not so much on variation in social valuation, for the need of saving human life was greater in earlier times, when there was less medical development than now. The primitive peoples certainly put forth effort, and their great men tried, as is shown by the practices of the shaman. Necessity has been called the mother of invention, but necessity did not produce scientific medicine among the primitive peoples. Nor does the need of great men in any endeavor necessarily bring them forth. The required cultural materials must be present.

Another interesting illustration is decorative art among primitive peoples. The patterns of a tribe, though varied and numerous, show little change, that is, invention. In this case, the absence of change would hardly seem due to the absence of the necessary cultural material, for the various possibilities of design would seem to be relatively independent of subsidiary materials. It seems rather more probable that the existing designs are sufficient for the needs or they are conventionalized to existing requirements.

In the case of great leadership in social movements or social organization, very little estimation is usually given to the importance of existing cultural elements in the social situation. The

lack or presence of great ability is customarily judged the important factor. It is probably, however, truer not to attribute the
failure of a League of Nations or the failures to escape the evils
of reconstruction after great wars to the absence of great men,
but to attribute these failures to the absence of the needed cultural
elements in the social conditions. For will power alone is no more
competent to produce a certain form of social organization than
it is to produce a flying machine. A flying machine depends upon
the contributory mechanical elements. So social organization depends upon contributory social elements. When a people is looking for a Moses to lead them out of the wilderness, the failure
of such a savior to appear may always easily be laid to a shortage
of exceptional ability, but it may be more realistic to attribute
the absence of a great leader to the condition of social economic
life.

But even granting that the times make the man one may wish
to ask, Does not the man greatly influence the times? Men influence the times because all cultural change must occur through
the medium of human beings. The eminent individual influences
the times, for one man is more influential than another, and there
is such a thing as leadership, even though the leader be the
medium through which the social forces play.

In discussing further how the individual influences his time,
I shall make another reference to the field of inventions. We may
say that the men who invented the steamboat influenced not only
their times but the whole future course of industrial evolution.
Shall we say it was the men who thus influenced their times, or
was it their invention? Men influence their times through their
work. So it was with the men who framed the Constitution of the
United States, a document which shaped the conduct of the
people for a long time to come. So it is with all great men.

It should be noted here, however, that the extent of the influence of great men depends not only on their talent but also on
the favorableness of the social conditions. There is a special time
that is favorable for the invention of a steamboat and for its adoption. So there is a particular time in the course of governmental
development that is favorable for the creation of a republican

constitution and its adoption. Great men thus appear as media in a social process.

The phenomenon of the great man, it is necessary to observe, varies a good deal among the different cultural activities, such as mechanical industry, art, religion, military affairs. For instance, in mechanical development, the psychological elements of personality hardly come into play as much as they do in religion. In those activities where there are opportunities for the influence of personal traits of leadership, the great man has an additional kind of influence, especially among his contemporaries. Also in painting, music, and literature there is opportunity for the influence of personal traits. So that in trying to appraise the role of the great man there is an error in generalizing for all fields of culture.

However, in some of the fields where the great man is very prominent, such as in art and in religion, much is credited to the great man that is due to other factors. For instance, the Christian who attributes to Jesus the invention of the Golden Rule does not know that the Golden Rule is a sort of proverb in a dozen or more different ethical systems. Also, the various schools in painting and in literature are hardly wholly explainable in terms of the great personality. Social valuations and existing cultural elements are also factors in greatness in religion and in art. The nature of military campaigns is such that the great leader has opportunities in such a crisis for spectacular achievement and lasting renown. But there are many other factors in wars than leadership. Economic factors and social organization are mighty influences. The social valuation of leadership in war is also great. So also in statecraft there are powers behind the throne. The Treaty of Versailles was determined by underlying group or public opinion in the respective countries rather than by great men as such.

The relative influence of the different factors in the foregoing illustrations are difficult to determine precisely by measurement. They are speculative and subject to claims and counterclaims. I should like to add one further illustration where the material has been subjected to measurement.

Professor Kroeber,[3] in working on this problem, considered the phenomenon of style and fashion in women's dress. The popular impression is that styles in women's wear are set arbitrarily by a few leading dressmakers. It would seem that here was a situation for a relatively free will. The leader does as he wishes, and the people follow like so many sheep—an extreme instance of the power of the great man. Professor Kroeber, in studying this matter, found a journal that had printed regularly pictures of styles in women's evening dresses for about one hundred years. He measured for each year a number of attributes of these dresses, such as width of skirt and depth of décolletage, and plotted the results on graph paper. If the styles were arbitrarily set we should expect no regular order to the plottings; the remarkable result, however, showed curves as smooth and regular, say, as the curves of business cycles, admittedly a product of social forces. Just what these social forces governing styles and fashion are, may not be known, but the leader certainly does not appear free to do just as he wishes.

The role of the exceptional individual in the social process and the relative dependence of social change and achievement on social forces or on the great man will no doubt be a subject of debate for some time to come. But these results of recent researches do seem to clarify the analysis. Our conclusions are that greatness must be conceived in terms of inherited qualities and environmental traits. The distribution of inherited qualities appears to be such that the inherited abilities of greatness should be plentiful and constant, facts which minimize the importance of the great man, biologically conceived. On the social-forces side, there are two important factors that affect great achievement— the existing cultural materials and the social valuations. These two factors vary greatly over time and by place and hence may be called causes of great achievement. They are of the nature of social forces. Great men are thus the product of their times. They in turn influence their times; that is, their achievements influence

3   A. L. Kroeber, "On the Principle of Order in Civilization as Exemplified by Changes of Fashion," *American Anthropologist*, XXI (1919), 235–63.

the times. The great man is thus a medium in social change. The phenomenon of the great man varies in the different kinds of social activities, and each situation should be separately analyzed as to the relative strength of the different factors. In some cases psychological traits of personality are more important than others. These factors at the present time are only with great difficulty susceptible of precise measurement. But certain extended observations indicate that the production of great men and their influence are strongly conditioned and determined by the particular existing stage of the historical development. The great man and his work appear therefore as only a step in a process, largely dependent upon other factors.

4

STATIONARY AND CHANGING

SOCIETIES *1936*

MODERN society has not made a successful shift to a
condition of change. Many ideas belonging to a time when change
was much slower or even imperceptible hang over into an era of
rapid change and act as a barrier to successful adjustment. There
is some practical advantage, then, in trying to note the traits
characteristic of stationary societies and those that will be found
in societies undergoing rapid change. The value of such a comparison is more than practical, though, in that it should constitute
a chapter in the growing knowledge of social change and, hence,
of society.

Methods and Concepts

There is no stationary society in existence today, and in
changing societies not all elements are rapidly changing. Hence
it is not possible to compare the traits of stationary and changing
societies by simple descriptions of existing phenomena. Nor is it
possible to make straightforward comparisons of societies that
have existed in the past, for the reason that the relatively stationary societies of former times and the changing societies of mod-

Reprinted from the *American Journal of Sociology*, XLII, No. 1 (July,
1936).

ern times have characteristics other than the absence or presence of the factor of change. Thus the simpler cultures are homogeneous as compared with the quite heterogeneous societies of modern times. Primitive societies are smaller in size. Modern societies are more highly organized. Hence observed differences between the relatively stationary societies and those rapidly changing may, theoretically, be due to heterogeneity, size, organization, or some factor other than change. For instance, the difference in attitudes toward morals in primitive and modern conditions is due in part to differences owing to heterogeneity as well as differences due to change.

The segregation of the influence of these other factors, to hold them constant in comparisons, is not possible because of the few cases. Hence resort has to be made to deduction. Thus it is possible to deduce the influence of change on morals as indicated later. Such deduction is not wholly without evidence, however. The data for these inferences and descriptions are drawn from readings of ethnographic reports on the simpler cultures and from observations on modern changing society in this and other countries. To extract from these voluminous materials traits due to change is not easy to do by direct observation. For instance, art has flourished in changing societies, as in ancient Greece or renascent Italy, more than in some stationary society; yet on the average the probable effect of change on art is one of hindrance. But any difficulties which change may make for the development of art are quite overshadowed sometimes by other more powerful influences favorable to it.

The traits covered in this paper are quite too numerous to present here a thoroughgoing analysis of them. Furthermore, the delineations are somewhat overdrawn in the interest of sharpness of presentation, since the purpose is to put a magnifying glass over the influences due to change. The paper therefore takes on the appearance of theory.

The conception of a stationary society is one where the cultural pattern does not change. There are the same tools, houses, economic practices, religion, and ceremonies from one generation to another. The human components change. Ambitions and intrigues flare up and die down. Leaders come and go. The individuals who deviate from the accepted norms will differ from time to time, but the norms remain. There is social movement, but not cultural change.

Experimentation

In a stationary society there is no experimentation with a culture trait, for there is no new cultural trait to experiment with. Long ago, when an invention was new, it was tried out in various ways, but the best way of using it had been tacitly agreed upon and accepted, and other less satisfactory practices were abandoned and avoided. Similarly, in the beginning, improvements were made on the trait, until a time when none others seemed possible. So the trait remained stationary, and the best usages of it were selected. The Hopi Indians plant ten or twelve grains of corn about a foot deep in the sandiest parts of the soil, about ten feet apart—a most unusual procedure in the planting of maize, as judged by the practice of farmers in the corn belt. Yet when Hopi culture of corn was studied by our modern scientific agriculturists there was no improvement that could be suggested, assuming their existing equipment. Indeed, their agricultural methods were considered to be the best under the circumstances. It may be that not every possible experiment had been tried, but the practice of experimenting, undoubtedly present at the inception of the trait, had been given up and forgotten. Hence the power in the rule that "we do it that way because it has always been done that way." In such a society one gets out of the habit of looking for the new.

On the other hand, a changing society is changing because new elements are being introduced. When any new trait is introduced it is tried out in all manner of ways, and modifications are made. Thus, the variety of ways of using a toothbrush, for illustration, are many, and all kinds of improvements are suggested. Many hundreds of patents have been made upon it. It may take thirty or forty years to settle on the best kind of brush and the best method of use, but in the course of time it will be settled. But when new culture traits are being introduced every little while the attitude naturally becomes one of looking for improvements. Instead of thinking the old way is best, one thinks the old way must be bad because it is old. A very good slogan for an age of change is: "There is always a better way."

Fate and Inevitability

A belief in fate is more readily acceptable in a stationary society. Of course, there are many elements that encourage the acceptance of the idea of fate other than an attitude of doing nothing about social conditions. Ignorance is perhaps even more of a determinant. The idea of fate is associated among the stationary societies with the incidents of life about which nothing can be done through changing the cultural conditions.

On the other hand, in changing societies the idea of progress arises. Man's egotism reaches the supreme heights of believing that he can control and direct social evolution. Pragmatism is a suitable philosophy. It also seems very probable that optimism would be more evident in changing societies, although this is a point on which the literature is generally silent. But in the development of the western part of the United States, where the changes were exceedingly rapid, there was a high degree of optimism, so writers generally testify. Nothing seemed inevitable or indeed impossible. It is recognized, of course, that other factors led to such attitudes, such as the favorable economic conditions and the presence of a selected young population. Rapid change put a slight emphasis on the speculative, gambling attitude, especially in business and legislative experiments. Bankruptcy in the less rapidly changing nations of Europe is viewed as a much more serious matter than it is in the United States. Daring may bring rewards, and its failures may not be very serious, since "a man may be down but never out."

It should also be mentioned that under conditions of change in the other direction, that is, under conditions of social disintegration, opposite traits may be found. Change may bring pessimism and despair as well as hope and optimism.

The Past and the Future

In stationary societies the prestige of the past is very great. We learn from experience, and the record of experience is found in the past. When there is no change, the future will be like the past. Hence the very great significance of history as a guide.

On the other hand, when conditions are changing, it is the role of the dead hand of the past which is impressive, rather than its reverence. The people want to get away from the past. This attitude is, of course, more noticeable among the less-favored classes, who want "to turn over a new leaf" in the book of life, like the immigrants who come to the United States looking to the future and wanting to start life anew. The vested interests holding favored positions are more disposed in a period of change to look back to the "good old days."

Elders and Youth

The records of the past are in the hands of the elders rather than the youth. This is particularly true in those cultures without writing. The experiences of the old men in the course of their long lives are the experiences of the ages, since conditions do not change. The wisdom which they have learned will be applicable to the years ahead for youth, since conditions are always the same.

When writing was first developed, societies were not changing as rapidly as now, and the wisdom of the old men was much honored, for they held in their heads all the history there was, together with a knowledge of the ceremonials, the religion, and the philosophy. Eventually, when one or several of them wrote down all this history and wisdom of the past, these particular persons or books acquired a most impressive veneration.

But with books and a future that will be different from the past, power shifts to the young, who have more daring by virtue of the phenomena of growth. There is often conflict between elders and youth in a changing society which could hardly occur in a stationary one. Conditions sometimes change so fast that the era of the parents is greatly different from the era of the children. Mothers and daughters hardly speak the same language. Because of this divergence in attitude and because the attitude of youth is closer to that which will be found in the future, the young people are often superior to the older ones in meeting the new problems.

Authority

As a social force, authority operates differently under stationary and under changing conditions. In the realm of daily behavior in a stationary society it is the authority of the past, of the elders, of public opinion, that disciplines the impulsive natures of the young and of the erring adults. In a changing society such authority is less impressive. There is a greater tendency on the part of the more sensible individuals to base conduct on reason or expediency. Less-social persons, who are not restrained by any respect of authority, must be disciplined by force where reason is not effective. Obedience was considered a great virtue under earlier conditions of less change. In the realm of scholarship, the authority of a great name and of wisdom or learning as such has been replaced by the authority of evidence. This shift in authorities is perhaps more the result of the growth of science rather than of change. Authority is much less in vogue in the schoolroom today than it was formerly. In the realm of religion authority is great, and any weakening of religion results in a weakening of authority. In the realm of action, authority seems the more emphasized in changing societies, because of the breakdown of so many other controls. It is a common saying that in a great crisis there is a tendency toward dictatorships and hence toward authority. When changes are exceedingly rapid, conditions approach a crisis, hence the opportunity for dictatorial authority. Under such conditions of change, when great things are to be done, coercive leadership comes to the fore. When emotional fervor is great, authority becomes respected, much as in religion.

Law

Reverence for law is reverence for authority. In the early part of the historical period, when change was much more slow than now, laws were, like the "common law," the long-established customs on serious issues, expressed in writing. These rules carried the authority of centuries of usage. They were like the laws of the "Medes and Persians," which did not change. Their prestige was almost hypnotic. Violations were probably few. The expression "majesty of the law" is suggestive of the high seat law occupied.

In modern times, invoking the law hardly carries the terror it once did, for most laws now are made by legislatures, often amended, and sometimes repealed. Since they are changed or since they are new, they no longer carry the veneration accorded the law of a more nearly stationary society. Respect for the law tends to decline, and it is difficult to see how it can be revived under rapidly changing conditions. In some cases the laws hardly have time to be learned before they are abrogated, as, for instance, in the case of the National Industrial Recovery Act of President Roosevelt's administration. The condition in which law finds itself is the result of other factors than change alone, notably, the heterogeneity of society; but the factor of change undoubtedly tends to take away admiration for laws and also to increase the violations. Law-breaking would seem to be proportionally greater in a rapidly changing society even if a uniform definition of law could be applied. Other things being equal, crime should be greater in a changing society as compared to a stationary one.

Morals

In a stationary society morals are almost completely different from what they are in a changing one. For in a culture where conditions are the same yesterday, today, and tomorrow, very specific rules of conduct can be laid down and they will be followed with success. But where conditions were different yesterday from today and will be different tomorrow, such detailed specification as to how we should behave in this or that situation can hardly be formulated. To meet the rapidly changing situations, ethicists attempt to generalize the principles back of these itemized codes of conduct, so that they will be applicable to any situation. An illustration is to "act in accord with the principle of the greatest good to the greatest number." But it takes a fairly high I.Q. to apply a principle of this sort to the problems of everyday life. The mid-Victorian rules of behavior were much more easily followed by the average run of human beings. Moral codes in a stationary society were somewhat like the rules of an army camp. They were very specific and so clear that the dumbest person could know what to do in each and every situation. But moral conduct under dynamic conditions is more like problem-solving and calls for intelligence. Problem plays and novels are thus a better way of teaching good conduct today than prescribing specific rules, because they furnish experience in solving problems of conduct, as an experiment in the laboratory, so to speak, in anticipation of a time when they may arise in actual life. The book of Deuteronomy and the Ten Commandments are not as effective today as they were in the time of the ancient Jews.

Mores

In preliterate societies, law, morals, and social-philosophical attitudes are not differentiated. The word "mores" has been used to denote a concept of such major customs and social attitudes found in these stationary societies. The binding nature of these mores over human conduct and viewpoints impressed William Graham Sumner very much. It is easy to see how dominating they may be, since they are something of a combination of social values, law, and morals. But like law and morals their force over human conduct is much more effective in stationary societies than in changing ones. Sumner never applied the idea with much success to modern times. Indeed, it may be questioned whether he realized the inapplicability of this concept, as he interpreted it, to rapidly changing conditions. Nor apparently are the sociologists following Sumner aware of why the concept is applicable only with difficulty to modern times. The conditions that produce the mores are different yesterday, today, and tomorrow; and hence with such rapidity of change, they can hardly be very binding on our conduct. Of course, not everything changes so rapidly in reality as in an assumed dynamic condition. Monogamy as a legalized form of marriage is the same yesterday, today, and tomorrow, and might thus be said to be a part of the mores. But back of the word as a legal expression there are, in reality, practices in connection with matrimony that are not exactly monogamous behavior, which are changing quite rapidly and about which the verdict and the binding power of the mores are not sure. Sumner's book on folkways is chiefly of value for behavior in stationary societies. The devastating effect of change is greater on folkways than on mores.

Fashion

The idea of fashion seems to have little meaning except against the background of change. Therefore in stationary societies there should be no fashion. The wearing of high copper collars by a tribe of Negroes is a custom, but if there were no change it should probably not be called fashion. Though by inference it might be said that it was a fashion found among Negroes but not among Indians. But if fashion is defined as a custom that varies with time, then with increasing change fashions would fluctuate more rapidly, while in stationary societies there would be no such thing.

Manners

Customs in regard to some of the little usages of non-economic life are called manners. They serve to routinize behavior and to keep the ego of the individual from impinging on the feelings of others in regard to these activities. Manners are like morals and laws, and hence the same analysis applies to them. It follows, therefore, that in stationary societies there are good manners, while in rapidly changing societies are found bad manners. Observers generally testify to the good manners of the primitive peoples, and it is rather easy to observe that manners in a modern city are not to be boasted of. Better manners are to be found in isolated rural regions than in the big cities. The words "good" and "bad," as used in connection with manners, have no moral implications. The word "good" in this connection probably means "many and definite." So that a people with good manners have simply many definite rules of conduct applied to certain sectors of life. But in a changing society, as the breakdown of moral codes leads to antisocial conduct and as the decline in the majesty of the law leads to crime, so the absence of manners leads to annoying expressions of the ego. The ego becomes less disciplined and restrained in a changing society.

Suppression of Human Nature

The individual who lives in a group must inhibit various actions that would encroach on the rights of others. So also any individual finds that many wishes and impulses must be denied. Group customs often impose restrictions that are not always in conformity with our animal or biological nature. Thus, Chinese bound the feet of their young females. Monasteries imposed celibacy. Indians fasted for long periods. The impositions in some cultures are much less in violation of biological health than those in others. It is possible that some of the cultures in Polynesia have fewer unhealthy inhibitions than do modern societies, for instance. It is, however, in the nature of group life within a culture to impose restrictions on human conduct. In stationary societies these impositions are fixed, obeyed, and little questioned.

But in changing societies, these inhibitory rules are being broken up by change. Bonds are loosed, as it were; and biological nature tends to break free from its cage. The ego expresses itself more directly, as it does when manners crumble. Sex is more restless against restraints of the specific moral codes. Also acquisitive tendencies are less disciplined. From these remarks it must not be understood that in a rapidly changing society there are no inhibitions. One cannot live in groups or in a culture without inhibitions. Indeed, there can be no controlled bodily movements or choices in conduct without inhibitions. But it is possible for one culture to impose on biological nature more than another. Change itself makes such impositions less probable, other things being equal. As change breaks up the rules, biological nature asserts itself. But since repression of the instincts is caused by many other factors than the one of change, in actual fact rapid change may be correlated at any one time with other factors that make new and stronger restrictions on biological expression. But it would seem that the influence of the factor of change alone is one to release the bonds holding back normal biological activity. Change thus helps to shape a culture more in conformity with biological nature.

Individualization

Walter Bagehot wrote of the "cake of custom" which encrusted mankind before the Greeks. This is so common a phenomenon in primitive societies that at first it was thought that there was little individual variation. Close study has shown, however, that in these primitive societies there is considerable room for temperament and individual display. The "cake of custom" which makes the individual conform is opposed by attempts on the part of the individual to break away and not only to express his wishes suppressed by custom but particularly to express his ego and his personality.

In a stationary society the idea never occurs that the situation of tension between custom and individual desire can be lessened by changing culture, because there is no idea that the culture can change. There is no outlet for the frustration in such a tension in changing the culture pattern, as there is in a changing society. It is highly probable that in these stationary societies religion often offers an outlet. The outlet in the form of a belief in a heaven is obvious. For life on this earth, the beliefs and rituals serve to socialize the deviant, even, at times, extreme types. Individualization is then found in religious practices.

In stationary societies, since there is no idea of changing the culture pattern and since religion as an outlet has a more or less fixed pattern, the adjustment between man and culture takes the route of adjusting man to culture and not culture to man. Hence the emphasis on morals, character, self-control, obedience, etc. Such is the only way. But in a changing society, with emphasis on progress and changing culture, there is less concern with discipline and more with self-expression.

So, as the rigidity of customs tends to break up with change, the individual, as contrasted to the institution, emerges more to the front. This is particularly noticeable in the family; in a stationary society the individual is known as a member of a family, oftentimes more than he is known as an individual, and carries the family stamp with him. But in a modern changing city, no one knows much about the family of a person; the individual is more prominent. So also in education the trend is away from discipline and toward self-expression and a consideration of the personality of the child.

Of course, it is recognized that no matter what the influence of the factor of change alone may be, changing conditions may be associated with more restraints, as, for instance, in the growing power of the state, for reasons other than change.

Caste and Class

A caste system of social classes can be imagined in a rapidly changing society, but it is much easier to see it in a stationary society. The reason is that culture is an integrated whole, and no two groups can hardly exist side by side without some intercorrelation of activities affecting the welfare of each. For instance, in the United States what happens to the Negro also affects the whites. Their wages are thus governed by the same forces. So if change is taking place in one part of society, it is likely to be affecting the other parts. In this way change tends to break up class systems. In a stationary society the barrier between classes is after all only a collection of rigid customs and can be maintained as long as there is no change. Though there are a larger number of classes and groups, the obstacles to crossing from one to another are probably not getting greater for a young person. In our society of great change, even if democracy should decline, it is probable that there will be rather less than more of caste and class.

Sentiment and Ceremony

Sentiment develops with repetition of some pleasant habit. Thus there is sentiment about particular places that we often visit or sentiment about a person with whom we frequently associate. Home and family, church and flag, are foci of sentiment.

A first experience, on the contrary, brings with it no sentiment. Adventure and sentiment are not commonly associated. Novelty is different, and it takes time for sentiment to develop. Hence a stationary society is one where certain culture traits encourage the development of sentiment. If the patterns change rapidly enough, the shifting culture traits may call forth little sentiment. We become sentimental about the old homestead. But we feel little sentiment for an apartment when we move every two years.

Ceremonies and rituals are a particular class of customs with a touch of sentiment. They are very common in stationary societies. And it would appear that the influence of change is to discourage ritual and ceremony. On the other hand, ceremony is associated often with the infrequent; hence, change affects it less. But ceremony is repetitive, and the conditions may be changed sufficiently to cause it to be discarded.

Sentiment and ceremony then grow up around the various social institutions. The family is a complex of sentiments and rituals in regard to home, mother, birth, death, etc. It is the pillar of society. So it is with the church and so with the community. But when the family is undergoing rapid change, the sentiment often weakens and sometimes is even turned into humor. The ceremonials of marriage, of mourning, and of christening of the infant become less widespread. Change then tends to divest the changing institutions and culture traits of sentiment, a fact often regretted by the poet and artist.

Art

Why art flowers at a particular time and why it does not among certain people have undoubtedly a variety of explanations, depending on the situation. Little is known on the subject. Art is, like any other culture trait, the result of many factors. How does the factor of change affect art? The answer is not at all certain or clear, but it seems probable that a stationary society favors art more than a changing one. First, it may be noted that art depends on an art tradition which may be more significant in a stationary society. Furthermore, the symbols which it employs are more likely to have wider acceptance in a stationary society. Certainly the symbols of much modern art have little common currency. Art is also associated with sentiment, ritual, and ceremony, which change tends to break up. Art forms and symbols are greatly enriched by the associations of ideas that cluster about them. A changeless art form or pattern gathers meaning as we experience it more. On the other hand, we easily get surfeited with too much sentiment, and there is undoubtedly a demand for the new in art. So, on the other side, change may bring something like fashion in art. Furthermore, the effect of change on art is to individualize it into more of the artist's own personal self-expression and to encourage the artist to be less considerate of the socialization of the symbols. This individualization is quite characteristic in modern art. In the practical arts a different sort of observation may be made. The first expression of a new invention neglects the art form, as, for illustration, the early automobile. It is only after most of the practical useful improvements have been added that the artistic side is then turned to and exploited. There is thus a good deal to be said for the theory that a stationary society favors art more than a changing one, other things being equal.

Religion

Social change is of course transcended by religion. Nevertheless, social change may modify greatly the form that religion takes. Religion is here conceived of in the social sense of being a complex of functions centering around a belief in some higher entity or entities, the conception of which is not scientifically determined, yet concerning which there are emotional reactions affording a relief and a comfort hardly found among the many frustrations of ordinary daily group life in the culture under which one lives. In a stationary society, when there is no conception of progress and no thought of social improvement, it is natural that the individual turns to religion as an outlet for hope. Furthermore, in a stationary society the particular set of institutions and customs that lead to frustrations are persistent, and the types of frustrations are standardized. Hence it is possible there to standardize a set of ideologies and beliefs which will afford an outlet to the frustrations. Furthermore, in so far as ethics is a part of the religious complex, the stationary society favors that type of religion more than does a changing society.

In a rapidly changing society it is difficult to guess the form which religion will take. But one would think that certain supreme values would be found associated with the idea af progress, and one would also expect these values to be attached to social institutions or movements effective in attempts toward progress. There are actually, in the changing society that we know, plenty of frustrations, not all due to the factor of change, of course. Perhaps there are more than in most of the very slowly changing societies. There is, on this score alone, much need of religion, though it is recognized that there are other outlets and that the psychological basis of religion is wider than frustrations. The religion in a changing society may be then less moralistic, less ritualistic, and perhaps more closely associated with social agencies of betterment.

Radicals and Conservatives

In stationary societies the attitudes of radicals and conservatives would hardly arise since there is no change to favor or disfavor. But in a changing society it is difficult to see how the issue of radicalism and conservatism can be escaped. Indeed, it will hardly be confined to politics or economics but should be found in regard to every social institution.

The Culture Pattern as a Whole

The different parts of culture are interrelated, of course. Recreation is related to religion. The family is related to economic structures. The state and family both govern. Custom and police exercise in part the same function. Culture, then, is somewhat like a watch in that the different parts must be fit nicely together. In a stationary society these interrelationships of the whole have all been worked out. The structure is nicely adjusted. It was previously noted that in a stationary society any particular trait, such as an invention, had already been improved to the limit (without assuming another invention), and that many possible usages of it had been experimented with, and the most effective one under the conditions had been chosen for use while the others were discarded as a result of the trial-and-error process.

As it is with a single culture trait, so it is also with the interrelationships of all the traits that go to make up the pattern of the culture as a whole. As one trait after another has come in, various relationships to the pattern have been tried out and the most suitable one adopted, so that there comes to be a balance to the culture configuration. This balance is good because it is the result of many trials. This nicety of balance is achieved, of course, not with wholesale experimentation with all the traits at once, as one might try out the blocks in a picture puzzle. But, rather, as each trait has been added, the balance has been shifted just a little back and forth until equilibrium has been restored. There may thus be said to be a true balance in stationary societies, and the presumption is that a better configuration is not likely to be found, given only the existing inventions and traits. There is thus a harmonious relationship. This harmony of the existing elements has, of course, persisted for some time, since it is by definition a stationary society. There has thus grown up a set of values and sentiments around the pattern, so that the whole has a certain artistic appearance.

In a changing society the situation is quite different. The new is being frequently introduced into the pattern. Before sufficient experimentation with the usage of a new trait can be carried out, still another new trait has come in which renders the other more or less obsolete, and the process of improvement, of trial and error, starts all over again, before any one trait can be properly assimilated. The arrangement of parts is in more or less turbulent motion, a sort of chronic imbalance.

This situation may be described in terms of change rather

than of pattern. What happens is that in one part of culture a new change is precipitated by virtue of some invention, social or mechanical. But this part thus affected is correlated with another part which has no such invention, causing it to change at the same rate of speed. So the harmonious relationship between the two parts is disturbed. There is said to be a maladjustment between the two parts, because one part has changed and the other has not. Thus, there may be said today to be maladjustment between religion and science, because science has changed more rapidly than religion. This imbalance in the pattern results in a series of maladjustments between the parts. In a changing society the different parts are changing at unequal rates of speed, thereby causing a series of maladjustments. There are stresses and strains in the whole structure. It may be true that any one new trait is an improvement and leads to a better adjustment between the individual and his culture, yet the effect on the structure as a whole is to produce a torsion. The whole pattern has then the aspect of the frontier, the first approximation, the behavior of the *nouveau riche.* It seems rough and unfinished and is particularly displeasing to the artist because the values and sentiments belonging to the stationary culture have not yet found their place in such a maladjusted society. There is, then, no maladjustment of parts in a stationary society, that is, of traits, though there may be much maladjustment of biological nature with culture. Maladjustment of parts, however, is a distinguishing characteristic of the culture in a changing society.

Characteristics of Stationary Societies

In stationary societies what is done is good because it has always been done. Experimentation or new methods would not be looked upon with favor if they should be presented. The prestige of the past is exceptionally great, and the elders who know it best are greatly respected. Fate and inevitability are accepted, and since there is little thought of changing conditions, efforts toward adjustment are directed toward modifying human behavior, particularly by inhibitions and control. Those who succeed have character. Authority of the past and of elders counts. Law is majestic; rules of moral conduct are set forth in detail and are followed. The mores are strictly obeyed, and deviation from them not permitted. The people have excellent manners. There is likely to be a good deal of sentiment attached to institutions. Ritual and ceremonialism are prominent. The conditions are favorable for art, religion, and for class lines. Especially is a stationary society a well-balanced, harmonious society.

Characteristics of a Changing Society

In a changing society the attitude is one of seeking improvement. There is always a better way. The new tends to be favored somewhat. Progress is a feature of the social mind. Optimism tends to prevail, and the social philosophy may favor pragmatism. The past is like a dead hand, something to get away from. The position of youth is strong, and young men often rise to influence. Authority as power yields to reason and evidence, but in crises dictators arise. There is no great respect for law, and crime is more frequent. Moral codes are ineffective, and good conduct rests upon intelligence in problem-solving. Mores are of slight significance. Manners are bad, and the egos of others become very annoying. Behavior is more in accordance with biological nature and animal tendencies. Sentiment about institutions does not flourish while the ceremonial tends to decline. Conditions do not favor rigid barriers between the classes, and the milieu is somewhat difficult for art. Traditional religion finds a more hostile environment. There is no great harmony in culture. The times seem out of joint, and there is much maladjustment between the different parts of culture, due to the lagging of some changes behind others. The different parts of culture are moving at unequal rates of speed.

5

INVENTIONS, POPULATION,

AND HISTORY *1942*

THE THESIS of this paper is that inventions affect the size of populations and in this manner influence history. That inventions have helped shape the events of past history is obvious, but not always appreciated. However, in the assessment of factors affecting the events of the past it is believed that invention has not received the emphasis it should have received if the various factors were given their proper weighting. For instance, America would hardly have been discovered and settled by white peoples if there had not been a boat of adequate size. Sails and a compass also were essentials in making the settlement of the New World, but the usual account gives no credit to these inventions, although the names of the ships are recorded. This is natural. Historians, of course, attribute this discovery to Columbus. Indeed, more credit is given to Queen Isabella of Spain than to the invention of the boat.

Inventions, of course, are not wholly neglected by historians. It is the custom, for instance, to mention in history how armies fighting with gunpowder overcame those equipped with bows and

Reprinted from *Studies in the History of Culture*, ed. Percy Long (Menasha, Wis.: Geo. Banta Publishing Co. for the American Council of Learned Societies, 1942).

arrows. But in the main, inventions are not greatly emphasized by historians in their concern with particular events.

In establishing the control of England over the seas in the nineteenth century, the deeds of her great naval heroes such as Lord Nelson are recounted, and properly so; but it remains a fact that the success England derived from her great empire rested in large part on attaching the steam engine to her ships, and the greatness of the premiers of England in foreign policy during the long reign of Queen Victoria rests in large part upon England's early attainment of the armored warship propelled by steam.[1] There is even a tendency to associate this Golden Age of England with the leadership of Queen Victoria herself. No doubt Queen Victoria was a good queen, but it is also probable that the greatness attributed to her is due to the remarkable success of England as a world power during her reign. The queen was the symbol of a great era; the achievements of the time really were determined by a series of successful inventions adopted by England before the other states of Europe acquired them.

I

That the success of leaders is sometimes due to possession of superior mechanical techniques on the part of their followers is one of the main points in the controversy over the role of the great man and of social forces in history. The tendency to explain history in terms of great men has been frequently discussed. Indeed, it is quite natural to describe achievements in terms of leaders. Medals are given to men for conspicuous deeds, but no one has ever heard of a medal being pinned upon an invention.

Such mechanical and hidden forces as inventions tend to elude the pen of writers. The working of some machine is not inherently as interesting as the human drama of war, debate, exploration, intrigues, or ambitions. These social forces are usually seen as economic, and there is a great body of literature concerned with the economic interpretation of history,[2] and there has grown up

---

[1]   Bernard Brodie, *Sea Power in the Machine Age* (1941).

[2]   E. R. A. Seligman, *Economic Interpretation of History* (2d ed. rev., 1924).

a great school of economic historians who are concerned with these impersonal and hidden forces that have determined the events of the past. But back of economic forces are inventional changes, as Karl Marx rightly emphasized. The inventional interpretation of history is, indeed, like the economic interpretation of history, only one step removed.

There are, though, two kinds of economic interpretations of history that have not in general been adequately distinguished in critiques of this type of history. One is the history which posits the movements of man as being essentially concerned with selfishness. This role of selfish interest is especially noted in class situations in society. An illustration of this type of economic interpretation is the work of Charles Beard on the origins of the Constitution of the United States.[3] Ordinarily the framers of the Constitution of the United States have been thought to be seeking, in a somewhat noble and disinterested manner, a document which would be the basis of the welfare of the common people of a democracy; whereas the work of Beard indicates that the framers were seeking selfishly their own class interest, which would prosper best without too much control being given over to the people.

The other kind of economic interpretation of history is one which does not emphasize the selfish motive so much as the force of economic factors. On this plane of analysis the great force in modern history was capitalism,[4] a monetary economy resting upon a great variety of economic organizations, such as corporations, banks, trust companies, exchanges, and labor unions. These economic structures were made possible by such social inventions as the division of labor, the wage system, and rates of interest. Thus, much of the activity of the nineteenth and twentieth centuries in Europe and America, which is the subject matter of modern historians, is to be accounted for in terms of these economic forces centering around capitalism.[5] This second type of

[3]   Charles A. Beard, *An Economic Interpretation of the Constitution of the United States* (1935).

[4]   Werner Sombart, *Der moderne Kapitalismus* (1928).

[5]   Louis M. Hacker, *The Triumph of American Capitalism* (1940).

economic interpretation of history concerns the materials of economic history. Usually, however, economic historians describe the economic trends without relating the superstructures of political and social organizations with this economic organization. Such a task of correlating cause and effect in economic forces and political consequences is very difficult if scientific standards are maintained.

If this analysis were carried one step further, back of the economic organizations, there would come a technological interpretation of history. The argument here presented is that the explanation of history would be somewhat better achieved if there were added a further explanation of the inventional influence back of the rise and variations of economic forces.

A very good illustration of the inventional interpretation of history is the history of the Great Plains[6] area in the United States, which in its early development was essentially an open range country for cattlemen. There were no woods, and the rainfall was too slight for agriculture. The westward movement of population passed it by because the woodland culture which they possessed was not adapted to the plains. Conquering of the plains came later, largely through three inventions—the six-shooter pistol, barbed wire, and the windmill.

II

Since the technology back of the economic organizations rests upon invention it is desirable to discuss the characteristics of invention. The word "invention," as used here, carries a broad meaning and covers not only the concept of mechanical invention but also discoveries in applied science. Thus the discoveries regarding antitoxins and the germ theory of disease would be classed under this broad concept as inventions. So also the domestication of cattle is of the general nature of inventions. In general, discoveries in pure science would not be thought of as inventions affecting history until these discoveries became practicable. Thus the discovery of the Hertzian waves did not become an influence in society until it acquired some practicable form as in the radio.

6   Walter Prescott Webb, *The Great Plains* (1931).

It is, therefore, the radio that influenced history rather than the discovery of the Hertzian waves.

The idea of invention is sometimes extended to include social invention. New types of social organization, of new art, or of religious forms—as, for instance, the League of Nations, or the literary essay, or the religious revival meeting—would then be called social inventions. It is quite desirable under some conditions to so extend the concept as to cover social organizations and new patterns in non-material culture. Such is particularly the case in studying social change, but it is necessary in this paper to eliminate from the idea of invention these extensions into the field of non-material culture.

Another characteristic of invention is its evolutionary nature. To most users of the term an invention appears to be born fully developed, like Venus out of the sea. In fact, however, the birth of an invention requires a period of gestation and a long period of development. For inventions to have widespread influence they must be relatively durable, simple to operate, and easy to repair. Hence, their appearance in the past is not quite as quick and dramatic as is customarily described. It took a long time for gunpowder to be used effectively in cannons. It seems to have been thus used as early as the fourteenth century, but gunpowder did not become a significant force in history until a century or more later, when it was influential in changing the feudal system. This slow development of inventions may be part of the explanation as to why their appreciation as forces in history tends to escape historians. The sudden, quick, and dramatic events of history, especially those centering around personal achievement and deeds, are more readily observable than these slow movements.

Particularly likely to be missed by writers is the influence of small inventions. The steamboat, for instance, was a large and spectacular one, and hence, difficult to overlook. The terms "large" and "small" in being applied to inventions do not refer to their physical dimensions but to their influence. Large inventions are those that are significant in their social effects. The small inventions are measured in the millions, while the larger inventions are measured in the thousands. While the illustrations and discussions that follow will be chosen mostly from the large inventions, it should not be forgotten that the cumulative force of small inventions is significant for history, too.

Inventions are seen in the theory being set forth here as a force. How can so material an object as an invention be a force? If the course of history is determined by social forces, how can technology be a social force? History is, by common agreement, the record of the behavior of human beings, and the forces of history are the activities of mankind. In other words, if there were no human beings and hence no human behavior, there would be no history. Social forces, therefore, flow from human beings and groups of individuals. When the phrase "the force of invention" is used, or when "technological forces" are implied, what is meant is that invention or technology serves as a new stimulus for groups of individuals to behave in different ways. The force is always resident in the physiological structure of the human organism, but inventions set up new customs and new social institutions because human beings react to inventions in new ways. Thus, railroads were a force in building cities. In fact, railroads ushered in the era of cities. Before then the proportion of the population in cities in any country was quite small. Now the railroad is the result of a mobile steam engine on a roadway made of two rails. Human beings react to these iron rails and mobile engines as stimuli by building cities. It is in this sense, therefore, that inventions become a force in history. They stimulate human activity.

III

The foregoing remarks sketch out quite generally a theory of inventions and history. The purpose of this paper, however, is not to explore this whole general field of the relation of invention to history but rather to discuss a limited part of it. This part concerns the effect of invention on population, that is, numbers of people. Since population aggregates of various sizes affect history, then inventions influence history indirectly by varying the size of human populations.

In exploring this thesis, populations are thought of as units of various sizes. At certain times in history the significant unit of population is the local community. At other times the significant unit may be the population of a large area, such as a state. Another population unit is an army. There are, then, a great variety of population units differing in kind and size.

The influence of population changes on history lies in the shaping of general processes instead of being the direct and immediate cause of unique events. The term "history" will be used not so much as a record of events as an account of social movements and of civilizational developments. A particular event, such as the decision of President Wilson to attend the Peace Conference in Paris, is not illuminated very much by any statistics of population. On the other hand, the rise of the United States as a power among nations distinctly rests upon population. That history, so conceived, is affected by population will be readily admitted. The population of France in the seventeenth century was probably four or five times the population of England at that time, while in the twentieth century they were about equal in numbers. The historical relationships of these two countries were undoubtedly affected by the ratio of their populations. For the exposition of this thesis it then becomes desirable to describe the ways in which inventions affect the sizes of populations and ensuing historical movements.

As a first point it may be observed that some inventions affect population directly. A very good illustration is contraceptives. This invention in its modern form was adopted in France in the early part of the nineteenth century and not in the other countries of the world until the latter part of the nineteenth century, thus producing differentials in population growth that were significant for history. Thus at the time of the beginning of the First World War the birth rate of Germany was very much greater than that of France and may have been a factor in causing the war. The population of northwestern Europe and, indeed, of the United States will become a diminishing population within a few decades largely because of this invention. It does not seem probable that this will be the case so soon with the Slavic countries or possibly with southern and southeastern European nations. Nor is the birth rate of Japan and the Orient likely to fall soon to so great a degree.[7] Consequently, it will produce new differentials between the sizes of the populations of the various states, which will undoubtedly influence the history of the coming years, especially in the competitive rivalry of states.

Another illustration is the epochal discoveries of the past century in medicine which have reduced the number of deaths. The result of these discoveries, plus the development of sanitation, has been a reduction of the death rate from 30 or 40 per 1,000 to almost a third these rates. The effect of the reduction of deaths has, of course, been compensated for in population growth by the reduction of births, which occurred at the same time and at nearly the same rate for a time; but in the future the death rate will rise while the birth rate will probably fall in the countries of the Western world. This control of disease makes possible, of course, the settlement of regions otherwise difficult, such as had been the area of the Panama Canal.

Another way in which inventions affect population is through food. At the time that Malthus wrote and earlier, variations in the food supply caused significant changes in populations. Today the actual changes in the amount of food probably do not cause such great changes in numbers, though always food is necessary to maintain populations. Hence, inventions affecting food affect population. There have been in the past thousand years many inventions relating to the supply of food, such as fertilizers, the rotation of crops, and the storage of food. These agricultural inventions applied somewhat more successfully to the population of France than to the population of Italy and led to the power of France during the late Middle Ages. Again, England's population has recently become the equal in numbers to that of France because of inventions affecting food. The British are able to obtain a much larger food supply by importation than they could if they were dependent upon their own agricultural land.

The idea of importation leads to a consideration of another way in which invention affects population, namely, transporta-

[7]   Warren S. Thompson, *Danger Spots in the World's Population* (1929).

tion. Transportation affects the size of an area in two ways—by bringing food and by moving human beings. Transportation, for instance, has abolished famines; and urban populations would be impossible if it were not for transportation, since the city is a local unit where the inhabitants are not able to raise the food they eat but must import. There are, of course, other inventions affecting the city, but food supply by railroads, boats, and trucks is quite essential. Cities are also a phenomenon resting upon the migration of human beings, that is to say, their transportation. Cities do not maintain their populations, since either the death rate is higher than the birth rate or the birth rate is lower than the death rate. Mathematically these statements are the same but not sociologically. In medieval London, for instance, it was impossible for the birth rate to equal the death rate, for the death rate was very high. In modern London the birth rate is so low that the death rate cannot be made to equal it. Hence, cities maintain themselves by migrations from farms and smaller places. Therefore, inventions affecting transportation affect populations. Other illustrations of more historical significance might be cited. The settlement of the New World could only have taken place under conditions of good transportation. In Asia and Europe the horse has led successive migrations from the Arabian Desert and from the steppes of Russia which have profoundly affected the course of European history. The coming of the Norsemen depended upon the excellent boats possessed by the Vikings. Thus, the role of the Norsemen in medieval Europe was the result of inventions related to transportation by sea.

Still another influence of invention on population occurs through the manufacturing of tools. This is very well illustrated by that great collection of inventions which gave rise to the Industrial Revolution of the nineteenth century. The population of Europe doubled during this century. At the same time it distributed her sons and daughters all over the world. This phenomenal multiplication of population during the past century and a half is attributed by students to the inventions centering around steam power and to the accompanying achievements in medical progress.[8] The development of manufacturing and the various organizations of the capitalistic system meant employment for larger and larger numbers of workers. This increase in workers could only have been possible with an increase in the food supply, either by imports or by agricultural improvements. That the coming of the machine age to the Orient will lead to a similar expansion of population is not certain, because of the spreading of another invention, contraceptives, which was subsequent to the Industrial Revolution in England. Birth control might even precede factories in China. It is possible to have an industrial revolution in the Orient without an increase in population, if numbers are kept down by contraceptives.

Still another way in which inventions affect population is through war. This is seen in the conquest of America by the whites. When the Spaniards came in contact with the American Indians, they possessed the horse, armor, sword, and gun; none of which the Indians had. It was, therefore, relatively easy for Cortez to conquer vast numbers of Indians with a handful of Spaniards so well equipped. The invention of the stirrup was especially significant in the development of cavalry, thus enabling the horse to play a very great role in history. Indeed, the domesticated horse, even without the invention of the stirrup, was one of the greatest war instruments known in early times, since it made quick attacks and quick getaways possible.

The bombing airplane and tank give an advantage to those larger countries possessing them in numbers which is comparable in some ways to the superiority of the Spaniards over the Indians or the horsemen of the Arabian Desert over the sedentary populations.

From the preceding paragraphs it can be seen that inventions affect population in a variety of ways, directly and indirectly, through birth rates and death rates and by migration and distribution. It is only by the recognition of the variety of ways in which these different inventions influence population that we can appreciate their significance for history.

[8]   Warren S. Thompson, *Population Problems* (2d ed., 1935).

IV

The subject has been discussed from the point of view of inventions that affect population. It is now desired to approach the subject from the other end, that is, to note certain significant changes in history and observe how they have been produced by changes in population and in inventions. The first illustration concerns the rise and fall of states. At any one time in history one state is predominant over another. Sometimes one people is thought of as carrying the "torch of civilization" which is later passed to another people. Thus Greece was at one time in the lead; at another, Rome; and so on. Perhaps the torch of civilization is not the right symbol; perhaps it would be better to speak of one state being an economic vanguard. In any case, the economic prominence of the eastern Mediterranean area rested upon a fortunate concurrence of a number of inventions occurring within a few thousand years. These were copper, bronze, iron, the alphabet, the horse, cattle, the wheel, and the boat. The peoples in other parts of the globe had no such happy concurrence of inventions. Hence, the Mediterranean peoples were given a tremendous lead over the other peoples of the world by the possession of such a remarkable set of great inventions. The definite proof and establishment of why one country takes dominance over another cannot be demonstrated, of course, without a great deal of research and investigation on the part of many workers, but the general theory can be illustrated quite briefly. It can hardly be questioned that England's priority in the nineteenth century was due to the power inventions producing the Industrial Revolution; to inventions in shipping plus the fortunate location, of course, of the island; and to the possession of coal and iron. This in no way minimizes the character of the English people. Explanations of the prominence in history of one people or country can be approached from this point of view rather than from the point of view of racial abilities. But Greece and Rome could not possibly have assumed the lead over England after the inventions using steam, because they had no coal and iron. Other inventions will produce other shifts among peoples in the future.

The history of the medieval and modern world was, as a further illustration, greatly affected by the inventions producing a series of agricultural revolutions. One of these is taking place at the present time. It is the application of mechanical power to the farms. During the Industrial Revolution mechanical power was supplied to the handicrafts. Farms were only indirectly affected, for mechanical power was not applied to the plow and hoe as it was to the handicrafts. Now, a hundred years later, farms are experiencing this same application of mechanical power through the gasoline engine, though, instead of through the steam engine.

In earlier times there was the agricultural revolution that attended the discovery of the three-field system. Indeed, it is argued that the practices that were developed with the transfer from the two-field to the three-field system in northern Europe increased agricultural efficiency enormously. Some interpreters of history, indeed, are disposed to explain the shifting of economic power from the Mediterranean to northwestern Europe as a result of agricultural revolutions, that is to say, of inventions improving agricultural production. The three-field system was not especially suited to low rainfall and general climatic conditions of the Mediterranean. The heavy plow also favored northern Europe, as compared with the Mediterreanean area. Parenthetically, the reader should remember that, although such great changes can be made only by clusters of inventions and writers have acquired the shorthand method of signalizing these by the central invention. Thus the Industrial Revolution is thought of as due to the invention of the steam boiler and steel-making. So the agricultural revolution rests upon various subsidiary inventions among which are the iron plow, which really might be considered a major invention as would also be the knowledge of fertilizers and the restoration of nitrogen to the soil by certain legumes.

Another phenomenon of history resting on population and invention is the shift of power from farms to great cities. The urban population of any large area before the railroads was probably never more than 10 or 15 per cent, if so much. It was the railroads and the factory system that brought in the cities. Today, of course, we have a great urban nation and a great urban civilization which has really furnished for man a quite new type of environment. Wealth is in industrial centers rather than on the farms. The cities are further being changed in the twentieth century by the automobile into what are called "metropolitan areas." The cities of the nineteenth century, produced by the railroad, are being changed into the metropolitan areas of the twentieth century by the automobile.

V

Great historical phenomena have then been brought about by clusters of great inventions. It is now desirable to go further back than the historical period and to see how certain developments before written records have been the result of inventions.

The earliest culture of mankind that we know is hunting and food-gathering without benefit of seed-planting and domestication of animals. Man in very early times hunted not only wild animals and game of various sizes, but he probably spent more time gathering roots and herbs than he did trapping, killing, and fishing, except in special localities. This stage of culture is usually known as the period of lower hunters. It rested upon relatively simple tools such as those possessed by the Australian natives or the Tierra del Fuegians. They had some traps, spears, and throwing sticks. There was no pottery, but some basketry. Their clothing was generally of the simplest. The effect of this simple technology on population was to maintain only very small groups, often five or six families of 20 or 30 individuals. With such small groups it can be seen that the elaboration of social life into other groupings, classes, and associations could not be very great. Furthermore, these small bands did not live generally in one place very long or, if they did, wandered out as hunters from a central location as a base. Hence, the wandering life meant a restriction of social institutions. This culture rested upon a simple technology with very few mechanical inventions. History was quite different with peoples on so slender a technological base from what it is with us, possessing such an elaborate structure.

Among other hunting people the technology became more elaborate. There were bows and arrows, sleds and other means of transportation, the domesticated dog, quite elaborate traps and fishing devices. In the case of the higher hunters the population unit was a good deal larger. It was sometimes a hundred or more individuals. Hence, there was more division of labor in their social system. A priest class began to arise. There were age societies and further elaboration of sex and age divisions in the group. As to more exact population statistics, Murdock has computed the average population of a community or band of hunters (lower and advanced) with no agriculture or herding. The average population of a band for ten such peoples was 45 persons. The population of a unit of hunting peoples was, furthermore, not very large because they had no way of storing food. Their economic life was essentially one of feast and famine.

Presently, however, a very important discovery was made, the domestication of large animals, which in a few localities led to a life of herding. These animals were not at that time located on farms. Herding of domesticated animals meant a more reliable supply of meat than could be obtained by hunting wild animals. The population unit increased in size. Murdock finds an average of 160 persons.[9]

As the domestication of animals led to a more continuous supply of meat, the domestication of plants led to a more abundant supply of plant food. The discovery of the planting of seeds and the invention of the digging stick led to agriculture in a simple form. The digging stick was used for resetting roots or for planting grass seeds. With such arts the food supply became more stable. Thus again the numbers of the population were increased. Villages were then the rule, and with a stable village life came possibilities of further specialization and division of labor among social groups. This type of agriculture is known as the hoe culture, and Professor Murdock's figures show an average community of 330 persons. Among primitive peoples who have both agriculture and hunting, the size of the population unit is still larger. It becomes, according to Murdock's figures, a village of about 450 persons.

Eventually there appeared another significant invention—the

9   From a paper made available to the author.

plow, which was quite superior to the hoe. It was more productive, led to a greater yield per unit of cultivated land, and made possible the applications of animal power to agriculture. The plow culture produced villages that are not greatly different from those we know today and a social life that was not so markedly different from that found in hamlets and villages in Colonial America, for Colonial America was a plow culture in the advanced stages. With the plow and domestication of animals, farming could support villages of several hundreds or even thousands of population. Consequently, a new order of social life was ushered in.

The boat became a very effective invention when coupled with the plow culture. Primitive peoples who live on water have some kind of water transportation. The simplest form is a log or a dugout, but when agriculture is fairly highly developed and when the wheel has appeared, the boat has by this time become a fairly elaborate instrument for travel. The combination of all these makes cities. The plow culture distributed civilization along the fertile river valleys. The hunting peoples lived, in main, on the edges of woodlands. The boat, wheel, and plow shift the population to the water edges either of big rivers, big lakes, or small seas. Thus the locale of historical events was again shifted in the direction of water transportation. Eventually came the steam boiler and steel, which produced another great shift already described. Mechanical power tends to move the center of civilization again to the regions which have access to coal and iron. The predominance of the river-valley nations is lessened with the coming of steam. The age of steam is not focused on any narrow area but rather shows its greatest manifestations in some big area that is relatively close or has access to coal and iron. The area is large because of the accompanying development of transportation.

VI

This theory has concerned history, history as a record of the past. Hence, it is not very appropriate to speculate concerning the role of invention and population for the future. But if the principle is once established and found to be widespread, namely, that inventions affect the size of populations and the size of populations affects historical developments, then it is to be expected that these same forces will shape the future as they have shaped the past.

It is beyond the province of this paper to say what the future may be like because of inventions, but it is certainly to be expected that the invention of electricity, which distributes power so easily, will be a factor. It is also thought that the chemical inventions, which are coming so rapidly to transform one substance into another, will be very influential. Steam power was able to transform the shape of one object into another. Chemistry transforms one material into another. Chemistry has greatly influenced the nationalism of Germany, for instance. Then again the inventions which are the most brilliant of our present era are the communication inventions—radio, television, facsimile transmission, motion pictures, sound-recording—all of which will be influential in the distribution of population. The twentieth century is also characterized by great developments in transportation. We are only seeing the beginning of the airplane. Its effect upon war is particularly spectacular, and it is apparently having an effect upon the amalgamation and enlargement of governmental units. When steep-flight aircraft are developed, a wider distribution of population around cities is to be expected. Indeed, significant inventions seem to be coming with greater rapidity than in the past, and it is hoped that the historians of the future will put emphasis on the social forces that arise from inventions.

6

TECHNOLOGY AS ENVIRONMENT

1956

AN AMUSING pastime is to visit a zoo and guess the natural
environment in which the animal lived before it was penned up in
a cage. The warm coat of the penguin suggests a cold climate, and
the big bodies of the bison indicate an area with plenty of vegetation. Without close examination, though, one might not guess
certain sheep as dwellers of steep, rocky mountains. A biologist,
of course, can make a more precise delineation of the habitat of
an animal.

The key to success in this guessing game is the idea of
adjustment between the animal and the environment, a concept
which Charles Darwin has immortalized. Indeed, environment
can be defined as something to which animals and plants adjust.

The environment to which plants and animals are adjusted we
call natural environment, and we think of it in terms of temperature, altitude, precipitation, atmosphere, soil, water, light, dark-
ness, other animals, and vegetation. But there are other environ-
ments. For instance, there is a social environment. Many insects
and higher animals live in groups, as do bees, termites, wolves,
cattle, apes, and, notably, human animals. Thus men must adjust

Reprinted from *Sociology and Social Research*, XLI (September–October, 1956).

to their community as well as to nature. The social environment is in addition to the natural environment.

I am now to introduce to you still another environment for man—technology—that is, the material products of technology, which is the implication of the word "technology" in the title. The word is used loosely to comprise the applications of scientific discovery and the material products of technology. In short, it includes the objects of material culture. Thus a technological environment consists of such fabricated objects as buildings, vehicles, processed foods, clothing, machines, ships, laboratories. As an illustration, an urban employee working with the machines in a factory would be working in a technological environment. A technological environment is not exclusive. Such an employee is also working in a social environment, for he interacts with his fellow employees and employers. He is also working in a natural environment, since he is working in nature's air and light and moisture and pressure.

Environment, as thus thought of, is seen as a sort of envelopment, a near-totality in which a man is immersed. Thus a man in a factory is surrounded by technologically produced objects. A wild animal is surrounded by nature. With this enveloping environment a living animal or plant must be in a relationship that is more or less harmonious to its environment. This harmonious relationship relates to the whole environment.

However, an environment consists of parts; that is, it is made up of elements, such as trees, water, houses, foods. Man's adjustment to environment is more appropriately viewed as an adjustment to the various elements that compose the environment. Particularly is his maladjustment seen in reference to some particular element in the environment. Thus an animal from the tropics is maladjusted to the cold of the Arctic. People have died for lack of Vitamin C or because of so small an object as the proboscis of the *Anopheles*, carrying even smaller objects, protozoans, that produce malaria. Animals adjust, as well as maladjust, to small elements of environment. Thus tens of thousands of sheep have been prevented from dying by adding one part of cobalt to two million parts of water and have thus become adjusted to those grazing lands where there was no trace of cobalt.

So, in thinking of our technological environment, it is well to think of it in terms of the individual elements to which we adjust. Thus the tin can is an invention of a century ago to which we adjust by processing food in factories instead of in the family kitchen and so letting the housewife spend more of her time elsewhere than in the kitchen.

The technological elements are many, counted in the millions, comparable to, though not so numerous as, the elements in our natural environment. They also vary greatly in size, from, say, a needle to a skyscraper office building. A large object like a skyscraper, however, may not bring about as much adjustment on our part as does the tiny needle. The extent of adjusting we do to a technological element is not closely related to its physical size, nor is the complexity of an element of technology an indication of the amount of adjusting we may make. The electronic digital computers that perform the seemingly magical functions of an electrical brain are an extraordinarily complex invention; yet they may call forth less adjusting than the simple invention of the wheel.

We have been using the expression "the amount of adjusting." That there are degrees of adjustment may appear strange to those who derive their concept of adjustment from biology, where the measure of adjustment is living and of the lack of adjustment is death. But the extent of adjustment varies, especially in the human individual. Being sick is not as good an adjustment as being well. A neurotic has a less satisfactory adjustment than a normal person. The word "adaptation" implies variation more than the word "adjustment." Thus varying degrees of adaptation are suggested by such terms as "strain," "tension," "nervousness," "vitality," "energy," "illness," "strength."

Another extension of the meaning of adjustment is necessary when such a term is taken from biology and applied to humans living in communities. In biology we think of an individual or an aggregation of individuals living or dying because of adjustment or lack of it. But with humans, aggregations are societies, and their group life is characterized by various institutions, such as schools, families, churches, states, clubs, economic and political organizations. When humans adjust to environment by groups, as well as by individuals, their group adjustment implies changes in social activities, such as those of religion, education, marriage, political and productive occupations. The lower animals have no schools and no churches, no parliaments, and no factories. Though the lower animals live in groups, their group adaptation is not greatly different from the adaptation of a group of plants. In either case the group adaptation to environment is something like the arithmetic sum of the adaptation of a collection of individuals.

But with humans, the adjustment of a collection of individuals is an adjustment of their group life and may mean an adjustment of their schools, factories, parliaments, and churches. In other words, with mankind, adjustment to environment means more than life and death of an aggregation of individuals; it means degrees of adaptation of social institutions and customs.

Thus when we added the steam engine to our technological environment and applied mechanical power to our tools instead of muscle, we worked in large buildings called factories, instead of in the family dwelling. Hence our adjustment to this technological element, the steam engine, meant an adjustment of the institution of the family and of our economic institutions.

One of the earliest technological changes in our environment concerned producing fire by friction. Before the acquisition of fire, the habitat of early man was Africa and southern Asia. He could not go outside this area because of the cold and the shortage of fruits. But when fire was used in cooking, the hard indigestible fibers of many plants and leaves were more edible. By migration, his food supplies could be increased greatly, and he could live outside the semitropics. Thus the adaptation to fire was migration, and men thus were spread more widely over the earth than any other animal.

For hundreds of thousands of years men were wanderers within a generally large though limited area. The little band of humans would eat a locality out of its supply of animals and wild plants and then move on to fresh food supplies. Then was added to this technological environment a most important implement, a digging stick, with which he would dig holes in the ground, drop in a seed, cover it, and then dig away weeds from the growing plant. This digging stick was a simple tool, a hard stick with a point or a flattened bladelike end, as in a small spade, or a stick with a joint at the end, which suggests a hoe. Yet the adjustment to this simple digging stick changed the wandering band of a dozen or more individuals to a more or less settled community of several scores of inhabitants. This was quite a change in the social life of man, and sociologists should recognize the influence of technology in this transformation of his society.

Various sociologists in the past have written of the influence of natural environment on our social life, but, strangely, few have studied the influence of the technological environment.

As the hoe evolved into the plough, food was raised from seeds of grasses—notably barley, oats, wheat, and rice—all of which could be preserved longer than fruits; and animal food, particularly milk, was produced from tamed animals. This increased food supply, based upon technology, made possible communities much larger than were possible in the hoe, or digging-stick, culture. Villages of several thousand inhabitants were possible where the climate and soil were suitable. In general, early agricultural villages were smaller than these. These early agriculturalists lived compactly in villages and went out to cultivate their fields and tend their flocks. But as the thickly cultivated plants annually took out of the soil chemical elements important for the growth of plant food, the soil became less fertile, and the villagers with their ploughs, domesticated animals, and seeds moved on to seek new lands. To find these lands they often cut and burned the forests. As they came in contact with the peoples living by hunting and gathering wild food, they killed them, conquered and married them, or enforced their culture on them. So the world became peopled by agriculturalists rather than by hunters and gatherers of wild foods. The adjustment to the technology of agriculture led to the replacement of the hunting people and to larger communities.

These adaptations I have just recounted—namely, migrations, increases in population, and stability of residence—are only the immediate adjustments that come directly from the uses of these technological elements. But the group adjustment to technological environment is more complex than the adjustment of the lower animals. Group adjustment to a technological element is made only in a few customs or institutions, not in the totality of them. The first adaptations are those coming from direct uses. But to these changed customs and institutions coming directly from their use, secondary, indirect, or derivative adjustments are in turn made.

Thus the first direct adjustment to the technology that increases the food supply and makes it more assured from season to season and from year to year is a larger population. But the adjustment in turn to a larger population may be a greater division of labor, a specialization of occupation, different religious ceremonies, a differentiation of age societies, or the creation of social classes. These are derivative adaptations to the original or direct adaptation to the technological innovation. The original or direct adaptation is a change in some element or part of the society which we may call A. A, then, has adjusted to T, the technological innovation. But in a society there are other parts or elements than A, as for instance, B, C, D, etc., where other elements, B, C, D, etc., may be interconnected with A. Hence B, C, D, etc., adapt to the new adaptation of A, which has resulted from an adaptation to T.

Men adjust to the steam engine by letting it drive their tools for them. Consequently, they work away from home in factories. Then the family, a social institution, adjusts to the absence of workers and to the new production and to the additional source of income. The adjustments in the family are the decline in the authority of the husband and father, the removal of economic production from the home, the separation of husband and wife, and the different type of education for the children. These are not the direct adaptations to the steam engine but are adaptations to the uses of steam-driven tools away from the homestead.

These derivative or indirect adaptations to the technological

elements in our environment are not usually recognized or appreciated, for many sociologists are interested more in descriptions
than in causes, and when they search for causes they look only
to the direct cause, not to the derivational causes. Causes are like
links in a chain and occur in a succession. A sequence may begin
with an adjustment A to a technological element T. B, another
adjustment in another element of society, is seen as an adjustment to A but not to T. The decline in the authority of the
husband and father in the family is not interpreted as an adjustment to the steam engine, but only as an adjustment to the transfer of production away from the home, which was in turn an
adjustment to the steam engine. The most numerous adjustments
to a technological environment are the derivative ones; for any
one direct adaptation to a technological element creates a change
in a custom or an institution to which several other customs or
institutions will adjust. But commonly these derivative adjustments are not seen as adjustments to the technological element in
the first instance.

However, there are some reports of both direct and derivative
adjustments to a technological element. Ralph Linton[1] has studied
the Tanala adjustments to the technology of a wet rice cultivation. Formerly the people had cultivated dry rice, which required
a large or joint family. Under the wet cultivation, a single family,
instead of a joint family, did the work, and the village became
permanent. The displaced families moved off into the jungle to
seek new fields, but the kinship ties of the joint family held, and
a tribal organization developed through intermarriage. With the
increased wealth and property came kings, slaves, and warfare.

Similarly, in several different parts of the world the adjustment to cattle-raising has led to increased stealing, to war, to
slavery, and to the creation of a nobility.

The most extensive adaptations to a technological environment
are not to a single element but to a cluster of elements. Thus
cities were a dramatic community adjustment to three basic tech-

[1]   Ralph Linton and Abram Kardiner, "The Change from Dry Rice
to Wet Rice Cultivation in Tanala-Betsileo," in the *Individual and His
Society* (New York: Columbia University Press, 1939).

nological elements: (1) an agricultural technology which enabled a farm family to feed more than its members, (2) a transportation technology which would bring food into the city and goods exchanged out of the city, and (3) tools of manufacture. With cities, as all sociologists know, came radical changes in many customs and institutions.

So also the modern family in the United States and western Europe is an adaptation to a cluster of technological and scientific elements, namely, the steam engine, contraceptives, and scientific discoveries affecting religion. Religious beliefs have made extensive adaptations to scientific discoveries which affected the forms of belief in miracles, healing, life after death, the location of heaven and hell, and creation.

The technological environment in modern times differs from natural environment in that it changes more rapidly. Natural environment has changed: four times northern Europe and America were covered with glaciers, but these glaciers came and went only a few feet a year; whereas in modern times there have come, within a couple of centuries, the steam engine, the internal-combustion engine, the dynamo, and now the atomic reactor. The railroad, the automobile, the airplane, and now the guided missile have come in an equally short time. Quite as rapid has been the advent of the telephone, radio, motion picture, television, microfilm, the tape recorder, and now the putting of vision on magnetic tape.

Unlike the natural environment, the technological environment is a huge mass in rapid motion. It is no wonder then that our society with its numerous institutions and organizations has an almost impossible task in adjusting to this whirling technological environment. It should be no surprise to sociologists that the various forms and shapes which our social institutions take and the many shifts in their function are the result of adjustments— not to a changing natural environment, not to a changing biological heritage—but adaptations to a changing technology.

7

CULTURAL LAG AS THEORY   *1957*

I SHALL begin with a definition. A cultural lag occurs when one of two parts of culture which are correlated changes before or in greater degree than the other part does, thereby causing less adjustment between the two parts than existed previously.

An illustration is the lag in the construction of highways for automobile traffic. The two parts in this illustration are the automobile and the highway. These two parts of culture were in good adjustment in, say, 1910, when the automobile was slow and the highways were narrow country roads with curves and bends over which had been laid a hard surface. The automobile traveled at not a great rate of speed and could take the turns without too much trouble or danger. It was essentially for local transportation. But as time went on, this first part, the automobile, which is called an "independent variable," underwent many changes, particularly the engine, which developed speeds capable of sixty, seventy, eighty miles an hour, with brakes that could stop the car relatively quickly. But the narrow highways with sharp bends did not change as soon as did the automobile. On these roads the driver must slow up or have accidents. A decade or more later we are building a few broad highways with no sharp curves, which

Reprinted from *Sociology and Social Research*, XLI (January–February, 1957).

will make the automobile a vehicle for long-distance travel. The old highways, the dependent variable, are not adapted to the new automobiles, so that there is a maladjustment between the highways and the automobile. The adjustment, as measured by speeds, was better for local travel around 1910 than it is for long-distance travel on these roads at present. The adjustment will be better on the new express highways. Since the adjustment is made by the dependent variable, it is that part of culture which adapts and is called "adaptive culture."

The concept of cultural lag, just defined and illustrated, was first published in 1922 in a chapter of a book on social change which carried this title, "The Hypothesis of Cultural Lag." Since I was not sure whether this term would be understood, I asked my colleague Lee McBain, then Dean of the Faculty of Political Science at Columbia University, whether he thought it was an appropriate title. He advised me not to use it because, he said, with a twinkle in his eye, it might be mistaken for a dance step. This was in the 1920's, when new types of dances in the night clubs of the Prohibition era were very popular. However, I did use the term, and I note with interest that it now appears in the dictionary and is in use in several countries in different parts of the world and has, in the United States, been found particularly useful by historians.

There is some interest always in the origin of an invention and how ideas develop. It therefore seems appropriate that I discuss briefly how this theory of "the cultural lag" was developed.

I am happy to discuss its origin, since I have been accused by some of taking the theory from Thorstein Veblen and by others from Karl Marx. I am quite sure there was no direct taking over of the idea from Veblen because I had never read him on this point. I had read Marx, and his materialistic interpretation of history was well known to social scientists and historians in general. This idea was a base, however, from which the theory of cultural lag was developed, but certainly neither the materialistic interpretation of history nor economic determinism is the same as cultural lag.

I first used the term in 1914, when I was a professor of economics and sociology at Reed College. I had for a long time been impressed with the economic interpretation of history, though as a user of partial correlation techniques I was appreciative of its limitations. The economic interpretation of history may be illustrated by the claim that the Crusades in the Middle Ages for the recovery of the Holy Land from the possession of the infidels were not a product of religious motives but resulted from the search for trade routes to the East. This economic drive utilized the religious fervor for purposes of enlistment. I do not wish to discuss the validity of the economic interpretation in this particular instance but rather to note that there was an economic factor in the Crusades and that it was obscured or disguised.

This word, "disguised," was widely current in the early part of the twentieth century because of the influence of Freud, all of whose writings I had read at the time. In his book *The Interpretation of Dreams,* he called the dream, as first remembered, the "manifest content," and the interpretation of the dream, the "latent content." Thus, if a person dreamed that a steam roller was about to crush him, that would be the manifest content, but if the interpretation showed that the steam roller was a symbol for a dominating father, that would be the latent content. The latent content was disguised. About this time, I read before the American Economic Association a paper stressing this point and entitled "The Psychological Basis for the Economic Interpretation of History," claiming that the economic factor was often disguised. But as I thought more about it, the disguise factor in social causation seemed less important than the time factor.

I noticed this time factor in unequal rates of change, particularly in the course I was giving on the family. I remarked that many changes were taking place in the family and that most of them seemed to be due to the economic factor, which removed production activities such as spinning, weaving, soap-making, and tanning of leather from the household and put them in factories, thus taking away many household duties of the wife. Yet the ideology of the position of the housewife persisted. It was said that woman's place was in the home. Also at the beginning of the twentieth century there was serious discussion as to whether women should go to college or not, because their place was in the home. I was impressed with the fact that the transfer of production from the home to the factory was precipitating a new locale for women outside the home. But there was a great time interval; that is to say, there was a lag in changing the position of women; so I came to see great importance in this lag, and, being active at that time in various reform movements, I was disturbed about the maladjustment in the position of women who were kept at home. I was an ardent feminist. So both lag and maladjustment impressed me.

I should like to digress for a moment and say that I do not consider all delays in taking up a new idea as being lags. For instance, I have been told that Queen Mary of England, who died in 1953, had never used a telephone. Well, she certainly delayed adopting a new invention; however, the failure to adopt a new invention is a delay—not a cultural lag. The theory of the cultural lag is somewhat more complex. It calls for the following steps: (1) the identification of at least two variables; (2) the demonstration that these two variables were in adjustment; (3) the determination by dates that one variable has changed while the other has not changed or that one has changed in greater degree than the other; and (4) that when one variable has changed earlier or in greater degree than the other, there is a less satisfactory adjustment than existed before.

I call attention to this series of steps in the formulation of the theory of cultural lag because it has sometimes been commented that the cultural lag is merely a concept. It is surely a much more elaborate concept than that, for instance, of primary group. I think it better to say that since it is a concept of a relationship, it is a theory. It is therefore more than merely a new term in the language.

This theory I had fully developed by 1915, but I hesitated to publish it, because I thought that theories should have some proof before publication. In order to prove a theory, one must set it up in a form that can be proved, with places for the relevant data. Thus, for proof, a theory evolves into a hypothesis. But the war came along, and it was only after the war that I took up the verification of this hypothesis by considering the adjustment of law to industrial accidents, which were increasing because of the introduction of whirling machinery with rapidly moving wheels. In this case, the independent variable was technology; the machinery of which, before the factory system, had been simple tools, such as those on early farms, to which the common law of accidents was very well suited. But after the coming of the factories in the United States, around 1870, accidents continued to be dealt with by the old common law and with much maladjustment, for where workers suffered loss of life or an injury to a limb, there was little compensation and long delay in paying for these disasters to the individual or his family. It was not until around 1910 that employers' liability and workmen's compensation were adopted in this country. So that there was a lag of about thirty or forty years when the maladjustment could be measured by inadequate provision for several hundred thousand injuries and deaths to which there would have been a better adjustment if we had had laws of employers' liability or workmen's compensation.

I still considered it a hypothesis because we needed more proof than one particular case. I attempted, though, to cite many hypotheses of cultural lag, and in nearly all cases the independent variable proved to be a scientific discovery or mechanical invention. For instance, the invention of the steam engine led to the factory and only afterwards to the change in the legal rights of women. Most of the illustrations given at this time were initiated by technological changes and scientific discoveries, and the lagging adaptive culture was generally some social organization or ideology. These illustrations led to a characterization, by some, of the theory of cultural lag as a technological interpretation of history. I stated, however, at the time the hypothesis of cultural lag was published that the independent variable could very well be an ideology or a non-technological variable. For instance, changes in the law of primogeniture, an independent variable, constituted a change in the legal system and not in technology. Changes in the law of primogeniture were accompanied, after a lag, by a change in the economic system related to agriculture and household production. So the fact that the technological change came first was simple observation of a temporal nature and not inherent in the theory as such. For instance, it is quite probable that religion and not technology was the cause of most social changes in India twenty-five hundred years ago, at about the time of Buddha. Also students of Stone Age techniques have pointed out the essential conservative nature of stone technology, that it was very resistant to change, and that probably the causes of changes then were ideological or social. But in our times in the Western world, technology and science are the great prime movers of social change. That this is so is an almost universal observation.

I did attempt to generalize the theory. It is this: A cultural lag is independent of the nature of the initiating part or of the lagging part, provided that they are interconnected. The independent variable may be technological, economic, political, ideological, or anything else. But when the unequal time or degree of change produces a strain on the interconnected parts or is expressed differently when the correlation is lessened, then it is called a cultural lag. The extent of the generalized applicability of the theory rests on how much interconnection exists among the parts of culture. That many connections exist is obvious. Religion is interrelated with science. Family is correlated with education. Education and industry have connections. Highways are necessary for automobiles. On the other hand, some interrelations are slight or do not exist at all between other parts. Painting is not related to the production of gasoline. And I was about to say that writing poetry is unrelated to aviation. But I recall seeing a sizable book of collected poems on aviation. To the extent that culture is like a machine with parts that fit, cultural lag is widespread. If, however, cultural parts are no more related than pebbles strewn on the beach, then cultural lags are rare. There must, of course, be change occurring at unequal time intervals. An indication that cultural lags are common phenomena is suggested by the incorporation of the theory in books on general sociology. There have been criticisms, however.

One in particular should be noted. It has been said that the hypothesis of cultural lag is not a scientific instrument because, it is claimed, it cannot be scientifically demonstrated. The reason why, critics claim, maladjustments (and presumably adjustments) cannot be objectively determined is that there is a subjective factor which exists because of a value judgment, and value judgments are not subject to measurement.

Values are truly difficult to rank or to measure. We can measure the temperature by a thermometer, but it is said we cannot measure the goodness in morals. This observation does not invalidate the hypothesis of cultural lag. It only concerns the difficulty of determining degrees of maladjustment. But, of course, many maladjustments are quite demonstrable irrespective of the variation in value systems. Maladjustment was an essential factor in Darwin's theory of evolution, and he had no difficulty in proving madadjustment. He used death as a test. But there are other tests. Sickness is one. So is insanity. Furthermore, maladjustment may be conceived as a deviation from a social norm. Certainly norms can be described and measured and hence deviations also. Even though maladjustment is difficult to demonstrate, and even though we fail to show it in some cases, it can be proved in many cases, and the hypothesis of cultural lag is not invalidated.

The application of the theory to modern times suggests a possible appendix to the theory which runs like this: The number of patents, discoveries in applied science, and inventions has been increasing in something like an exponential curve. Most of these are minor; but important ones have been coming very rapidly, as, for instance, the magnifying of light or the putting of vision or the isotopes from nuclear fission on tape. As these discoveries and inventions are adopted, we must adjust to them; we must adapt ourselves to this changing environment, but we do it with a certain amount of lag. So an addendum to the theory of cultural lags is that lags accumulate because of the great rapidity and volume of technological change.

However, there are certain events that tend to cause cultural lags to crumble. One of these, I pointed out in my book, *Social*

Change, is revolution, and the reports we get from the revolutionary movement in China in the 1950's indicate that there are many lags having to do with the family and rural life and Confucianism that have been toppled over by the revolution. For instance, women are less in bondage since the revolution. Also, feudalism has been overthrown. An observation closer to home is that war causes a decline in the pile of accumulated lags. For instance, the war has taken more women out of the home and put more of them into industry, offices, and stores, where they tend to remain after the war is over. Similarly, the position of Negroes has been changed by war. As Negroes have been differentiated into upper classes, middle classes, professional groups, it becomes obvious that the whites cannot treat these upper-class, educated Negroes in the same way that they formerly treated Negro field hands or domestic servants. Yet many Negroes in the twentieth-century cities, with their middle and upper classes, are being treated as they were in villages of the South when they emerged from slavery, shortly after the Civil War. The war, however, broke some of the old lags because it put Negroes into association on the basis of equality with the whites of the armed forces, and the Negroes were drawn into the cities of the North. So war tends to break down cultural lags. It may preserve a few, too. This is a matter for empirical observation.

Even though war and revolution are breaking down cultural lags, there are many that persist. For instance, one such lag that is clearly demonstrable regards our foreign policy. In the eighteenth century the advice of President Washington to avoid entangling alliances with foreign powers was very appropriate because of our isolation, because of the abundance of our natural resources, and because of slow transportation. But in the twentieth century there have come the airplane, the fast steamboat, the radio, the telephone, and also the search for raw materials, which are needed for our industries and which are widely but universally distributed over the world. The old foreign policy of isolationism is a maladjustment to the changed technological situation. Isolationism, however, is diminishing. How long it may persist is a question. In the 1950's non-isolationists are the most influential in guiding our foreign policy. Yet for a large part of the twentieth century, isolationism in foreign policy was a lag.

Another illustration which, I think, is clearly demonstrable has to do with the death rate and the birth rate in their relation to the increase in population, particularly in southeast Asia. Throughout the great period of written history, the birth rate and the death rate have tended to be the same, except for intermittent periods when the death rate fell and the birth rate stayed high. When that occurred, there was, of course, an increase in population. Such is occurring now in India, where the birth rate is probably around 35 per 1,000 and where the death rate is about 25 per 1,000. The result is the increase in the population of India of 4 million per year. Occurring in an agricultural country where the farms have an acreage of about three acres, this pressure of population upon the food supply will bring hardships and may result in great human tragedies and will certainly make it very difficult for the standard of living to be raised.

This imbalance of births and deaths produces a maladjustment in other countries also, as, for instance, in Egypt and probably, if we had the figures, in China. The adjustment could be restored by raising the death rate, which of course we do not wish to do, or by lowering the birth rate, which is resisted by some moral and religious groups and by customs. However, the imbalance in the birth and death rates represents a cultural lag in some densely populated countries.

A long-continuing lag is in the adjustment to cities, which were produced in great numbers and in large sizes by the factory and the railroad. In many ways we were better adjusted to rural life. For instance, a greater death rate exists in cities than in the rural districts. There is also more crime in cities. Thus in several respects we have not adjusted well to this urban environment.

I have time to mention only one other lag, the lag in adjusting to the atomic bomb. The atomic bomb brought the possibility of great destruction to cities in a war. The atomic bomb was produced in two and one-half years. And yet, a decade later we have developed no defense against the atomic bomb, nor have we made an adjustment either in the dispersion of urban populations or in controlling atomic energy or in agreeing to ban the atomic bomb. Possibly many decades may pass before we will adjust to the atomic bomb—a lag of great danger.

If there were time, dozens of cultural lags causing very serious problems could be listed, lags which arise largely because inventions and technology have increased in volume and rapidity faster than we are making adaptations to them. The great need of our time is to reduce this lag. Cultural lags are one characteristic of the process of social evolution, which occurs in a closely integrated society in periods of rapid change. In the long perspective of history, though, lags are not visible because they have been caught up. They are visible phenomena largely at the present time.

II. Social Trends

8

THE RESPONSIBILITY OF THE

SOCIAL SCIENCES *1929*

IF PRIMITIVE peoples are asked why they do certain things the way they do, the usual answer is, "Because it has always been done that way." The late Dr. W. H. R. Rivers wrote a book in 1906 describing the culture of the Todas, a hill people of southern India. He included as an Appendix some brief observations of these same people written by a Portuguese missionary in 1603. These two descriptions seem to be describing, in so far as they go, the same society and the same culture, although several centuries had intervened. In other words, within about three hundred years the changes in the Toda culture seem to have been very slight. How different it is with us! What vast changes have occurred in the area of the United States in three hundred years! Even in the times of our great-grandfathers social changes were slow, but now they come with great rapidity. What a gulf separates even two generations! Mothers and daughters often understand each other's viewpoints so little that it seems as though they are not speaking the same language. Our industrial techniques— to choose one illustration—are being so revolutionized that it

Reprinted from *Recent Social Changes in the United States since the War and Particularly in 1927* (Chicago: University of Chicago Press, 1929).

would be a confession of incompetency to say that a thing is done a certain way because our forefathers did it that way. The more common remark is that it used to be done that way, but now we do it differently.

Changes are occurring throughout our whole social system. The education of youth in school and college changes from year to year, so many are the suggested improvements. Religion is no longer the unchanging Rock of Ages. We hardly know what is to be the future of the churches. The family is becoming smaller. It is losing many of its former functions to industry and to the state. Young people are marrying earlier and getting divorces more frequently. Restaurants and hotels are increasing rapidly in number, and apartments are becoming smaller. More and more women are working for pay outside the home. Their occupations are myriad, while formerly the only respectable occupation for widows who had to earn money was to run a boarding house. In government, we still have Tammany Hall and the Constitution of the United States, but even these two ancient political instruments have changed. The automobile, the airplane, the moving picture, the telephone, the radio, and television are multiplying a thousandfold the frequency and rapidity of communication. Machinery is capturing farming; the villages are declining; and the rural habits are changing in the direction of urban customs and manners. A decade ago we were fighting bloody wars; today we are (for the moment) signing treaties to outlaw war. We are not quite certain what is going to happen to the labor movement. The old radicalism itself seems to be preparing to wear a different garb. And most perplexing seems to be our changing morality itself, for the detailed application of moral codes gives very uncertain advice on the new problems of conduct. We look upon years before the War of 1914–18 as a different era, so great are the changes of the past dozen years.

These are certainly years of great and rapid change. This means that they are years of great uncertainty. They bring gain to some and loss to others, but to virtually all they bring uncertainty. The primitive people, the Todas of India, could pretty well guess what the next year would be like; they would know that the world their children and grandchildren were to live in would be about the same world they lived in. But we have no such certainty about the future of our children and our grandchildren, nor indeed of our own future or that of our business. And many of us of little faith are not very certain about whether these changes are in the direction of progress or not. This uncertainty becomes very acute with some of us at times and indeed with whole peoples. Within most European countries particularly there exists today, ten years after the war, very great uncertainty about the course of events. Even in the United States we erect, almost hysterically at times, the notion that we are safe with, say, Coolidge as President. This tendency to choose a President under whom the country will be safe is very suggestive of a subconscious unrest, underlying the surface of things.

The social sciences ought to render aid in these times of change and uncertainty. Unfortunately, as sciences, they are young. Indeed, their achievements in the exact measurement of the relationships of social phenomena are meager, too much so for much reliable prediction. Nor do we know that the social sciences will ever attain the state of accurate prediction in the whole realm of sociology. But one generalization does stand out sharply in our social and historical studies. It is that there is a continuity in cultural change; one event grows out of another. An invention is a co-ordination of existing elements. Discoveries are based on previous knowledge. Miracles do not occur, and revolutions are few. The greater our knowledge, the rarer are unheralded changes. Indeed, sudden, dramatic, and complete changes are decidedly the exception. The principle of continuity in social change is very reassuring. Our various studies of statistical time series show a very important thing, namely, that the measured trend of events and phenomena is the best guide that we yet have for the prediction of the future. Knowledge is the antithesis of mystery and uncertainty. And the knowledge of what has occurred and of what is happening is the safest guide we have. With more complete statistics and with better measurement we shall attain fuller knowledge of what is happening to us and where we are going. Only with these shall we be in a position even to begin to speak of control.

9

SOCIAL TRENDS *1957*

THE EXPRESSION "social trends" has only recently come into our scientific and popular vocabulary. What does it mean? Originally the word "trend" meant the direction which a river takes. Later it was used to designate the course which events take. But before the term came into its present-day usage, the idea was expressed by other words. One such expression was "social movements," as for instance the woman-suffrage movement or the trade-union movement. The more general word "history" sometimes meant trends, as for instance the history of prison reform, though such a history may have emphasized persons and events to the neglect of trends. For a time sociologists called such a history "natural history," thus de-emphasizing heroes and great events and stressing processes. Again the word "evolution" described trends, as for instance in the evolution of the family, but it implied more in that it carried the suggestion of improvement. Thus the phenomenon of social trends has had various expressions to designate it. Is the term "social trends" an improvement over these older terms, or is it merely another label? There are several ways in which it is a better term. It is more precise and less general, which makes it better fitted for scientific usage, as I shall proceed to show.

Reprinted from *Sociology and Social Research*, XLII (September–October, 1957).

Trends came into scientific usage with the application of statistics and curve-fitting to past data which were reported regularly. This usage occurred in the first and second decades of the twentieth century. An illustration is the production of pig iron which was reported annually over a period of many years. Such annual data were called a "time series." In the United States the amount of pig iron produced increased as time passed, though there were brief periods when it decreased, as in a business depression, or when the increase was less than at another period, such as a war or preparation for a war. If annual pig-iron production is plotted as upright bars on graph paper, the succeeding bars are in general taller than the preceding, though there will be exceptions, for the production of pig iron fluctuates from year to year. When a line is fitted through the tops of these bars by the method of least squares, and therefore is running through the middle, this line curves upward. It is called a "trend line." The trend was upward and showed increasing pig-iron production over the years.

One of the reasons for drawing a trend line was to show the annual fluctuations above and below it. In this illustration these fluctuations indicated ups and downs of business conditions. And so fluctuations around certain economic trend lines were used as measures of business cycles. To measure business prosperity and depression it was necessary to meaure them from a trend line. So the trend must be determined exactly.

A trend, as has been said, is like the course of a river, which is likely to be in one general direction but with various bends. Thus the Mississippi River flows southward from Minnesota to the Gulf but with many curves around the trend.

The scientific nature of the study of social trends is shown by the fact that accounts of trends are impersonal and without the dramatic coloring of heroic personalities. Nor does the term have any necessary moral implications. Thus when the trend of marriage is increasing or when the trend of birth rates is downward, these are impersonal statements of facts without any suggestions of progress or the reverse, though, of course, they may be interpreted as good or bad. To some, a decreasing birth rate is regretted; to others, it is desirable. But the trend line alone does not say which.

Having been accepted in science, the word "trend" became the possession of the people shortly thereafter. An event that helped to give it widespread acceptance was the publication in 1933 of a series of studies made by the President's Research Committee on Social Trends, appointed by President Herbert Hoover in 1929. The publications of these studies, called *Recent Social Trends,* were distributed widely and found frequent use by students in universities, colleges, and high schools. They became standard reference books in libraries. Not all of these studies were based on statistics with trend lines measured, as was the case for instance in the volume on population. Measurement was used where quantitative data were available, as in the publications in the series on crime, education, and the family. In some areas quantitative data were scarce, as in the case of the studies of religion and of government. Where data were missing, the concept of trend line was valuable, nevertheless, even though the study was in non-quantitative descriptive terms. These trends in religion could be described, though they could not be measured. Such descriptions are not as precise as those based on measurement; yet such approximations are useful. Thus we may speak truthfully of trends in painting or in music based upon verbal description and illustration without any statistics.

It is verbal description rather than statistical description that has made possible the popular use of the term "social trends." We may say that the trend in rearing children is toward less discipline without knowing any statistical measurement but relying on impressions or descriptive illustrations.

When there is no statistical measurement there is danger, however, of misstatements about trends which are based upon impressions and illustrations. Who can say, for instance, without statistics whether there is a trend toward increasing church attendance or not? Another danger in the loose usage of the term "trends" lies in the difficulty of distinguishing a fluctuation around a trend from the trend itself. For instance, is the recent increase in the birth rate a new trend in the birth rate, or is this increase merely a fluctuation around a downward trend in the birth rate which has been going on for a century and a half in this country and which may continue downward during the remainder of this century? It is difficult to say.

The answer depends upon how long a time is needed to determine a trend. How long a time is required to call a movement, for instance, in the stock market, a trend? Five years, fifteen years, or fifty years? In the case of suicides, I have heard it said that the trend was downward on the basis of a decrease in suicides over a period of one year. The person who made this remark evidently was not aware of the difference between a trend and a fluctuation around a trend. One year is too short a time to determine a trend on data reported annually.

As to how long it takes, the general practice is not to determine a trend until there have been several cycles of fluctuations in the time series around where the trend line will be. A cycle is a fluctuation from above the trend to below and then up again above. A trend line is more stable if it is constructed from say five or six or more cycles. If a cycle averages three years, then the period required would be at least fifteen years. Not many statistical trend lines exist for more than fifty or seventy-five years, for earlier statistical reporting of many series did not exist.

But in some cases we know trends have existed for many centuries, even though we have no measurements. Thus the trend of scientific research has been upward for four hundred years. In the case, for example, of temperature, to determine any trend upward or downward may require time measured in thousands of years rather than in hundreds. Yet, to some persons, a couple of very cold winters coming together is enough to establish a trend, and we are told on this basis that the earth is getting colder and a new Ice Age is on the way.

These remarks I have just made show the scientific nature of the concept of social trends. Such a scientific term is readily diffused among the people because ours is a scientific age, and the average man on the streets is accustomed to scientific speech from physicians, architects, farmers, automobile mechanics, and gardeners. It seems that everyone wants to be scientific—even preachers, painters, and poets.

A very important characteristic of social trends which I discovered several years ago but have never published is that social trends seldom change their direction quickly and sharply. This is a simple statement, but the implications are great. First, let me present the evidence.

I searched the records of America and Europe and found some three hundred time series, running back several decades, from the fields of production, marketing, finance, population, vital statistics, transportation, government, and various other social phenomena. To these three hundred time series I fitted trend lines, and an examination of them showed that over 90 per cent continued their course without any quick or marked change in direction. A quick change was one that occurred in less than, say, fifteen or twenty years. The replacement of the horse-drawn vehicle by the automobile did not occur rapidly. Even the trend in immigration to the United States did not change quickly, though legislation restricting it was passed quickly. Some of the changes which occurred suddenly and radically were from England during the war.

When the causes for this persistence of a trend in its course are examined theoretically, there are several reasons which make us think that more cases than the three hundred would corroborate the finding. In other words, a theoretical examination of causes leads us to think that the finding is universal. I regret that I have not the space now to set forth this examination of causes.

One use of this discovery is of great significance—that the projection of a trend line into the future has some trustworthiness and tells us with some degree of probability what the future will be. This property of a trend line is due to the fact that it seldom changes its direction sharply. This guidance as to its future course is good only within limits. Hence it does not pinpoint the future precisely, and a projection of the trend line of population change in the United States into the future may not predict exactly the population twenty years from now. But even if the projection missed it by ten or fifteen million either way, that is an error of only 5 or 6 per cent. In any case, there is assurance that the population will continue to increase during the next twenty years and that it will not suddenly begin to decrease. Of course, if an atomic war should destroy our cities, such a sudden reversal might occur. In the case of population, it should be said, there are other ways of making forecasts than that of projecting the trend line of population growth.

Three cautions should be observed in extending trend lines. One is that the past trend should be of some duration. Thus in projecting the future of passenger miles flown by airlines, it is desirable to have enough data to establish a trend. A record of a few years is not enough. Otherwise, the error is great.

The second point to be observed is that the further the projection is made, the greater is the error. Thus the range of error in the projection of the increase in per capita income to the year 2000 is greater than the projection to the year 1975.

The third observation is that the projection of trend lines into the future is not a forecast of what the time series will actually be. It is only a forecast of what the trend line will be, not of the fluctuations around the trend line. Thus a trend line of the national income to 1960 may not indicate even for so short a time as four years what the actual national income will be, for there may be a business depression which would bring the fluctuation of national income well below what the trend line will be in 1960. Thus a projection of the trend may forecast 350 billion dollars. But even if this is an exact prediction of the trend for 1960, the actual national income might be only 325 billion, if there is a business depression.

Where exact forecasts are needed, as for instance in the airplane industry, that is purchasing transport planes for future use and planning schedules and seeking capital, the projection of trend lines does not meet the requirements. But there are probably thousands of instances where great exactness is not needed. In these instances projections of trends may yield about as much information as we care about. For instance, to build a new city hall it is not necessary to know the exact population of the city in 1985. Nor in building an express highway is it necessary to know the precise number of automobiles that will pass over it in 1970. Since so much of knowledge desired about the future need not be exact as to quantity nor precise as to date, trend lines can be very useful. Also in this uncertain world we often act on plans whose probability of materializing is less than 95 out of 100. In projecting trends, probabilities, though not 1, that is 10 out of 10, are often high, say of the order of 9 out of 10.

We conclude our remarks with two thoughts on the meaning for us of our knowledge of social trends. The first general message that knowledge of social trends brings to us is that there is much stability in society, even though there be a period of great and rapid social change. It gives us a feeling of confidence that our habitation is not built upon shifting sands. It means a sense of certainty that revolutions are rare and that evolution is the rule. With this knowledge there should be dispelled the fear that the bottom will drop out of things. We do not have the same comfort in social trends that the religionist has in the Rock of Ages, but there is some comfort in knowing that social institutions are essentially stable, like, say, climate; though in the long run they change, as we well know from history.

The second lesson we learn from our knowledge of social trends is that there is a sort of inevitability about social trends. "Inevitability" is perhaps too strong a word. Yet our evidence indicates that an individual is not likely by his own effort to change the direction of a social trend quickly nor very much. No individual or group is likely to stop the trend toward planned parenthood, or the trend toward bigger business, or the extension of governmental function, or the increasing employment of women outside the home, or to return the authoritative power of the husband. A knowledge of trends keeps us from believing in fairy tales.

It is difficult to buck a social trend. It may be slowed up a bit, but generally a social trend continues on its course. It should be realized that if a social trend is to be opposed successfully, even temporarily, a mighty effort is required. For instance, to slow the trend of the movement of city dwellers out of the city to the suburbs, city chambers of commerce will have a very hard time of it and are not likely to be successful for long. Even a Winston Churchill could not stop the breaking-up of the British Empire.

Success is more likely to come to those who work for and with a social trend than to those who work against it. There is, for instance, a trend toward nationalism in Asia and in Africa. Success is more likely to come to Russia if she works with this trend than to the colonial powers of Europe that work against it.

It may be argued that we should work for principles, whether they be with or against social trends. This position can be defended. But should our principles dictate that we work against social trends, we would do well to appraise the size of the effort needed, unless we wish to be martyrs.

The same lesson should be heeded by city and national planners. They should not start with a utopian urge and a clean slate and a belief in the unlimited potentialities of human will. Rather they should see clearly what the trends are. Only then can they approach realistically their task of planning. As the materials with which the architect works are stone and steel, brick and glass, the materials with which the statesman works are social trends.

10

PROGRESS AND UNIFORMITY IN

CHILD-LABOR LEGISLATION

1912

Preface

THE STUDY of comparative legislation is of importance
for the improvement of state laws. This monograph is a comparative study of the field of child-labor legislation. It presents detailed information regarding each state and measures the progress
and the uniformity of legislation on child labor. The period of
time covered is approximately one-third of a century, and thus
tendencies are shown. The attempt has been to make the description accurate and thorough, and to this end it has been necessary
to use many tables and statistical terms. It aims, in fact, to be a
statistical description. For the foregoing reasons, it is recommended to the legislator and to the student of practical affairs in
the important field of comparative legislation.

Uniformity in state legislation is discussed with increasing
interest. If interest in uniformity be for the purpose of future
activity, then it is desirable to know how much uniformity there is

Reprinted from *Progress and Uniformity in Child-Labor Legislation*
("Studies in History, Economics, and Public Law," Vol. XLVIII, No. 2
[New York: Columbia University Press, 1912]).

and what its tendency is. If uniformity is of importance, it would seem that it should be measured. Until it has been measured, knowledge of it must remain vague. This study calculates uniformity in one field of legislation. The methods represent the amount of uniformity at a definite time in a single term. It is hoped that these methods will be of interest both because they will prove to be applicable to other fields of legislation and to other social data and also because, to the student whose viewpoint is that of science, the methods used and their application are, it is thought, important and suggestive of the possibilities in quantitative method.

Sociological Aspects

RELATION TO SOCIOLOGICAL THEORY   The intention has been to make this study also of value to sociology in its theoretical and scientific aspects. It is expected that sociology in the future will be concerned largely with inductive studies in the theory of social control. Many phases of social control are instanced by Professor E. A. Ross in his book bearing that title. Professor Franklin H. Giddings has emphasized the importance of social self-control in an article in a recent issue of the *Political Science Quarterly*.[1]

Social control is secured by means of forces which are designated as "social pressure." The theory of social pressure that is current among sociologists may be best explained by reference to a similar theory of environmental pressure familiar to biologists.

It has been known since the writings of Quételet that the measurements of certain physical traits, as, for instance, height and weight, follow what is known as the normal law of distribution. The normal law of distribution is represented graphically by a bell-shaped curve. For instance, if the scale of measurements of heights of persons is marked on a horizontal line and the frequency of each measurement of the scale is indicated by a vertical line erected to a length corresponding to the frequency, then the resulting curve has the shape of the perimeter of a bell. The individuals whose measurements lie at the center of the scale included

1   *Political Science Quarterly*, XXIV, 569–88.

in the curve are the most usual, the average individuals. They are sometimes spoken of as the "type." Those whose measurements lie at or near the ends of the curve are the rare, the most unusual individuals, and are spoken of as the "extreme deviations," or "deviates," because they deviate considerably from the average. These bell-shaped curves are not all of exactly the same form. Some are tall and narrow; others are low and broad. The measurements whose distribution forms a tall and narrow curve are described as clustering closely about the average. The extent of the clustering about the average has been measured by a term known as the "standard deviation." A tall and narrow curve has a small standard deviation, and a low and broad curve has a large standard deviation. This kind of distribution of physical traits has been found to be true not only for the measurements of mankind but also of other animals and of plants.

The form of these distributions of physical traits of animals and plants is related to environmental influence in a manner shown by the following illustration. A rainstorm washed a large number of sparrows out of their nests. These sparrows were picked up, and a large number revived. Measurements of all these sparrows, both dead and revived, were taken; and the curve showing their distribution was plotted. Then the measurements of the revived birds only were represented in a curve. The curve representing the birds which survived was a narrower curve, showing that the birds killed were more largely the unusual, the extreme, those widely deviating from the average. The curve of the measurements of the surviving birds possessed a smaller standard deviation than did the curve of the measurements of all of the birds. Thus, it is argued that in the process of adaptation to environment, the extreme variants from the normal are less likely to survive a rigorous environment, and the more normal are more likely to survive. Thus, a smaller standard deviation means that the environmental pressure has become more rigorous. Such has become the theory even with some distributions other than the bell-shaped curve. These, then, are, in brief outline, the essential points in a theory of environmental pressure affecting data biological in nature.

With regard to social pressure, it is argued that there are social types which are the result of purely social forces, as there are biological types which are the result of environmental forces, and that there are deviations from the normal, or type, in social phenomena as there are deviations from the normal in biological phenomena. It is argued that there are distributions of social phenomena of similar nature to the distributions of biological phenomena and that these distributions are the result of purely social forces, as the biological distributions are the result of environmental forces. Social forces such as imitation, tradition, and governmental control, like response to stimuli, tend to mold a type and tend to eliminate extreme deviations from type. Then, in distributions of social phenomena, smaller standard deviations indicate a greater social pressure, and the size of the standard deviation measures the amount of the social pressure.

It is readily seen that this theory is of great importance for sociology. Its importance makes studies in its inductive verification highly desirable. There are two difficulties, however, in such inductive studies. One is that many social phenomena cannot be measured because there is no scale of measurement. Another is that it is sometimes difficult to extricate the purely social forces from the biological and the psychological—all of which shape the product. So far as the writer knows, no study has been made in the manner outlined in the inductive verification of this theory. This monograph on child-labor legislation is such a study. Child-labor legislation is a result of purely social pressure. This study measures the standard deviations of certain features of the child-labor laws. It is known that there has been a powerful social pressure on these features of the child-labor laws within the past ten years. Have their standard deviations, or, as these measures are termed in this monograph, the "indexes of uniformity," decreased? It is found that they have. Thus the theory is supported by fact. The results of this inquiry are of importance for sociology in showing the possibilities of measuring social pressure by standard deviations and of interpreting their significance.

AS A STUDY IN MEASUREMENT This investigation in its purely scientific aspect aims also to be a study in measurements, and it is considered of value to the extent that it succeeds in measuring the phenomena concerned. The importance of measurements has been very admirably expressed by Lord Kelvin in an address on "Electrical Units of Measurement."[2]

I often say that when you can measure what you are speaking about and express it in numbers, you know something about it, but when you cannot measure it, when you cannot express it in numbers, your knowledge is of a meager and unsatisfactory kind; it may be the beginning of knowledge, but you have scarcely in your thoughts advanced to the stage of *science,* whatever the matter may be.

No science has progressed far without basing its conclusions on measurements. Progressive sciences have, of course, been in the possession of instruments and systems of measurements. Distances and lengths are measured in meters and fractions of meters. Weights are measured in grams and multiples of grams. Sociology is unfortunate in that, for many social phenomena, there are no scales of measurement. Professor Giddings has attacked this problem in a paper on the "Social Marking System," which appeared in the *American Journal of Sociology.*[3] Mr. G. Udny Yule has devised a scheme of measurement, applicable under certain conditions, which he calls the "theory of attributes." It is found in the first part of his *Introduction to the Theory of Statistics.* Professor Karl Pearson has formulated a method of determining correlations between attributes not applicable of quantitative measurement. This appears in his recent memoir, *On the Theory of Contingency.* Although a beginning has been made on the problem of measurement in social phenomena, much remains to be done. In the measurement of the laws of the states, great need is felt for the proper systems and instruments of measurement.

For many of the problems in measurement there are supplied the tools for measuring, and for many problems the materials to be measured are essentially simple in nature. Yet, on these simpler problems, there is a great body of writings, the accumu-

2   Sir William Thompson, *Popular Lectures and Addresses* (London, 1889), I, 73.

3   *American Journal of Sociology,* XV, 721–40.

lation of which has extended over centuries. To measure the height of a person seems simple because of familiarity, yet back of such an attainment are a perfected method and a perfected system. To measure the height of a person with accuracy is very difficult. Back of such attainment is thought contributed by the greatest intellects. While for most practical purposes great accuracy in the measurement of the height of a person is not necessary; in astronomy, in physics, and in chemistry, measurement is fundamental. To measure the height of a people is a task that has proven worthy of profound reasoning. The science of measurement becomes more difficult, the more complex the nature of the measurement.

The complexity of legislative enactments on child labor and their peculiar nature make peculiar difficulties in measuring them completely. Particularly, their nature makes accuracy difficult to obtain. So far as the writer knows, no previous attempt has been made to measure laws quantitatively. For these reasons, this work may be looked upon, from the standpoint of science, as a new experiment in measuring. Since hitherto no quantitative measurements have been made upon laws, it is interesting to observe the nature and forms of their distributions and the characters of their variables. This is all the more interesting, since the laws are so largely the product of purely social forces.

Average Age Limits

INTERPRETATION OF THE AVERAGES   The meaning of an average does not appear on the surface but is dependent upon several considerations. In order to know the meaning of an average it is necessary to know the method by which it has been computed. It is necessary to know the nature of the data from which it has been computed, the nature of the units of the data, and whether the data are homogeneous from the point of view from which the average is being interpreted. An average is a numerical figure, and the meaning that it has is the one the reader puts into it, and that meaning should be dependent upon the above considerations. This is particularly true of the averages presented here.

The averages presented here are arithmetic averages. The units from which the averages are deduced are the age limits of the individual laws of the states; and the number of units is, in each case, not the number of states that have a general age limit or the number of laws, but the number of age limits, which is quite likely to be larger than either the number of states or the number of laws. No weights have been used in computing the averages. All that has been said regarding the nature of the age limits, when the fact that a state may possess more than one age limit was explained, is, of course, applicable to the averages. In forming comparative estimates of averages it is desirable to bear in mind the number of cases from which the average was computed. These are printed in the tables, above each individual average.

It is necessary to explain further what is meant by homogeneity or heterogeneity of the units. Let it be imagined that the average height of a people has been ascertained. Thus far the conception seems simple. Now, if one-half of the people are of a tall race and one-half of a short race, then the conception of the average is less simple, because the people are not homogeneous; and this fact should be borne in mind in order to understand clearly the average. Suppose further that only one-tenth of the people are females; unless this fact were known there would be a wrong meaning attributed to the average. It would be desirable to know also if any who had not reached full stature were included in the measurements. There may be many other considerations that enter into the conception of the average height of a people. These various considerations that enter into the conception of the average explain what has been referred to as the homogeneity or heterogeneity of the units.

These considerations enter largely into the conception of average age limits. This is so partly because of unavoidable features of classification and partly because the conception of the average age limit is not familiar to the general reader. To illustrate, take the average age limit in the manufacturing group of occupations. The age limits in some laws apply to a wide range of manufacturing industries; in other laws, to a narrower range.

A few laws in the earlier years assigned one age limit for girls and another for boys. At one period a state may have a modern child-labor law with a high age limit and at the same time retain on its statute books an old law with a low age limit. These factors tend to make the units entering into the average unlike. However, these disturbing influences are comparatively small, and it is estimated that in the main the age limits in the manufacturing occupations are homogeneous.

Units and averages are matters of concept. If every state possessed the same number of children; if the occupations consisted of nothing but cotton manufacturing; if every state possessed the same number of cotton factories, employing the same number of children under hours of employment and educational requirements and other conditions the same, differing only in the matter of age limits; then the concept of average would be simpler to grasp. Thus, it appears that in situations that differ from this simple case, the concept of an average is less simple. Averages may be deduced from more or less heterogeneous units, but only those attributes that are common to the units will enter into the conception of the average. If one has the habit of considering the differences in the units more than the likenesses, to that extent is the conception of the averages complicated.

Occupation groups A, B, C, D, E, and F are in the main of homogeneous units. The street-trades occupation group is to a certain extent heterogeneous, since in the later years a few states have enacted two or more different age limits for two or more different occupations which have been classified in this group. Similarly, in the mining industries there are a very few cases where there is one age limit for working within the mine and a different one for employment about the mine. One state has different age limits for anthracite mines and for bituminous coal mines. Occupation group G, the group of dangerous occupations, is essentially different in its constitution from the other groups. It consists of a number of subgroups. The average age limit for this occupation group is based on units homogeneous in the sense that all of the occupations included in it are essentially dangerous, but is heterogeneous in the sense that the various occupations differ in the degree of their danger, so that varying age limits are applied to the various dangerous occupations.

The average age limits for all of the occupation groups taken together have been found, but in understanding these averages the above-mentioned considerations should be fully considered. The method of finding the average age limit for all the occupation groups taken together is as follows: All of the units in the data of each group of occupations from which the average age limit of each occupation group was constructed are taken as the data from

TABLE 1. *Average Age Limits for the Occupation Groups*

		1879	1884	1889	1894	1899	1904	1909
Occupation Group A	No. of cases....	7	11	25	32	31	43	54
Manufacturing	Av. age limit....	11.00	11.64	12.20	12.50	12.77	13.05	13.50
Occupation Group B	No. of cases....	1	......	7	8	14	18	31
Mercantile	Av. age limit....	10.00	......	11.86	12.50	12.86	13.28	13.84
Occupation Group C	No. of cases....	......	......	1	2	2	7	20
Hotels, offices, etc.	Av. age limit....	......	......	13.00	13.50	14.00	13.68	13.85
Occupation Group D	No. of cases....	......	......	1	......	3	11	31
Street trades	Av. age limit....	......	......	10.00	......	14.00	13.55	13.97
Occupation Group E	No. of cases....	7	10	24	37	32	38	46
Mining	Av. age limit....	12.29	12.80	13.00	12.87	13.09	13.32	13.89
Occupation Group F	No. of cases....	......	......	......	2	6	8	22
Any gainful occupation	Av. age limit....	......	......	......	12.50	14.00	13.87	14.04
Occupation Group G	No. of cases....	20	26	42	57	81	107	197
Dangerous occupations	Av. age limit....	15.70	15.38	15.59	15.56	15.90	15.93	15.00

which an average has been found. This average is called the average age limit for all of the occupation groups taken together. The difference in the nature of the units in the dangerous-occupation group from the nature of those of the other occupation groups has suggested the advisability of constructing the average age limits for all of the occupation groups, except that of the dangerous occupations, taken together.

PROGRESS IN AVERAGE AGE LIMITS   In Table 1, the average age limits for each of the occupation groups at each five-year period are shown; in Table 2, the average age limits for all of the occupation groups taken together are shown. The average age limits for all of the occupation groups except the dangerous occupations are shown in Table 3. The changes in the age limits for each occupation group and the amounts of change are represented graphically in Figure 1. It is seen that in almost every case there has been a continuous advance in the size of the average age limits. Also, the rates of increase in the size of the average age limits have been fairly constant for the three groups of occupations in which there has been most legislation, and consequently the most social pressure, namely, the manufacturing group, the mercantile group, and the mining group. The group of dangerous occupations, because of its complex nature, is here excepted.

TABLE 2. *Average Age Limits for All Occupation Groups Taken Together*

		1879	1884	1889	1894	1899	1904	1909
All Occupation Groups	No. of cases....	35	47	100	138	169	232	401
	Av. age limit....	13.49	13.70	13.78	13.88	14.43	14.51	14.87

TABLE 3. *Average Age Limits for All Occupation Groups Taken Together, Excepting the Dangerous Occupations*

		1879	1884	1889	1894	1899	1904	1909
Occupation Groups A, B, C, D, E, F	No. of cases....	15	21	58	81	88	125	204
	Av. age limit....	11.53	12.14	12.46	12.69	13.06	13.29	13.80

In the manufacturing industries, which have been essentially the focus of social pressure, the average age limit in 1909 was 13.5 years, while thirty years previous it was only 11 years. The rates of increase over each preceding five-year period are, beginning in 1884, 5.8 per cent, 4.8 per cent, 2.5 per cent, 2.8 per cent, 2.2 per cent, and 3.4 per cent. In the first few years the increase was greatest. Again, in the last five-year period, the increase was great. In most of the occupation groups, the period of years from 1905 to 1909, inclusive, was unusual not only in the increase of legislation but also in the advance in age limits. In occupations in which legislation is small, the amount of fluctuation in the development of the average age limit is great. The presumption is

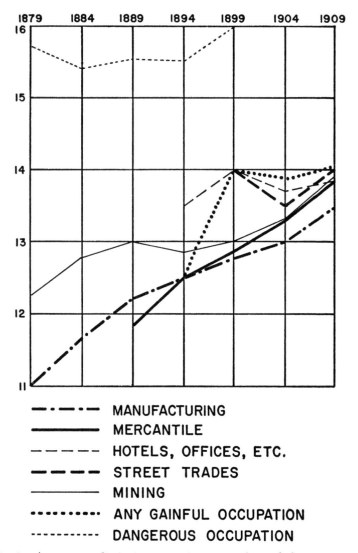

Fig. 1. Average age limits in occupation groups for each five-year period

that where there is little legislation the social pressure is slight and more random influences are in play. Figure 1 reveals the interesting fact that, in 1909, the average age limits of the occupation groups, excepting the dangerous occupations, are closer together than at any preceding period. The widest difference is only a little more than six months. This shows the tendency to uniformity among the occupation groups. For occupation groups A, B, C, D, E, and F, the average age limit was 13.8 years, in 1909; in 1879, it was 11.53 years; the rates of increase over each preceding five-year period, beginning in 1884, being 5.3 per cent, 2.6 per cent, 1.8 per cent, 2.9 per cent, 1.7 per cent, and 3.4 per cent. Here again the development in the last five-year period is relatively large. The average age limit for all occupation groups taken together, in 1909, was nearly 15 years (14.87 years); and in 1879, it was 13.49 years. The average age limit here is comparatively high. This is due to the influence of the age limits of the dangerous occupations, which throughout the period studied have been well over fifteen years and usually nearly sixteen years.

THE TYPICAL AGE LIMITS   The average is a number which in reality is practically never found. It is interesting and valuable to know a number, similar to the average, which is found. Usually, such a number is that unit which occurs most frequently in a series of units. This number of greatest frequency is here called the "type." For instance, it is desired to know which one of all the age limits occurring in 1894 is possessed by most of the state laws. Twelve years is such an age limit; this then is the typical age limit.

What, then, are the typical age limits from time to time in the various occupations? In the manufacturing industries, for the first ten years studied, 10 years was the type. For the next decade it was 12 years, and for the last fifteen years it has stood at 14 years. In most of the employments, except the dangerous occupations, the most frequent age limit before 1894 was 12 years. Since that date in every case it has been 14 years, a considerable uniformity. These data are shown in Table 4.

During the period investigated there has been a considerable growth in the number of states with legislation containing age limits, and at the same time there has been a considerable increase in the size of the age limits. Theoretically, there are two ways in which this may occur. First, the pioneer states may begin with a low age limit and throughout a period of years gradually evolve higher ones. The states which year by year initiate legislation may on the basis of adaptation and experience follow the same course as the pioneer states. This must result in a slow advancement of the age limit. On the other hand, the states which

TABLE 4. *The Typical Age Limits for Occupation Groups*

	1879	1884	1889	1894	1899	1904	1909
Occupation Group A Manufacturing.......	10	10	12	12	14	14	14
Occupation Group B Mercantile..........	......	......	13	13	14	14	14
Occupation Group C Hotels, offices, etc.....	......	......	......	......	14	14	14
Occupation Group D Steel trades.........	......	......	......	......	14	14	14
Occupation Group E Mining.............	12	12	12	12	14	14	14
Occupation Group F Any gainful occupation	......	......	......	......	14	14	14
Occupation Group G Dangerous occupations	16	16	16, 14	16	14	14	16
All Occupation Groups..	16	12, 14	12	12	14	14	14
Occupation Groups A, B, C, D, E, F..........	10, 12	12	12	12	14	14	14

year by year initiate legislation may adopt, at each year of their initiatory legislation, age limits which are approximately the same as the average age limit or the typical age limit at that time. This process must result in a more rapid advancement of the age limits. This latter process illustrates the force of imitation and the spreading influence of the mores. It is more largely the latter process that has been followed by the states in their advancement of the age limit and their increase of child-labor legislation.

Uniformity in Age Limits

THE CONCEPTION OF UNIFORMITY   The expression "uniformity in child-labor legislation" possesses several meanings.

The term is popularly used with two distinct meanings. One is the following: If more states have enacted child-labor legislation by 1909 than had enacted it in 1904, there has been an increase in the likenesses among the states in the matter of possessing child-labor legislation, and there has been more increase of uniformity with respect of that likeness. In reality this idea of uniformity is simply that of increase. The other current meaning of uniformity refers to laws rather than to states. For instance, are the state laws that exist in 1909 more uniform than those that existed in 1904? Here the idea of increase in legislation is eliminated. This latter idea of uniformity is the one that appears in the further discussions.

It is well to inquire what is meant by the word "uniformity," when the uniformity in the state laws of one period is compared with the uniformity at another period. Does it mean the amount of similarity? Does it mean the amount of exact resemblance? In analyzing the idea of uniformity for the purpose of measuring it, several possible meanings appear: (1) Uniformity may be looked upon as the amount of likeness or resemblance that exists among the individual laws. It may be that no two laws are exactly the same; it may be that no two laws are identical even in certain essentials; yet considerable likeness may exist. And at one period of years there may be more likenesses among the laws than at another, though at each period no two laws are identical even in certain essentials. If then the laws are more alike at one time than another, may it not be said that they are more uniform? If this be accepted as an idea of uniformity, then to measure the uniformity the amount of likeness would have to be determined quantitatively with regard to the various attributes of the laws. This would be difficult to do, particularly if it were attempted to express the amount of likeness or uniformity in a single term or expression. Because of certain difficulties this method has not been developed in this section or in the discussions of any of the sections of this study. (2) Another idea of uniformity is as follows: In any number of child-labor laws, it is possible to find a law—it may be an imaginary one—which all the other laws closely resemble. The amount of resemblance which each law bears to this law may be calculated. The average resemblance which all of the laws bear to this law may be looked upon as the amount of uniformity that exists among the laws. Thus the uniformity of the laws may be found for any period. Certain difficulties are found in measuring uniformity according to this conception. It is necessary to decide what shall be taken as the law to which the resemblance of the other laws is measured; how this resemblance can be measured; and how it can be put in a scale so that the averages may be found. This conception of uniformity has been used in this study as the basis for measuring uniformity; it is further developed in the pages which immediately follow. The aim is to present in this paragraph only the conception of uniformity. (3) Still another conception of uniformity is that of the amount of identity that exists among the individual laws. Some exact resemblance will exist if the attributes in which resemblance is measured are sufficiently broad. On this basis, then, there can be calculated the greatest number of laws that are exactly alike, that is, an actual one-formness among the laws. The amount of this uniformity, or one-formness, can be calculated for any one time; and, in order that it may be compared, the amount of one-formness may be expressed in proportion to the total number of laws. This idea of uniformity has been used also as a basis for measuring uniformity throughout the study. It is further developed in the pages which immediately follow. This method is generally applicable.

It is now obvious that the conception of uniformity is not simple—not so simple as the conception of the height of a person nor so easily measured. Consequently, it has been necessary to analyze carefully the idea of uniformity from the point of view of a possible basis of measurement. For purposes of illustration, the problem of measuring the uniformity in a body of child-labor laws may be compared to the problem of measuring the uniformity in a number of individual persons. A group of persons are alike or unlike in many attributes—height, weight, hair color, eye color, memory, temperament. Child-labor laws are alike or unlike in many attributes—age limits, occupations affected, hours of labor, educational requirements. It is simpler to estimate the uniformity in a body of persons with respect to one attribute than it is to measure the total amount of uniformity. It is easier to estimate the uniformity of child-labor legislation with respect to the attributes taken singly. The uniformity of child-labor legislation with respect to age limits is considered here.

THE CALCULATION OF UNIFORMITY IN AGE LIMITS   The indexes of uniformity for age limits in the state laws as presented in Table 5 have been calculated according to the second conception of uniformity mentioned in the foregoing pages, namely,

TABLE 5. *Uniformity in Age Limits for the Occupation Groups*
   (*Larger numbers mean less uniformity*)

		1879	1884	1889	1894	1899	1904	1909
Occupation Group A Manufacturing	No. of cases.... Uniformity.....	7 1.19	11 1.45	25 1.33	32 1.27	31 1.38	43 1.22	54 1.10
Occupation Group B Mercantile	No. of cases.... Uniformity.....	....	....	7 1.33	8 1.12	14 1.41	18 1.14	31 0.72
Occupation Group C Hotels, offices, etc.	No. of cases.... Uniformity.....	....	....	....	....	....	7 0.68	20 0.65
Occupation Group D Street trades	No. of cases.... Uniformity.....	....	....	....	....	....	11 1.56	31 2.01
Occupation Group E Mining	No. of cases.... Uniformity.....	7 1.28	10 0.98	24 1.08	37 0.95	32 1.04	38 1.22	46 1.30
Occupation Group F Any gainful occupation	No. of cases.... Uniformity.....	....	....	....	....	6 1.29	8 0.33	22 0.71
Occupation Group G Dangerous occupations	No. of cases.... Uniformity.....	20 1.83	26 2.20	42 2.66	57 2.61	81 2.68	107 2.63	197 2.26

uniformity as an approximation to a specific standard. In this case the standard, resemblance to which is measured, is the arithmetic average of the age limits. The closeness of approach of the various age limits to the average age limit is calculated and called an "index of uniformity." This closeness of approach is calculated by extracting the square root of the arithmetic average of the squares of the individual differences between the respective age limits and the average age limit. This is, approximately, the average amount of resemblance to the standard age limit. It should be remembered that the smaller the index of uniformity thus calculated the greater the uniformity. This method needs no further discussion as it is the method commonly used in measuring variability. It is applicable only in cases where the differences can be measured in a scale.

Figure 2 presents graphically the changes in uniformity of age limits in the various occupation groups from period to period. In all the occupation groups except that of mining and that of street trades, there has been an increase in uniformity during the past ten years. The lessening uniformity in the age limits in the mining industries seems to be due in part to the fact that some of the states have raised their age limit for this occupation to 16 years, while others retain on their statute books old laws with very low age limits. The low and decreasing uniformity in

TABLE 6. *Uniformity in Age Limits for Combinations of Occupation Groups*

(Larger numbers mean less uniformity)

		1879	1884	1889	1894	1899	1904	1909
All Occupation Groups	No. of cases....	35	47	100	134	169	232	401
	Uniformity.....	2.60	2.51	2.52	2.07	2.47	2.35	2.03
Occupation Groups A, B, C, D, E, F	No. of cases....	15	21	58	81	88	125	204
	Uniformity.....	1.41	1.47	1.31	1.12	1.28	1.20	1.24

the street trades is due to the fact that several different occupations in this group have called for different age limits, also to the fact that for street trades, a higher age limit is sometimes set for girls than for boys. In the earlier years, in all the occupations, the number of cases is so small that very little significance can be attached to the indexes of uniformity found for these years. During the period of years studied there has been a continuous change in the average age limit for each occupation; hence it would seem reasonable to expect fluctuating indexes of uniformity, the uniformity being an approximation to the changing average. The indexes of uniformity for the dangerous occupations mean little, since different age limits are expected for some of the different occupations in that group. This yields figures which mean little uniformity. The same is true for the uniformity in the occupation groups taken together, as is shown in Table 6,

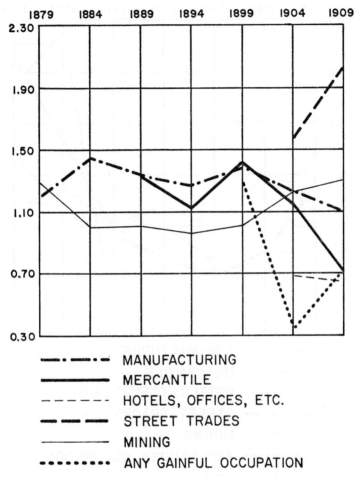

Fig. 2. Uniformity in age limits for occupation groups by five-year periods. (A downward slant to a line means increasing uniformity. The figures to the left of the diagram are indexes of uniformity.)

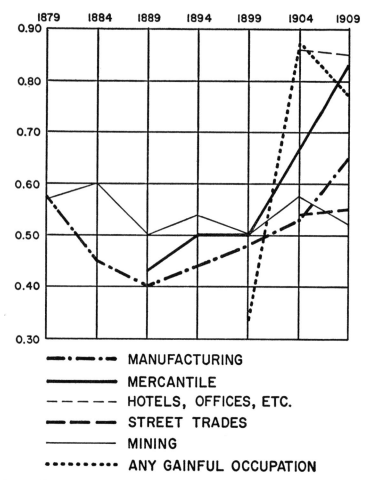

Fig. 3. Uniformity in age limits as percentages of exact resemblance to
types for the occupation groups by five-year periods. (An upward
slant to a line means increasing uniformity. The figures to the
left of the diagram are indexes of uniformity.)

because there is a large influence of the dangerous occupations. However, there has been a considerable increase in the uniformity in the occupation groups taken together since 1899. In conclusion, then, it may be said, speaking generally, that there has been an increase in uniformity in age limits during the last ten or fifteen years.

ANOTHER METHOD OF CALCULATING UNIFORMITY   Further knowledge may be gained of the uniformity in age limits by

TABLE 7. *Uniformity in Age Limits, as Percentages of Exact*
Resemblance to Types, for the Occupation Groups
The Ratio of the Number of Cases of Greatest Frequency
to the Total Number of Cases

(*Larger numbers mean more uniformity*)

		1879	1884	1889	1894	1899	1904	1909
Occupation Group A Manufacturing	Total number.......	7	11	25	32	31	43	54
	Ratio in per cents...	0.57	0.45	0.40	0.44	0.48	0.53	0.65
Occupation Group B Mercantile	Total number.......	.....	.....	7	8	14	18	31
	Ratio in per cents...	.....	.....	0.43	0.50	0.50	0.67	0.84
Occupation Group C Hotels, offices, etc.	Total number.......	.....	.....	.....	.....	.....	7	20
	Ratio in per cents...	.....	.....	.....	.....	.....	0.86	0.85
Occupation Group D Street trades	Total number.......	.....	.....	.....	.....	.....	11	31
	Ratio in per cents...	.....	.....	.....	.....	.....	0.54	0.55
Occupation Group E Mining	Total number.......	7	10	24	37	32	38	46
	Ratio in per cents...	0.57	0.60	0.50	0.54	0.50	0.58	0.52
Occupation Group F Any gainful occupation	Total number.......	.....	.....	.....	.....	6	8	22
	Ratio in per cents...	.....	.....	.....	.....	0.33	0.87	0.77

attempting to measure it by another method. The conception of uniformity here measured is the third conception, briefly outlined on a previous page, namely, the conception of uniformity as one-formness. That age limit which most of the state laws have adopted is the one-form, and the extent to which it is adopted is the extent of one-formness, or uniformity, in age limits. Thus, if the number of typical age limits is 40 per cent of all the age limits at one time, and if at another time it is 60 per cent, then it may be said that the uniformity has increased. According to this idea of uniformity, figures have been calculated showing the extent of uniformity in age limits for the different occupation groups. These are presented in Table 7. These figures were calculated as follows: It is seen from a previous table that there are fifty-four age limits in 1909 for the manufacturing group of occupations. The most common age limit is 14 years. There are thirty-five age limits that are 14 years. This number of age limits is 65 per cent of all the age limits, and this 65 per cent may be taken as indicating the uniformity in age limits in 1909. The other figures are similarly derived. It will be observed that, in these figures, the larger the percentage, the greater the uniformity.

Figure 3 presents graphically the changes from time to time in uniformity for the occupation groups. In this figure, an upward slant of the line means increasing uniformity. The conclusions that may be drawn from this figure and from Table 7 are in accord with the conclusions drawn from Figure 2 and from Table 5. Uniformity and tendencies to uniformity thus seem to be the same, whether deduced by one method or the other.

11

TECHNOLOGY AND GOVERNMENTAL

CHANGE   *1936*

THAT social changes are rapidly taking place today is a truism. The daily newspapers carry cartoons proclaiming it. Moving-picture films illustrate it. Why is the social current moving so rapidly; why is the torrent so much disturbed? It was not always this way. Among isolated primitive peoples, the years that come and go are very much the same. A mother knows that her granddaughter will be doing about what her own grandmother did. No doubt such a relatively static condition existed among the Europeans of prehistorical times. But today no mother can predict five generations ahead what her offspring will be doing.

The volume of rapid social change is the outstanding, basic fact of modern times. No field of social life escapes its influence. No social phenomenon can be discussed without considering it.

Why is there so much social change today, and why was there so little in ancient times? The most probable answer, the result of quite extensive study, is mechanical invention and scientific discovery. There is no doubt that useful inventions and researches

---

Reprinted from the *Journal of Business of the University of Chicago,* IX, No. 1 (January, 1936). This is the first of a series of lectures given in 1935–36 at the University of Chicago under the general title, "The Shifting Borderline between Government and Business."

cause social changes. Steam and steel were major forces in developing our extensive urban life. Gunpowder influenced the decline of feudalism. The discovery of seed-planting destroyed the hunting cultures and brought a radically new form of social life. The automobile is helping to create the metropolitan community. Small inventions, likewise, have far-reaching effects. The coin-in-the-slot device changes the range and nature of salesmanship, radically affects different businesses, and creates unemployment. The effects of the invention of contraceptives on population and social institutions is so vast as to defy human estimation. It is obvious, then, that social changes are caused by inventions.

Not everything new, of course, comes from mechanical invention. There are social inventions also, as, for instance, proportional representation, social insurance, the holding company, and the League of Nations. Some social changes originate then from social inventions. Social inventions may have been precipitated by mechanical inventions, as, for instance, the Interstate Commerce Commission was caused by the railroads. The connection between the social invention and the mechanical is not so close in the case of the juvenile court, which results from changes in the urban family due in turn to the mechanical forces that produced city life. Some social inventions are so far removed from mechanical invention that any connection is scarcely discernible. Such would be the case with the invention of the parole of prisoners. On the other hand, some social inventions cause mechanical inventions. Thus, a sales tax may bring out a new token money. A zoning law, as in New York, may force architectural devices to be used to modify the skyline, or an antinoise campaign may cause the invention of a rubber horseshoe used in connection with milk wagons on early-morning deliveries.

Indeed, the more one studies the relationship between mechanical and social inventions, the more interrelated they seem. Civilization is a complex of interconnections between social institutions and customs, on the one hand, and technology and science, on the other. The whole interconnected mass is in motion. When each part is in motion and banging up against some other part, the question of origins seems artificial and unrealistic. If one pushes the question to the extreme, origins are lost in a maze of causative factors.

The analysis can be carried further and clarified more, but at a cost of time. Such an effort would be beyond the scope of this paper. It may be said, however, that new contributions in technology and science are more accumulative than new contributions to customs and social institutions. And the bigger the accumulation of technology, the more probably there will be a greater number of new inventions. So in the course of time a great technology has developed, accompanied by an enormous number of inventions which occasion social changes. But it is not necessary to accept completely such an analysis for the purpose of this paper. All that it is necessary to admit is that there are a very large number of inventions and patents every year and that many of these cause social change.

If an invention causes social change, then the invention must come first. Sometimes the consequent social change may come very quickly, almost immediately. Thus consolidated rural schools followed shortly after the coming of good roads and the automobile. In other cases, the social changes follow very slowly, requiring a century or more. As an illustration, the general property tax, that is adapted to a system of agriculture where property is visible, has persisted for a century after inventions increased greatly the proportion of our property that is tangible and rendered the general property tax unjust and inadequate. One may say, therefore, that technology moves forward and the social institution lags behind in varying degrees.

As to why so much time elapses between a technological development and the social changes it causes, there are a great variety of reasons, only one of which will be mentioned now. It is that the contact of the social institution with the technology is not direct but takes place through a varying number of intermediaries. A change in A will not effect a change in D directly but must effect a change in B first, which then changes C, which in turn reaches D. Time is required for such a process of change. Thus the invention of the elevator increases the number of homes in apartment houses, which leads to increased density of population, which tends to lower the birth rate, which sets free more of a married woman's time, which finally increases the number of women employed outside the home. It takes some time, therefore, for the invention of the elevator to affect the employment of women or otherwise to spend its force as one social change after another is affected.

A very common pattern is for the technological change to affect, first, an economic organization which, second, causes a change in some social institution, such as the family or government, and which finally causes a change in the social philosophy of a people. Thus technology brings the factors which take occupations away from the home; which cause a loss of other functions of the family, such as caring for the old; which causes the government to provide old-age pensions; which in turn tends to weaken the social philosophy of laissez faire. It is not claimed that such a process is universal, has been true in all history or prehistory, or that there are not other different social processes. All that is claimed is that observation shows such a process to be fairly common today. Observation of the phenomena of the social change of modern times also reveals that governmental institutions are often the third link in this four-chain sequence, to wit, technology, industry, government, social philosophy. The statement of sequence is an elaboration of the theory of the economic interpretation of history, made by placing a technological factor before the economic factor. The economic interpretation of history really is a technological interpretation of history.

This theory then means that technology, through the media of other institutions, is forcing changes in government, if we may focus our attention on that particular institution. It follows also that changes in government come later than the precipitating technological changes. Our interest may now be turned to the questions of how much later do changes in government occur and is such a delay a serious matter? These questions may best be pursued by considering some illustrations.

That governments are slow to change is shown by a consideration of county government. In the early history of the United States, when the great majority of the population followed farming as an occupation, when cities were rare and villages many, the county was a very significant unit of government. The size of the county was a convenient one, having been laid out in terms of the horse and buggy and the inferior roads of the time. The distance of chief concern was that to the county seat, where the courthouse was located. The taxation base was largely farm wealth, and since the family of that time performed so many social functions, what the government did was not extensive. The social services were not developed very much at the time, and county government was not expensive.

But the situation became changed because of the factory and because of the transportation inventions. The effect of the factory was to differentiate the sources of wealth and concentrate it in cities, particularly the intangible forms of property. At the same time the factory transferred many governmental functions, formerly exercised by the family, over to various agencies of local government, thus increasing the cost. The county government became unable to meet modern problems and, as a government, drifted into a subsidiary position among the various other forms. At the same time the automobile and the steam locomotive were perfected, which made it theoretically possible for a county government to serve a much larger area as readily as it served its present area in earlier days. If the county were, say, ten times its present area, it would have a much wider base for raising revenue, a very important matter. The situation is further illustrated by a comparison with the wards of a city. One would not recommend that each ward of a city have a separate government financed from funds raised only from within the boundaries of the ward. The poorer wards would not be able to supply their own governmental needs. With the changed methods of transportation, counties are now somewhat like the wards in the preceding illustration. The expense of trying to maintain so many county offices in a state of efficiency is a burden on the taxpayer which could be alleviated by consolidating counties, as was done with rural schools.

Technology thus brings about a condition where fewer and larger counties are needed. But the county government does not change to keep pace with the advancing technology. This delay is quite long and costly. In a severe depression, such as we have just experienced, it is a very serious handicap.

This resistance of a social pattern to change is so common that social scientists have given it a scientific name, "cultural inertia." Boundary lines between counties and states are peculiarly resistant to modification. Boundary lines of cities also are difficult to enlarge, but less so. If the boundary lines of counties are not changed so that a number of them may be consolidated, the governmental functions will tend to leave the county and go to units with a larger tax base, such as the state and the nation.

A governmental pattern that is very inert may persist so long that it loses all its old functions and takes on an entirely new set. Such is the case with the persistence of the Monroe Doctrine, which has a function different from that it had a century ago.

The government of peoples within the present areas of counties will have to make some kind of adjustment to meet the new technological situation. Certainly the technological situation is not going to be changed backward to make an adjustment to an unchanged county. So there will be an adjustment in one way or another. But the question is, How costly will be the delay, how inefficient? The longer the delay, the greater the cost, the more inefficiency there will be, the more maladjustment will result.

A somewhat similar illustration, but less obvious, is the selection of representation for legislative assemblies. The basis of selection in this country is geographical, which was quite appropriate at the time the assemblies were set up, for differences were largely geographical. Distances were great and communication undeveloped. Andrew Jackson fought the Battle of New Orleans three weeks after the War of 1812 was over and the treaty signed. He had not heard the news. The relative isolation of different districts meant that customs, manners, interests, and even dialects developed peculiar to different localities. But transportation, communication, and advertising have greatly changed these differences. The newspapers are surprisingly alike as one travels from Atlantic to Pacific. Towns and cities show the same advertising; and the store windows, the same displays.

Meanwhile, other technologies have differentiated society into a vast number of occupation and interest groups: laborers, farmers, bankers, cotton-growers, the foreign-born, the professions, etc. Formerly, nearly everyone was a farmer. Society has become more alike horizontally, so to speak, but vertically more differentiated. Yet, the basis of representation is still geographic in this country. The logical step to take, it is thought, would be to give representation to the interest groups. But the governmental patterns stay fixed. We have, then, a changing technology with consequent changes in economic and allied institutions, but a rigid governmental structure. What happens? In this case legislative lobbies, affording some sort of representation to these special interests, grow up outside the formal structure of constitutional government. Indeed, they have been called the "Third House." They are not recognized officially, as in Italy and in Russia. This sort of roundabout adjustment has led some observers of the governmental process to think that a flexible people with ingenuity can make any governmental structure work. According to this attitude, it doesn't make any difference what kind of a governmental structure we have; the right spirit in the people will make it click. This conclusion is only grossly true in wide limits. It simply means that the people will have some kind of government. But if we make more refined observations on degrees of adjustment and maladjustment, it would seem to be clear that a more flexible governmental structure would enable a happier adjustment to a rapidly changing technology, which goes its own way without having to make adjustments to government.

The slowness of governmental structure to change is quite impressive as one studies the situation, at least so far as the United States is concerned in the course of its brief history. A very simple illustration of quite a minor character was accidentally observed recently in noting the comparisons of characteristics of rapidly growing cities with those of cities with declining populations. The number of police per unit of population was quite consistently fewer for the rapidly growing cities and greater for the cities with a declining population. Why does a rapidly growing city have fewer police than a declining one of the same size?

Quite probably, when the budget is made up for the coming year, the estimates are based on the known past rather than on a problematical increase (or decline) of population. Furthermore, policies in regard to tenure of office may be against the practice of dismissals and possibly of increases of staff. But, no matter what the reason, the government does not change quickly enough in increasing or decreasing the numbers of police to adjust to population changes. Again, it may be noted that population increases or decreases of cities are due largely to economic changes, as has often been shown, and these in turn rest on technology.

One of the most important sources of extensive changes in government is the decline of the family. Let us consider more fully this relationship, since it is not generally appreciated by students of political science or by students of sociology. The major changes in the family organization are due to technology. The steam engine as a source of power was too large for the dwelling house with its home industries, and the larger buildings that were built were called factories. Spinning, weaving, furniture production, soap production, medicine-making, canning, baking, tailoring, sewing, laundering, followed the steam engine into the factory. When these economic functions were in the home, the family as an institution regulated and controlled industrial production and the conditions of labor. But with the transfer of production to the factory, industrial conditions were uncontrolled for quite a time by any outside institution; but later the state took over certain regulations, such as those dealing with child labor, accidents, working conditions, and hours of labor, which were formerly handled by the family. Whether government in exercising such regulations has made a satisfactory adjustment to this loss of economic functions by the family will be questioned by many persons who protest the existing order. There are those who argue that the Supreme Court still blocks the proper adaptation, and it may also be argued that the persistence of old boundaries to local governing areas delays a proper adaptation on the part of government to an industry that has sprawled over state lines. But most everyone will agree that the government delayed much too long in shortening the hours of labor of children and in general in preventing the excesses of unregulated industrialism.

With the loss of the economic functions from the family, there was a corresponding loss in other correlated functions. A very good illustration is the protective function exercised by the family over its members. For instance, the police now afford families a protection once rendered by the adult males of the family with their swords. So, also, the family's recognized obligation was to protect its children. Yet in many families under the condition of life in the city's slums, where mothers are wage-earners and where gangs thrive, the protection of children is shifted to governmental agencies, such as juvenile courts, reform schools, playgrounds, and day nurseries. So, also, caring for the old was almost exclusively a family function before the modern technological development, except in those accidental cases of badly broken kinship groups among the very poor, when the county poorhouse was provided. But now the transportation system scatters the members of the family groups to the different corners of the nation. The invention of contraceptives means that often there are no children to care for the old. The factory system brings more mobility of labor over longer distances than does household agriculture. Furthermore, the crowding of families in multifamily dwellings puts a premium on living space, which makes the adjustment to the care of the aged more difficult, as does also the absence of a vegetable garden in cities. Private insurance companies have not met the problem, so this family function of caring for the old is being taken over by the state through the medium of old-age insurance.

Indeed, it may be said that all forms of social insurance are functions taken over by the government from the family, because technology first changed the family, which in turn forced a governmental change as new technological developments grew up outside the homestead. This transfer of functions from the family to the state is not appreciated by the laissez-faire-ists. The family was once the chief regulatory agency over production; but as technology moved production outside, it was more or less unregulated, until it was found that the state had to do what the family once did in regulating working conditions. So, also, much of the proliferation of the functions of city governments, so well described by many political scientists, is really the collective handling of functions that were done by the farm families before technology changed the face of society. The breakdown of the family accomplished by technology is, then, in a way, the cause of the socialistic and fascistic trends of the state.

From this analysis it follows logically that there must have been a delay in the transfer of functions from family to state. How serious the maladjustment was can only be determined by examining each transfer separately. But the delay was quite seriously prolonged in the case of workmen's compensation and no doubt in the case of caring for the old and in unemployment insurance, as well as in other services.

Another illustration of technology forcing a change lies in the field of international relations. Here the steamboat, the cable, and radio have meant trade and travel, investment, and the flow of short-time securities. Yet "Washington's Farewell Address" about entangling alliances is still quoted in support of an isolationist policy. An adequate governmental development, to keep pace with the technology that is forcing contacts between nations and nationals, would include the ambassadorial and consular service, trade and investment information bureaus, well-thought-out creditor and debtor policies, monetary programs, as well as more than an isolated attack on such an international problem as war. We have in recent years greatly improved the consular service and made much better provisions for information about trade. But in most other relations, it is easy to show rather conspicuous inadequacies. In this particular illustration it is quite difficult within the limits of this paper to prove that changes in our governmental machinery dealing with contacts with other nations have not kept pace with the technology that has increased there. But a brief examination of the situation makes the hypothesis quite probable.

The most convincing illustrations in support of the idea of governmental inertia against the pervasive force of technological change are naturally historical rather than contemporary. From the practical point of view there are many acute situations today apparently owing to the slowness of governments to change, but this causal relationship is difficult to prove. Quite similar to the crisis in county government is the situation in reference to the suburban areas of the very large cities. The problem of government in suburban areas is precipitated by the automobile and rapid rail transportation, both of relatively recent origin. They have dispersed population and factories outward from the metropolitan center, but not yet has the city government been extended outward. Instead there has grown up a multiplicity of local governments, educational boards, sanitary commissions, park committees, health units, town governments, and dock commissions, presenting overlappings as well as interstitial areas. The advantage of a larger central government made by consolidation of these smaller local governing units is easily argued. The advantages of consolidation are not difficult to see in dealing with crime, where the narrow boundary lines of city governments are quite inadequate to hold the criminal. He has learned the use of the automobile in making his escape, and his search for hideouts has taken him into outlying regions where police surveillance is weak or non-existent. What is happening is the creation by technology of a new population unit—not a city, not a village, not a county. Indeed, there is as yet no name for it. For want of a better designation it is sometimes called a "metropolitan area." But while technology has created this new population unit, there has not yet been created an adequate governing unit for it.

An inquiry into the relations of technology and governmental change should include illustrations of governmental change producing new technologies. Perhaps the best illustration is that of wartime governmental organizations developing military inventions and machines useful in war. Here the governmental change would seem to precede the technology. War, however, is also accompanied by a slowness to import military inventions found in other nations. Military establishments are not always up-to-date.

There are, of course, many cases where governments take up directly a new invention and make use of it. Such is the case with the airplane. In such instances the reaction of government to technology is somewhat similar to industry. In these cases of direct use of tools by governments, adaptation is quite rapid once the government decides to adopt the new machine. The situation is different, though, in those cases where the influence is less direct, but comes indirectly from the infringement of some other social institution which has felt earlier its direct influence. Thus the government seems to be slow in adjusting to the monopolistic industries that technology is encouraging and in recognizing the public-utility status in several industries that appear to have reached that status today, again owing largely to technology.

There is one type of governmental activity that very definitely encourages resistance to change. I refer to the courts, in their practice of following precedent when interpreting a particular law. Law, itself, is in a peculiar position as regards social change. Common law is the codification of certain old customs on vital matters. Hence the common law crystallized the old and would, of course, be essential in stationary societies. New situations are dealt with by new laws from legislative bodies. The purpose of new laws, like the old, is to make rules that society is to follow. But naturally, rules, in so far as they are specific, as most legal rules are, are only applicable to situations that are continuing. Thus, law-makers and law-administers seem to have the functions of laying out grooves for the flow of human behavior and of trying to force human beings to fit into the grooves. Such an assignment is quite in conformity with life as found in a stationary society. But in our changing society, technology is continuously breaking up many of the grooves that law makes and administers. Thus law and technology are opponents as in a battle. So it is natural that the courts should hark back to precedent, and the administrator is under oath to enforce the law, no matter what the changes may bring about. The lawyer loves the orderliness of his pattern of law and does not like to have it disarranged by invention. Meanwhile, in our rapidly changing society, the legislatures have a difficult task, with their large membership and their tradition of deliberation, of keeping up with the new and changing conditions brought in by technology.

The courts are thus an extreme case of special resistance to change, but other structures of government have also special forces operating on them to resist change. The Constitution of the United States is thus too revered and hallowed an instrument to tamper with. The utterances of the fathers of our government are to be followed as literally as possible, so great is their halo, although they lived in a comparatively simple household economy, while ours is a quite complicated machine age.

Some governmental structures are thus an unusual obstacle to change. Meanwhile, technology develops, is let loose on society, sweeping all before it. Time on the clock of technology cannot be turned back. We cannot return to the Stone Age, or to the horse and buggy, or to the plantation days of a rural economy. Technology rolls on like a huge tidal wave, while governmental structures stand like the Rock of Ages in a world of disorder—an irresistible force meeting an immovable object. If governmental structures won't change and technology can't be stopped, what will happen? The answer is that the impasse may be avoided, after delays long and painful enough, by developing practices not officially recognized as governmental or political. These do the functions which a governmental structure would do if it had changed. Thus the legislative lobby performs, perhaps less well, functions which would be performed by a reorganized legislature with a more adequate basis of representation. The basis of legislative representation does not change; the influence of technology in reclassifying social groups cannot be stopped; hence, a new liaison body develops to make the old governmental body work, somehow, under the new conditions. Of course, it is not strictly true, either, that governmental structures do not change. The Constitution is amended from time to time, and new administrative bodies do develop and even exercise legislative functions. But the tragedy lies in the delay. In conclusion, then, we may say, technology cracks the whip, but because these extra liaison bodies do not develop rapidly and properly in the effort to make the lethargic governmental structure work, the institutions of society slip out of gear, and humanity suffers because of it.

12

ON INVENTIONS AND THE STATE

1949

THE PURPOSE of this introduction is to develop a possible frame of reference for the reader of the chapters, varying in approach and range, which constitute the text of this book. The development of this frame of reference consists in the exposition of three themes. The three movements described have existed throughout all history, and in each a crisis exists at the present time. They are the shifts in the relative power of states, the evolution of states in geographical size, and the pursuit of peace. All three movements are related to and affected by technology. The presentation is wholly introductory and consists of the presentation of ideas and the indication of significances rather than the drawing of conclusions and the presentation of evidence.

The Ranking of Powers

We may begin with a consideration of the ranking of states on the basis of their military power. In a world in which war is frequent, nations have a ranking order of power. They are like the chickens studied by biologists, which are found to have a definite pecking order when a feed pan is set down among

Reprinted from *Technology and International Relations* (Chicago: University of Chicago Press, 1949), pp. 1–15.

them. The rank is perhaps not so definite among nations as it is among chickens, for the competition, even in peacetime, is not settled to the agreement of all concerned. The new inventions and population changes cause shifts in ranking after periods of struggle. For example, Britain fought it out with Spain on the seas in the sixteenth century and in the eighteenth and nineteenth century again with France. Britain's rank in the order of power was top during the nineteenth century.

Britain's top position was strengthened by her early acquisition of the steam engine and of modern methods of steelmaking. These inventions were applied to her navy and to her merchant ships. Her trading vessels carried the products of her factories to various parts of the world and brought back foods and raw materials. Britain, about the size of the state of Oregon, was thus enabled to support a population of forty-five million, whereas in 1800 her population had been only ten million. The Industrial Revolution, produced by steam and steel, occurred first in Britain and is credited with strengthening her navy and her finances and increasing her population.

Inventions have a way of spreading after a time from one part of the world to another. But the use of coal in engines and the making of steel from iron ore cannot be done just anywhere. Coal mines are required, with iron mines not too far away. These requisites of military might are found in the United States, Russia, India, northern China and Manchuria, Germany, and, to a certain extent, in France, Poland, and Japan, but not so satisfactorily in other countries of Europe or in South and Central America. The use of steam engines and the making of steel spread from Britain to Germany, the United States, and Japan. These techniques spread later to the Soviet Union and will be adopted by India and China. Germany, the United States, and Japan have become great powers. Indeed, Germany may be said to have challenged Britain's rank as a power.

Steam and steel do not alone produce a nation high in the rank of power. Belgium had steel mills, but not many; and her population was small. Also, an area, to be the seat of a great military power, must have political coherence. The western and central parts of the continent of Europe have both coal and iron. If the peoples of this area had had political unity, the rank of this area as a power would be greater. Continental Europe may yet acquire the necessary political unity to become a great power.

One of the problems of policy for non-Continental European powers, arising from the spread of steam and steel to Europe, is whether to encourage the continuance of a Europe made up of many small states or whether to favor consolidation. Consolidation would mean a stronger ally if the alliance could be guaranteed to last. The defeat of Germany had the effect of preventing a Europe more tightly organized around Germany as a center. There may be some fear on the part of other powers that a consolidated Europe might become too strong a power.

The industrial revolution is beginning to revolutionize the great area just east of Europe. The Soviet Union is organized politically and has both coal and iron and a large population. Indeed, with her heavy industries only partially developed and with her nationalism strongly assertive from the Second World War, Russia is already high in the rank of powers.

An interesting question is whether the acquisition of steam and steel makes a nation warlike. Sometime in the near future India and China will have much production done by mechanical power in mass amounts from assembly lines. Will these two relatively peaceful peoples then become fighting states?

The question seems at least doctrinaire, if not absurd, for is it not the will of a people and not steam power that makes them fight? And the will of a people is subject to persuasion. We shall not attempt to answer the question; and, of course, it cannot be answered definitively. But the idea may be a very important one, and we should like to present enough discussion to show that the question is not absurd in view of the probabilities in the practical world. The idea that industrial revolution may make a state warlike is really a question of the response of a people to machines which hold out the prospects of increasing wealth, which in turn calls for a search for ever more raw materials and for expanding markets. Both Japan and Germany became aggressor nations after they began to use steam in large amounts. Britain was, however, a relatively peaceful nation after she became industrialized. There were few, though, to challenge her supremacy. Nor has the highly industrialized United States been an aggressor nation. Although she was in the last two world wars, she entered late. The United States has had territory, natural resources in abundance, a small population, and no nearby challengers.

The theory that an industrial revolution may fan the spark of war into flames is based upon a sequence of attitudes—optimism, confidence, and aggressiveness—that is found in many situations. We shall present first this theory independent of international relations.

First is the attitude of optimism that often comes with a sudden increase of wealth. The fact that rapidly growing cities are optimistic has been frequently observed. Cities that double their population in a decade are places in which incomes expand quickly. Among nations the agricultural states are relatively poor compared to the industrialized ones, and when a nation whose occupations are largely farming and handicraft becomes possessed of power-driven factories that turn out products in profusion, the leadership, industrial and political, is likely to be optimistic.

The optimistic attitude is frequently correlated with the spirit of confidence, for optimism is often a result of achievement. A ruler or a political party claims credit for good times, though they be due to the forces of the business cycle or to the weather. Newly industrialized nations, like new cities, tend to have confidence.

Furthermore, these new and large rewards come as a result of initiative ("the early bird catches the worm"); and expanding factories, transportation systems, and merchandising establishments are the products of enterprise. So with optimism and confidence goes aggressiveness.

This aggressiveness need not display itself in war. It does not in cities, of course. When it does start a war, we call it "aggression." But newly industrialized nations feel many needs—for raw materials, for new areas to exploit, for favorable trading conditions, for additional markets, and, in general, for expansion. It is sometimes easy for these needs to lead to war, particularly where war is in the national tradition.

The foregoing theory is hardly well enough established to forecast a warlike India or a China on the march for conquest when it become industrialized, or a more militant Russia, when her heavy industries become greatly expanded after several more successful five-year plans. But such a contingency should be contemplated. This sequence of attitudes of optimism, confidence, and aggressiveness has been witnessed in Chicago, Seattle, and Los Angeles, on the Pacific coast, and in Texas, Germany, Japan, and Britain. It may well be expected in India and China. New struggles for position in the ranking of powers may follow the spread of the power inventions.

Policies are generally based not upon such long-run forecasts but upon more immediate issues. Logically, a policy of a large, highly industrialized power state that wished to maintain its rank at the top would be to try to prevent the industrialization of a large, populous, potentially rival state. Britain, however, did not try to prevent the industrialization of Germany or of the United States. On the contrary, she advanced India on the road to mechanization. Indeed, the policy of such states is rather that of exporting technology. Britain helped finance the economic development of the United States. Such foreign investments are the source of immediate income to the investors, and such interests far outweigh the fear of the growth of a rival and challenger. Even if the policy of a state should be to prevent the industrialization of a potential rival, as, for instance, Russia or China, such a policy could not be successful, though it might cause a little delay in the process.

For a large industrialized power the spread of blast furnaces to small states presents little challenge. On the other hand, if the small states of an area unite, they may become a danger. Britain was aware of such a danger on the European continent. If Britain wants a union of western European states now, it is probably as an ally against a much stronger power or as a zone of security. If the Germans had won in the Second World War, there would probably have been a good deal of integration of the various European states around Germany at the center. The combination might have been a very strong one. Indeed, there seems to be some fear from those that fought Germany in two world wars that if a European union is formed, it will be dominated by a Germany which may turn aggressor again. Others view the struggle between Russia and the Anglo-Saxons as a fight for control of a united Europe; at the same time, there are forces operating to split Europe in two, one part leaning toward Russia and the other toward Britain and the United States—a split which might prove costly in economic terms.

Policies of division or union in India and China have not been discussed. India, united under British rule, later became divided. China, which has had a long history of unity, probably could not be permanently so easily divided. On the other hand, China is not knit closely together by the contact inventions—and hers is a system with a very great loyalty to family, possibly a priority over loyalty to the state—and, in fact, is divided now by civil war.

The military power of a country depends not upon mechanization alone but, among other factors, on population. Manpower is still a source of fighting strength. But technology affects the supply of manpower also. In the past the spread of the industrial revolution into a country has been accompanied by an increase in population, as was the case in Britain, in Germany, and in Japan. A natural question then is, Will the expansion of power-driven industries in Russia stimulate an unusual increase in population; and, if so, how much will the population be increased? This same question may be asked about India and about China, in which countries the populations are already large.

Further inquiry into this question of population increase accompanying industrialization suggests a breakdown of the problem into the influences that affect the balance of the birth rate and the death rate. The death rate was lowered in Germany and in England by sanitation and medical progress as well as by the growth of factories. Hospitals and plumbing can be diffused into various countries more easily than blast furnaces and, indeed, without them. So the forces operating for the reduction of the death rate have preceded, in a measure, the industrialization forces. The death rates in India and in Russia have decreased for these reasons, and this decline has already meant an unusual rate

of population increase in these countries. Thus the forces associated with the coming of the industrial revolution to a country,
which affect population growth through the lowered death rate,
increase the strength of such industrialized nations as military
powers.

Later, however, the spurt of population growth of newly industrialized states has lessened, and these states in maturity face
a population decline. The slowing of the increase in population is
due to a decreasing birth rate, particularly in cities. The reduced
birth rate has been the result of birth control, which rests in part
on the invention of contraceptives—simple inventions, but vastly
important in social consequences. While historically a rise in
population growth due to industrialization and its accompani-
ments has preceded a fall in population growth due to birth control, it does not appear that this sequence is inevitable for the
areas to be industrialized in the future. It is possible that the
birth-control inventions could precede, rather than follow, the diffusion of the inventions of steam and steel. There is, however, no
statistical evidence to indicate that this is likely to occur.

The influence of contraceptives on the ranking powers may be
very great, though perhaps, not quite comparable to that of the
power inventions.

It appears that the birth-control inventions are about to create
in western Europe and in the United States either stationary
populations or declining ones. The spread of contraceptives into
the Soviet Union and to the Slavic peoples of eastern Europe has
not gone very far, and before their wide adoption a considerable
growth of the population, even without industrialization, is to be
expected over the next thirty or forty years. Hence this technological influence favors the relatively greater rise of the Soviet
Union as a military power.

There are, of course, many other technological influences,
such as the airplane, that affect the ranking of powers; but these
rest on a foundation of heavy industries. Finally, it is to be noted
at the present time that the two leading great powers, the Soviet
Union and the United States, are both large in area and in population. We raise the question as to whether at this stage of history
the top-ranking powers can be other than very large ones.

The Growth of States in Size

We now arrive in our introductory outline at another great phenomenon of history—the tendency of political units to grow larger. We wish to inquire how this trend is likely to operate in the near future. The question is particularly interesting at this time because of the expressed desire of many observers, who want to avoid the destruction of an atomic war, for a world government—one large political unit encompassing the earth.

The trend toward larger political units has been observable since preliterate times. The political groups of the American Indians, before the advent of the white man and the horse, inhabited quite small areas, though there was a good deal of territory included in the empires of the Mayas, the Incas, and the Aztecs. Before the Treaty of Westphalia there were nine hundred sovereign states among the Germanic peoples, which afterward were reduced to three hundred and fifty. When the Germanic Confederation was founded in 1815, the number was thirty-six; finally, in 1871, there was only one. Spain, France, Britain, Italy, Russia, and the United States are all unions of smaller political units. The same area, thus, tends in the long run to have fewer states.

These political entities may be thought of as of two types. One is the empire, held together generally by force, often attained by extensive conquests due to military superiority over the conquered peoples. The other is a nation, with greater coherence and often less heterogeneity in language, ethnic stock, and customs.

The growth in size of both empire and nation has been achieved generally by military force, though the size has become greater also at times by the marriage of rulers and by federations based on agreements. Even when the Thirteen Colonies combined by agreement to form the United States, they sought strength in unification against possible military aggression from the outside.

In the expansion of states by conquest, technology plays a role, as does the size of the army and the quality of its courage. For instance, in the acquisition of colonial empires by Spain, France, and Britain in the sixteenth and seventeenth centuries, after the development of the boat and the compass, their superior technological equipment as compared with that of the natives made the conquest relatively easy. The advantage of the western Europeans in metals, horses, and gunpowder enabled vast empires to be created by conquests over peoples with only weapons of stone and wood, much inferior to guns and armor.

Conquests are not always enduring. Empires dissolve and states are split by civil war. So the growth of political units in size is met by reverses from time to time. The breakup of empires in particular is due to the weakness of the cohesive forces and to a rise in power of some coherent part of the empire. This dividing of empires is to be seen not as a trend but as a variation around a trend.

An interesting question is the part played by transportation and, lately, by communication inventions in the evolution of states in size. Where transportation of humans is accomplished solely by their own muscle, the state cannot be very large; though, with the boat and waterways and with good roads or paths, the area of a state can be considerably enlarged. The addition of sails to boats and the domestication of the horse make still larger states possible. Indeed, very large empires have been built with the aid of sailboats and the horse. The steamboat has increased the possibility of great empires based upon sea power, while the railroad has helped in making more cohesive large nations of land power. We are naturally curious as to whether the airplane will be used for further increasing the size of the nation or empire.

The relationship of transportation to the size of political areas is not so simple as is implied in the preceding paragraphs and needs further analysis. We have already indicated that thinking on this subject must continually differentiate two concepts: the unstable empire built upon conquest but with not enough solidarity to endure without force and the more stable nation with many linkages other than force holding the peoples of the nation together. In either case transportation inventions are only means, which may or may not be used for the enlargement of the area. When the transportation techniques used are poor, such as human muscle, the nation or empire cannot be very large. The stage of the transportation systems sets a limit somewhere on size. On the other hand, with big ships, horses, and railroads, larger, enduring nations are possible. Thus the stage of the transportation system makes states of varying sizes possible, depending upon the transportation inventions in use.

Since the transportation inventions are only a tool, an improvement in transportation is not automatically accompanied by an increase in the area of a state. An increase in the speed of railroad trains of 10 per cent is not automatically followed by an increase in area of the state of 10 per cent. Both small nations and large nations have railroads. Then, too, there are many factors affecting the growth of states in size other than the transportation inventions. One of these is wars of conquest. Where the differential in the tools of war is very great between the contestants, large areas may be brought under one rule. But first there must have been a war of conquest.

Another reason why transportational development is not soon followed by the increase in the size of states is the phenomenon of the resistance of political boundary lines to change. Over very long periods of time there is a correlation between transportation and size of political units, which were much smaller in Europe twenty-five hundred years ago than now. This is obvious, yet the point is important. Over short periods of time, perhaps hundreds of years, the correlation is not so clear. One reason is the resistance of political boundary lines to change. For instance, in the United States the political boundaries of counties, cities, and states, when first determined, bore a closer relation to economic and cultural conditions than at present. Now the economic city is larger than the political city, and we call it the "metropolitan area." County lines have not the social significance they had in the days of the horse and buggy, and many economic regions in the United States are much bigger than the states. A review of changes of boundary lines in Europe over the past several hundred years shows that most of the changes occur after wars. Therefore, in peacetime we should not expect transportation systems to be very effective in changing the boundaries of states. The influence, therefore, of the transportation inventions—which are only media—on the size of states would be effective only after a considerable lag, perhaps measured in hundreds of years.

When we speak of the evolution of nations in size, we mean durable nations, not transient empires. And when a one-world government is spoken of, it is an effective government that is wanted, not one that will be split by civil war or by secession.

The durability of a nation is a function of cohesive ties. What are these forces of cohesion? They are the magnetic force of common interests, but to be felt and made known as common to the people of a community, there must be communication through contacts. Over a large area, where the face-to-face contacts of a single person are with only a small fraction of the population, contacts are made with the aid of the transportation inventions or by the use of the communication devices. In modern times a great agency of communication is the printing press, the use of its products depending upon literacy.

These various contact inventions make for homogeneity through imitation, social pressure, intermarriage, trade, mass production, dress, topics of conversation, etc. It takes time for these similarities to occur. Religious differences, for instance, are very slow to break down. Hindus and Moslems living side by side have killed each other. More difficult to obtain is the cohesion of heterogeneous peoples having different languages, religions, customs, traditions, heroes, and loyalties.

The contact inventions are necessary, then, for the cohesiveness of peoples living over a large area. This is not to say that homogeneous groups may not have grave dissension. There may be religious differences, class friction, and economic conflicts in an area with many contact inventions. Indeed, the communication inventions are only tools which may be used for various purposes, for creating disruption as well as consensus. But, even when these inventions are used to foster homogeneity, there is delay due to resistances of race, of skin color, of religion, and of economic conflict.

We conclude that extensive use of the many contact inventions makes possible a greater solidarity of a large nation in much the same way in which the transportation inventions, together with the military ones, make possible nations with larger boundaries.

The question that follows this analysis concerns the significance of this theory for the present situation. In the airplane, which is still evolving, we have a transportation vehicle that is quite extraordinary as compared to ship, railroad, and automobile in its ability to cover immense distances with tremendous speeds. It would seem to make possible, when its use becomes extensive, a very large political unit, perhaps as large as the earth's surface. The domestication of the horse did not lead at once to the empire of Genghis Khan, about one-fifth of the land area of this planet.

Modern war inventions also make possible a very large nation. The atomic bomb, the air bomber, and the tank are very powerful weapons. The superiority of a state possessing them over a state not having them is great indeed. Speaking quite generally, does it not now appear possible for one state, after one or more wars, to conquer the world?

If these suggestions seem fantastic, the more modest claim that the new transportation inventions and the new war inventions make possible a very large political unit does not appear to be exaggerated. Small nations are quite at the mercy of the large mechanized ones. Twice the Germans made a bid by war for a larger territory. Without defeat we do not know how extensive their control might have been. Extensive conquest seems often to lead more readily and first to the empire type of political structure, which has less inherent stability than a unified state.

If, then, a world government is possible by virtue of the transportation and wartime inventions, we may ask whether this world structure can be administered and controlled successfully. The heterogeneity of the peoples of the world is very great, but so was the heterogeneity of the Roman Empire and of the British. To reduce the heterogeneity into the degree of homogeneity required for a nation, the contact inventions are needed, for they make possible the spread of similarities.

There does exist now a wonderful assortment of contact inventions, comprising the airplane, radio, television, facsimile, telephone, teletype, and printing press. The effective reduction of heterogeneity depends not only upon their existence but upon the extent of their use and the amount of resistance of localisms to their impact. The statistics on telephones, airplanes, automobiles, and radio sets show much less use of these in other parts of the world than in the United States. Furthermore, the varieties of language, religion, and the extent of illiteracy argue for the resistance to the spread of uniformities for a long time to come. The various states of Europe, although now fewer in number than a thousand years ago, are still not united into one single state. Important in these considerations, also, is the strength of local power groups which we now call "nations." They have the potentialities, by virtue of their ability in collective action, to break away from a world state.

If, then, a durable world state seems remote, the forces which help to produce the very large durable state are in existence. But, as we have seen, the existence of a set of contact inventions is not necessarily followed in a reasonably short time by an expansion in area of states. Yet these contact inventions are being used more and are more available to speed the evolution of states in size. Even the mechanized war inventions have been recently employed in two world wars in an effort to expand a large state. That the effort was unsuccessful for that particular state does not deny the fact of two world wars in a quarter of a century. Also we observe that after the Second World War, the top-ranking powers were larger than were the top-ranking powers before the First World War.

Before closing this theme of the evolution of political units in size, the question may be raised as to whether a new type of political unit may not be in the making. We have referred to two types—the nation and the empire. The possible emerging type may be a large nation with surrounding zones of influence. The large states want to have the nearby states friendly. As centers of dispersal of economic and cultural influence, these large states may integrate fairly closely, through the medium of the contact inventions, with the bordering friendly states into a regional grouping with the large state at the center. This may be done without any special formal political integration but with much the same functioning in international matters as if they were integrated politically.

This political arrangement of a large region may prove to be too unstable to be called a new type of political unit. Yet, even if it be not enduring, it may be a phase in the evolution of states in size.

However problematical the forecasts may be as to the growth of states in size, the existence of such a trend over the historical period indicates an important phenomenon as a frame of reference, set forth as a basis for the interpretation of the relationship of technology and international relations.

The Increasing Destructiveness of War

There is a third phenomenon, of recent origin yet of great importance, on which some comment is needed. The comment, though, may be brief. It is the vast devastation which wars now bring and which may be increased even more in future wars.

This increase in the destructiveness of wars is the result of science. Technology is applicable to war as well as to peaceful pursuits. So there are miracles of destruction as well as miracles of construction wrought by the marvels of science. These facts are well known. They are symbolized by the atomic bomb. But, before the atomic bomb, the chemical bombs were very destructive. Whole cities have been destroyed by them.

We have referred to the extreme devastation of modern war as contemporary rather than as characteristic of history. Some primitive peoples, however, have been almost exterminated by superior war power, especially of the white peoples; and some European wars in the past have been very destructive, as was the Thirty Years' War. But modern science has made the total mass of destruction vastly greater than ever before in history. We should, however, be looking toward the future on this problem of the human cost of wars, rather than toward the past or the present.

A point to be remembered but often overlooked is that new inventions do not remain as they now are but evolve. Atomic fission is only about a decade old. Many new discoveries are to be expected in nuclear physics, though now we do not know what they may be. We already have prevision of long-range rockets, of guided missiles, of radiating dust, of bacteriological warfare, and of superior atom bombs. Other elements than the heavyweight thorium and uranium may be used for explosion, fire, and radiation. We are sure that science will make the potential destructiveness of wars much greater in the future, though we do not know the details, provided we continue to follow the pursuit of war.

It is possible that science will also create a defense of some kind, mechanical or social, for this new offensive power. Historians tell us that eventually defense has always caught up with offense. The explanation of this tendency for offense and defense in war to come to a balance is found in the great power of the factor of demand in the inventive process. As inventions accumulate, we are able to invent almost anything we want to. This statement is not wholly true, of course. We have been a long time trying to discover a cure for cancer. So we do not know absolutely that a defense will be found for the new war weapons. But, if defense does catch up with offense, it may be long delayed; and the costs of defense may be as great as, for instance, the dispersal of city populations, which involves a remaking of a large part of civilization.

The nature of mechanized warfare of the present and of the future has become so horrible to contemplate, and it seems so suicidal to wage such wars, that we naturally ask, Why fight at all? Why not abolish war altogether? The search for peace is not new. It has existed during all history, through treaties, agreements, the resolution of conflicting interests, and the limitation of armaments. Today this search takes a more generalized form, in addition to the old procedure, of a peace movement to prevent war forever everywhere.

In the past the adjustment to new discoveries and inventions of metals, cutting tools, vehicles, and explosives has been to incorporate them into the warring activities. If precedents of history are followed, we shall use bacteria and radiating particles, rockets, and guided missiles in the wars to come. But using them in war is not the only adjustment to the new technologies. The adjustment to such lethal inventions could be to change our habit of going to war. So the effect of the new technology could be to abolish war. Certainly the effect has been to stimulate movements toward a lasting peace. The question, of course, is how effective such a movement would be.

The obstacles are very great, even though the objective is sensible and desirable. Most difficult of these obstacles are the awareness of ruthless attacks and invasions of the past and the fear of them in the future, the remembrance of broken agreements, the great desire for the security thought to be afforded by military preparation, and the theory that the best defense is attack. Then there are such obstacles as conflicts of interest, particularly economic; the effectiveness of power in various international activities; and the tradition of prestige and glory. Contemplation of these resistances by those who have read their history carefully makes them seem very difficult indeed to overcome.

Some have thought that a less difficult objective is some restriction of the use of these agents of destruction in warfare. We have tried to restrict the use of the atom bomb but have met so far with failure. But war, like all collective activity, has rules. In many wars of the past there have been rules against atrocities. Even with the breaking-down of codes today, we do in general conform to the rule of not killing prisoners. It may be that later we shall try again to prohibit the use of atomic bombs or set up a rule of not bombing cities which do not have military objectives, such as factories within their borders. Such agreements may be broken, of course, but not all new habits are established at once without fail.

Along with the attempts to restrict the use of atomic energy, there occurred a movement to preach peace into practice by persuasion, particularly through the motive of fear. Success of such a movement in the country of only one of the potential contestants would be dangerous without the development of a similar attitude in the other. This is not to say that education for peace is not a proper accompaniment to our efforts to abolish war.

The development of an international organization based upon such beginnings as are found in the League of Nations and in the United Nations is generally viewed as a more effective approach.

However, the obstacles to attaining a world political unit make one realize the magnitude of the task. Especially is it important to realize that the attainment of a single world political unit must be concerned with the processes of power.

A world federation of states with considerable power still has the problems of disruption due to heterogeneity of interests, the weakness of the agencies of cohesion, and the power of local groups with nationalistic traditions. The purpose of these remarks is, however, not to pass judgments or to reach conclusions but rather to indicate the various possible effects of the new inventions on the attempts to find peace.

Another effort to adjust to the new technology of war is to try to postpone war as long as possible without attempting to set up at once an effective organization to abolish war forever. With the present geographical distribution of bipolar power, if the conflict of national and ideological interests could be workably adjusted and a greater sense of security from attack could be had and guarded, war might be postponed for a long time. Perhaps the most serious difficulty in maintaining a very long peace is the rise of new powers among the states and the decline of old ones. These shifts often occur, as we have seen, with new technological developments and necessitate changes in boundaries and expansion in areas. These changes have always been difficult to handle by the peaceful methods of negotiation. The effort to postpone war would make use of the familiar historical skills with which states of the past have dealt with one another. The skills which have failed in the past (though they have succeeded for fairly long periods) may fail again in the future. The idea this time, though, is to utilize the time gained by the postponement of war to build up new international organizations for peace, for it will probably take some time to give them the strength needed.

In conclusion, then, one social effect of the new destructive agencies of war is to stimulate several different movements to avoid the great destructiveness of war: restriction of weapons, the adoption of peace through fear and persuasion, the strengthening of the United Nations, a world federation, a one-world government by conquest, and a postponement of war to gain time to strengthen the movement for peace. However these various movements may develop, the impact of the destructive weapons is to increase greatly the efforts for peace.

The chapters which follow deal in varying degrees of emphasis and approach with contemporary crises in international relations; each one, however, is concerned with the three themes common to history and set forth in this introductory frame of reference, namely, the shifts in the ranking of powers, the growth of states in size, and the movement for peace.

13

TECHNOLOGY AND THE STANDARD

OF LIVING   *1955*

A PREVIOUS article[1] showed that the standard of living in the United States was twice as high at the mid-century as at the beginning. A few of the important effects of this spectacular change in the level of living are now discussed and the probabilities of a continuing rise during the second half of the century are considered.

I

THE REDUCTION OF POVERTY   So great an increase in incomes must have reduced poverty in the United States, unless the incomes of the poor had remained low while the average income was being doubled, which is unlikely. Actually, the rich are less rich, which means that, since the average has doubled, the incomes of the poor have more than doubled. For instance, in 1919, the earliest date for data, the top 5 per cent received 22.9 per cent

Reprinted from *The American Journal of Sociology,* LX (May, 1955), 541–46.

[1]   William Fielding Ogburn, "Technology and the Standard of Living in the United States," *American Journal of Sociology,* LX, No. 4 (January, 1955), 380–86.

of individuals' incomes before taxes, while in 1948 they received 17.9. These data are for the highest incomes.[2] For the low incomes, in 1935–36, the lowest fifth of families and single individuals received 4 per cent of the money income, while in 1948 they received 4.2 per cent.[3]

Poverty cannot be defined solely by the lowest position on a scale of ranking of incomes; for, then, no matter how high the distribution of incomes is raised, there would always be the same amount of poverty if the distribution remained the same in shape. Poverty, rather, is the condition of life on some low quantity of consumption. It has been variously conceived at different times and in different countries, as, for instance, by such terms as "stark" or "naked" poverty or merely the condition of the "poor." A good many minimums have been drawn for the United States or for localities in it (particularly during the second decade of the twentieth century, when minimum-wage laws were being passed) and have been called "minimum standards of living." The expression "minimum standard of living" suggests that those who try to live on less cannot do so. The idea is that those who are so trying are dying less slowly than those whose consumption levels are above this standard. The line of demarcation has not been drawn objectively: the standards are estimates of persons or families with living conditions and prices in various localities at a given time. Such estimates have the approval of opinion and are accepted by wage boards and by charity organizations. Adopting this conception we shall call those trying to live on less than a living wage as "poor," that is, living in poverty.

The problem, then, is to find this minimum standard in 1900 and in 1950 and the number of those living below these standards. For 1900 only one attempt to determine the numbers living below it has been found: Dr. Hazel Kyrk made such an estimate based on the family expenditures collected by the United States Bureau of Labor in 1901. Allowing $100 as the minimum expenditure

2   Simon Kuznets and Raymond Goldsmith, *Income and Wealth of the United States: Trends and Structure* (Cambridge, Eng.: Bowes & Bowes, 1952), p. 142.

3   *Statistical Abstract of the United States, 1953*, p. 289.

for a child and $400 or $500 a year as the minimum for a married couple, "then it might be said that from 60 to 40 per cent . . . had money incomes adequate at an acceptable standard."[4] She finds 40 per cent of families with two children living on less than $600 and 75 per cent of families with three children living on less than $700 (and 37 per cent on less than $600). Professor Kyrk does not present any evidence to support these particular amounts of money as minimum standards. She is, however, a lifelong and well-known authority on family consumption. For a husband, wife, and three children, her budgets for 1901 would be $700 and $800.

From 1910 to 1920 the question of minimum wages was a lively one, and several minimum–standard-of-living budgets for a family of 5 were submitted with detailed expenditures by items in quantities and prices. They were widely accepted. Because of the care and thought put in drawing them up, it is important to see what they were worth in 1901 dollars. The budget used by the National War Labor Board in 1918 set a standard of $1,386 for a family of 5. In 1901 dollars this would be $700. The Chapin standard budget of 1907 and the Streighthoff budget of 1914, both for New York City, were a little over $700 in 1901 dollars; and the standard set by the National Industrial Conference Board, an organization of employers, in 1927 for Marion, Ohio, was about $720 in 1901 money. In these budgets and in Dr. Kyrk's estimate the minimum standard for a family of 5 in 1901 was set at around $700.

These minimum-standard budgets, though realistic in prices and amounts, were not set for an average family but rather for one of 5, for which it was thought the income should be enough to provide. The average family in 1901 was smaller than 5, and in 1950 the average urban family was about 3.4 persons. For a family of this size in 1901 the minimum-standard expenditure would be $540 (if a minimum standard for 5 was $700), which would be equivalent to $1,728 in 1950 dollars.

The important question is: What percentage of urban wage-

[4]   Hazel Kyrk, *Economic Problems of the Family* (New York: Harper & Bros., 1933), p. 210.

earners and low-salaried clerical workers were trying to live on less than this minimum in 1950? That about 9 per cent of all families with incomes of less than $10,000 ($3,100 in 1901) living in urbanized areas had incomes below it is shown in a survey of 15,000 urban and rural households made by the United States Bureau of the Census for 1951.[5] The percentage was probably smaller for families of wage-earners and clerical workers, since the income of the families of self-employed of these income levels is less. The percentage would be still less if the data were for expenditure rather than income, since the low-income groups often have a deficit. Income here is before taxes.

Somewhat less than 9 per cent of urban wage-earners and clerical workers, then, were trying to live on less than $1,700. This $1,700 was an estimated standard for a family of 3.4. But some of the families surveyed were smaller and some larger. The ideal would have been to set a standard for each size of family (instead of for the average) and then to find out the percentage of each size living below its minimum. But the data did not permit. However, for the 1901 data, which were more flexible, the percentage of all those living below the several minimums set for each size was about the same as the percentage of all the families living below the minimum standard for the average size of family.

Another study was made in 1950 by the Bureau of Labor Statistics[6] for 10,813 urban family households. Of wage-earners and clerical workers with less than $10,000 a year, about 5 per cent of those reporting were living on less than $1,700.

The data indicate therefore that in 1950 from 5 to 10 per cent of the families of this income class in cities were trying to live on incomes below a minimum standard. In 1901 about 40 per cent of the families of this income class of wage-earners and clerical workers were trying to live below it.

5   *Family Income in the United States, 1951* ("Current Population Reports of the United States Bureau of the Census," Series P-60, No. 12 [Washington, D.C., June, 1953]), Table 1, p. 16.

6   *Family Income, Expenditures, and Savings in 1950* (United States Department of Labor Bulletin 1097 [Washington, D.C., June, 1953]), Table 7.

The rise in per capita income in the first half of the twentieth century seems, then, to have reduced poverty in cities (as set by a minimum-living income) greatly, probably by 80 or 90 per cent.

IMPROVEMENT IN HEALTH   If sickness is more prevalent among the poor, then a reduction in poverty will improve health. Woodbury showed that the infant death rate was higher among the poor and that the general death rate is higher in areas where the infant death rate is high.[7] The correlation is .64 for community areas in Chicago in 1950. Where the death rate is high, the sickness rate is high, deaths without preceding sickness being rare. Hence, infant mortality gives some indication of illness.

In 1900 the infant death rate of wage-earners' families was probably about 110 per 1,000 infant births. This figure was determined by applying Woodbury's specific infant mortality rates for annual earnings of the father to the distribution of families supported by earnings of the father, by expenditure, from the 1901 survey, after some interpolation and adjustment, and then increasing the result by 20 per cent, which shows the increase of the general death rate in 1901 over the rate in 1915.

What would be the infant death rate of such a distribution of families by expenditures were their incomes raised by the percentage increase in family incomes between 1900 and 1950?[8] By applying the Woodbury rates plus some extrapolation to this new income distribution, the infant death rate is shown to be 80. In other words, if the medical progress and sanitation had been the same in 1950 as in 1900, the rise in the standard of living would have resulted in a lowering of the infant mortality rate by around 25 per cent. Since infant mortality rate is correlated with death rate and death rates with morbidity rates, the decline in infant mortality is an indication of the improvement in health.

A LESSENED APPEAL OF SOCIALISM   Socialism arose from

[7]   Robert M. Woodbury, *Infant Mortality and Its Causes* (Baltimore: Williams & Wilkins Co., 1920), p. 131.

[8]   The actual distribution of wage-earners' families by incomes in the 1950 survey of the Bureau of Labor Statistics was very similar to the projected distribution of 1901.

the recognition of the inequality in the distribution of wealth and the desire for a program to redistribute it so that those with low incomes received more. Such a redistribution of wealth has occurred in parts of different countries where the wealth was largely land; thus large landed estates have been partitioned, either with or without payment to the former owners, and made the property of a large number of owners. In an industrial society the redistribution of property is planned by having the government, by the people, take over the agencies of production and distribute the income therefrom less unequally. Other objectives in socialist programs include increased production, power readjustment, and more justice.

The average factory worker in 1900 received about $450. If the net national product had been distributed equally among all the labor force at that time, each member would have received $525 per year, or about $75 a year more. (Such a redistribution could not have occurred without doing violence to the productive system, for the costs of government and savings for new capital would have to be made.) But, without any redistribution through socialism, the factory worker could have expected to have his income increased by about $75 in about eleven years. The worker sees production increasing and wages going up under the present economic system, and, with so sure an expectancy, he may question whether so radical a change in the economic system would promise him much that he could not expect under a system which brought increases in wages. Besides, it is not demonstrated that a socialistic government would increase production as rapidly as privately run businesses. Thus, without elaborate calculations, the worker can expect increases in income in the future as he has in the past because the factories are producing more. The promise of socialism is not as certain as the promise of greater production has proved to be in the United States. The socialists' vote for President of the United States dropped from 6 per cent of the total vote in 1912 to 0.3 per cent in 1948 and to a negligible fraction in 1952, though the vote in the depression year 1932 was 2 per cent.

II

FUTURE RISES IN THE STANDARD OF LIVING What will the standard of living be at the end of the second half of the century?

During the first fifty years the increase was at the rate of .014 per year. Should this rate continue, the standard of living would be twice as high in the year 2000 as in 1950. The median family income for the United States, both urban and rural, in 1950 in current prices was $3,300 a year; and the arithmetic mean for urban workers, largely wage-earners, was $3,900.[9] If this rate of increase continues, in the year 2000 the median family will have an income of $6,600 with the purchasing power of 1950.

It is very rare for a trend line to change its course radically within a short space of time, and rarely does it change its direction suddenly. We also know that the further a projection is extended, the greater is the error, and fifty years is a rather long time for a projection where the unit of measure is the year. Furthermore, exponential curves cannot go on increasing at the same rate for long. After a while the rate lessens and the curve tends to flatten out, and we have then the common S-shaped curve, frequently called the "logistic curve."

That the rate of growth of national product per worker is slackening is indicated by the analysis of Kuznets of his data from 1869 to 1948.[10] His annual net national products per worker are averaged for ten-year periods beginning with 9 as 1869 and with 4 as 1874. Moving averages of five of these averages of ten-year overlapping periods are made. These moving averages, going back to annual data of 1869, show a slower rate of increase over the whole period, particularly during the latter part, which includes the years of the deep depression of the 1930's, when there was an actual decrease in the net national product per worker.

[9] *Family Income in the United States, 1951,* Table 12; *Family Income, Expenditures, and Savings in 1950.*

[10] Kuznets and Goldsmith, *op. cit.,* p. 71.

For 1900–1950, however, the percentage rate of change of Kuznets' averages for overlapping ten-year periods shows a slight increase: 10, 6, 4, 9, 13, —3, —1, 13, and 14. A straight line fitted to them gives a plus sign for the slope, indicating that for the first half-century, the rates of increase were not declining but rising slightly. This does not foreshadow a decreasing rate of growth for the next half-century of net national product per worker; on the contrary, a slightly increasing rate is suggested. This means that the per-worker net national product may more than double from 1950 to 2000. Against this result are Kuznets' moving averages for a longer period, which do point to a decreasing rate.

Future inventions and discoveries.—Since a projection of a trend fifty years hence, based on annual data, is at best only loosely approximate, with chances of considerable error near the end of the projection, it is well always to consider the factors that shape its course. In the previous article on the rise in the standard of living in the United States, 1930–50, and its causes,[11] by far the most important factors bringing about the increase were found to be technological development and new discoveries in applied science. What is expected from 1950 to 2000 in technological development and scientific discovery?

In the first half of the twentieth century three indicators of technological development increased at rates commensurate with or superior to the rise in the standard of living: the annual number of patents granted, the value of reproducible equipment in industry and on farms, and the supply of mechanical energy. Hence their projections indicate an increase in technological developments.

Patents are for the most part of rather trivial importance for the standard of living, only a small proportion being significant. Until about twenty-five years ago the number of patents was increasing exponentially, but since then there has scarcely been any yearly increase. However, there are important inventions in recent years that are not patented at all, and an increasing number of inventions, it is said, are never patented. Also

11   Ogburn, *op. cit.*

there could be a decrease in patents of trivial inventions that do not affect the standard of living.

A long time is required after an invention is patented or made for its adoption to be sufficiently extensive to affect the standard of living of a whole people. If there were no more new inventions from now on, those now in existence would for some time influence the rate of production per worker. However, one would be rash indeed to forecast a stoppage of inventions and scientific discoveries now and for the next fifty years at the eve of the atomic age and the dawn of automatism. Inventions increase at exponential rates, though the great difference in the significance of inventions indicates a considerable fluctuation around any such trend. A casual glance at the new discoveries and inventions in chemistry, electricity, nuclear energy, engineering, and physics certainly suggests the coming of many new technological influences on production.

The annual supply of mechanical energy for industry will probably be greatly increased by nuclear reactors of the breeder type. This may mean the release of some coal, natural gas, and oil for those vehicles and other machines for which atomic energy may not be well suited.

NON-TECHNOLOGICAL INFLUENCES   A variety of other factors may affect production. Obviously, a long destructive war in which the industries and cities of the United States are bombed would invalidate these forecasts. But there were two world wars in which the United States was a participant between 1900 and 1950.

A long, severe industrial depression would also affect adversely a favorable rate of production. But the standard of living doubled during the first half of the century in spite of the severe depression of the 1930's and several minor ones.

Another influence that should be considered is the necessity of maintaining a military establishment of some size and the diversion of the flow of some production from the consumer to it. It seems very probable that we shall have to continue preparation for war and that it may have a retarding influence on living standards. However, during the first half of the century we prepared for two world wars, though our participation in each was brief. Indeed, it could be argued that the preparation for them resulted in raising the standard of living.

There is the possibility of a scarcity of the raw materials of industry with the depletion of natural resources. No such scarcity was appreciably experienced from 1900 to 1950. We do not know that such a scarcity is probable during the next fifty years. Some of the resources coming from outside the United States could be cut off, but there is the possibility of substitutes (atomic energy for power from coal and oil, titanium and aluminum for some iron and steel). Further development of chemistry and metallurgy could overcome possible shortages.

As long as there is enough food and rising costs of natural resources do not interfere, an increasing population is not a deterrent to a rise in the standard of living in an industrial and commercial society. An unusually large increase in population is not expected in the United States during the next fifty years. On the controversial subject of the course of the birth rate (which, aside from immigration, is the determinant of the future size of the population), the author is inclined to look for further decreases during the remainder of the century, since the fall appears not to have run its course yet in certain large segments of the population.

A slower rate of capital formation can retard the rise in the standard of living. But a high productivity rate is favorable to savings. There seems to be no particular reason, short of wars and severe depressions, for expecting any special difficulty in the supply of capital, which is in reality expressed in capital goods, much of which are technological equipment.

III

What are some of the social implications of such a great rise in the standard of living?

MASS PRODUCTION OF HIGH-PRICED GOODS   The expected rise in incomes means great marketing possibilities for a class of products that are now sold only to the middle and upper classes. A market will be opened for the mass production of higher-priced products, which, because of mass production, should be cheaper. There has always been mass production of cheap products like pins or soap. A mass market for automobiles was the surprise of the first half of the century. Perhaps a mass market for roadable helicopters will come in the second half.

SOCIAL CLASSES   If we think of social classes in the first half of the century as economic classes and in terms of the articles they can and cannot buy, then the working class, as previously known, will cease to exist and will move up to the middle classes, as defined in terms of purchases. In other words, the working classes of tomorrow will have the standard of living of the middle classes of yesterday.

POVERTY   If per capita incomes double again, poverty should be reduced to a minimum. There may always be a few poor because of mental inability, improvident habits, sickness, and prolonged unemployment, unless some sort of collective action, as by a government, provides care for them. But, barring this type of poverty, we should expect poverty to disappear.

HOW THE INCREASED INCOME WILL BE SPENT   In order to learn what we would be likely to do if our incomes were doubled, the expenditures of those with incomes of $3,800 have been compared with the expenditures of incomes of twice that size, namely, $7,600.[12] How do families with $3,800 more to spend than families with only $3,800 spend that extra $3,800, and how is it apportioned among the various items of purchase? The largest portion of it is spent on the house, its furnishings, and its operation. The percentage is 35, slightly over one-third. About one-sixth, or 16 per cent, is spent on clothing and personal care. Fifteen per cent is spent on food, either for greater amounts or for better quality. The percentage spent on automobiles is the same as the percentage spent on education (including reading), 9, or nearly one-tenth for each. Transportation and recreation

[12]   The data are taken from the consumer-income survey of 1935–36, published by the Natural Resources Planning Board, from expenditure breakdowns, where the totals are equivalent to $3,800 and $7,600 in 1950 dollars.

(rather narrowly defined) claim 6 per cent each, and 3 per cent is spent for medical care.

How much expansion is there in the money spent for a particular item when the income is doubled? The amount spent on housing is increased 110 per cent, so also is the amount spent for clothing and personal care. For food the increase is only 60 per cent. Very large increases occur in expenditures for education, including reading (300 per cent), and for transportation (500 per cent). But the total spent for each of these items is small as compared with the expenditure on housing, clothing, and food. The increase for recreation, as defined, is 145 per cent; for automobiles, 78 per cent; and for medical care, 62 per cent. It would have been interesting to have had smaller classifications. Sometimes an item is difficult to classify. Is reading recreation or education? Perhaps the automobile and transportation might be classified in part as recreation. A finer breakdown might have shown a great increase in travel, which includes more than transportation in a vacation period. Various reflections may be stimulated by examination of certain items. For instance, the amounts spent on personal care and on clothing are probably more for appearance than for comfort or for health. If so, the average family will spend more than twice as much on appearance.

The foregoing analysis is for a supposedly average income. The apportionment and increases will be different for families with incomes smaller or greater than the average.

14

WHY THE FAMILY IS CHANGING

1954

THE FAMILY as a social institution is changing, as are other institutions. These changes differ somewhat in countries according to the degree of their industrialization, of their urbanization, and of their isolation. But whatever these changes may be, they can be better seen after an analysis of the factors that affect the form and functions of the family. Five such factors are selected as of especial importance.

Community Size

The first factor is the number of people living within the area of the community in which the family exists. Among many peoples who hunt and gather food without cultivation of plants and domestication of animals, the community is small, sometimes consisting of very few families, say, five or six. The community is a band that often occupies an area for only a short time. In other cases the number of families may be twenty-five to fifty, and the occupation of a site, as for instance near the sea coast or a waterfall, may be larger.

In any case, the population is not large enough to support

Reprinted from *Sociologus* (formerly *Journal of Sociology and Social Psychology*), New Series, IV, No. 2 (1954), 160–70.

many social organizations. A band of twenty-five persons with six or seven men and eight or nine women, living in relative isolation, could not support a baseball team, a debating society, or a luncheon club. Since, say, ten such single-purpose organizations must necessarily have the same personnel in membership, it is more probable that there will be one organization with ten functions.

Among such primitive hunters there are always two social organizations, the family and the community. The functions that people have are then divided between these two organizations. These functions are such as eating, working, loving, procreating, fighting, playing, educating, safeguarding, and worshiping. Theoretically, the family could have had only one of these functions, procreation, and the community all the remainder. Actually the family in such small communities is an organization that procreates, educates, prepares food, eats together, with members working for it, and thus has multiple functions. So does the community, which may organize hunting parties, make provision for worship, provide recreation, aid in informal education, and furnish the parties to feuds or factional disputes. There may be other organizations, such as men's clubs or age societies. But in general most of the activities of life are divided between the family and the community, the proportionate distribution varying among different peoples according to situations and circumstances. The emphasis to be noted is that in such small communities the family is a multipurpose organization with many functions and not one for procreation and child-rearing only.

In a large community such as a modern city, these various human activities may become functions of specialized institutions. Thus, factories produce cloth and clothing; restaurants serve food; churches are places of worship; and schools educate. Hence many family functions either leave the family for such specialized institutions, as when spinning and weaving left the family for the factory, or the family function may be surpassed by those single-purpose organizations, as when recreation in the family is relatively less common than in places of commercial recreation such as motion-picture theaters, athletic events, school playgrounds, or parks. Large communities therefore make it possible for various other organizations to take over and develop functions exercised by the family in very small communities. Hence, relatively, it is possible for the family to lose functions to outside organizations.

The Economic Factor

There is one activity in society that has proved to be of exceptional importance in affecting other activities. This is the production of food and other goods and services, which we call the economic function. For instance, it may determine the location of a community, as for instance in a fertile valley or near to the fish beds of the ocean, or where a person lives, as in a city or the open country or in a mining community in the hills. The economic factor provides a standard of living of a family either of wealth or poverty. It is a source of power socially, politically, and militarily. It is a factor in the choice of a mate, in the rearing of children, in the provision of recreation, in safeguarding against life's adversities, and affects status in a society.

The extent that the family as a social institution has an economic function, then, is of great importance. The family has an economic function in all societies and in all sizes of communities in that members of the family work and provide for what the family consumes, and some are better providers than others. The variation that is important is in the relative extent that organizations other than the family exercise the function of production of goods and services. Thus in cities today, the great centers of production—and trade is a production of place utilities—are factories, stores, offices, banks, railways, and highways; while in farms that are isolated, the family is a center of production, which in commercial farming is yielding to other economic institutions.

By contrast, self-sufficient family farms of the open country are the main economic centers. The household is the forerunner of the factory. Where farming families live in villages, as is the case in most of the agricultural nations, some economic functions are shared more readily with non-farming families of handicraftsmen, who make wheels, model iron, tan hides of animals, etc. Before trade was very much developed and technology had advanced very far, where the agricultural family possessed the plow and had domesticated animals and some knowledge of fertilizers, the family was the outstanding economic organization. That is to say, in the household economy, few other economic institutions could compare with the family as a producing organization. Some families took on a military function and with private armies were able to levy upon other families for their produce and labor. In such cases these military farmers, the lords and dukes, became the centers of very powerful family organizations. Out of such families grew kingship, which was modeled after the authoritarian head of a family. The status of families was at its zenith.

There were at this time some families that existed without farming—by trade, by handicraft production, and by transportation of goods, especially in boats and sometimes in caravans. There were at this time towns and an occasional city on a waterway which had developed specialized organizations, such as guilds. Traders used market places, and peddlers carried goods from place to place, but manufacturing was much in cottages, and hence manufacturing tended to remain in the family even in urban communities. Since the handicraftsmen worked in their homes, the economic function of the family was still an important one as compared with the economic function of other institutions, as, for instance, those of religious organizations such as monasteries.

Not a great deal is known about family life in towns and cities in the era of the household economy. We may infer, however, that there was more division of labor between families in towns and cities than on farms in the open country or perhaps in hamlets and small villages, and hence more purchase or exchange there. Yet, if the population of towns and cities was drawn from village and rural areas and if much handicraft was a family function, then very likely the customs of marriage and the family in towns and cities were not greatly different from those of the general culture area which was predominantly rural. The type tended still to be set by the conditions of the predominant occupation, which was farming with a moderately high grade of equipment and knowledge and with a variety of domestic animals, some of which may have been fairly numerous.

We assume that the high development of the economic function of the family of the farming population and very probably of the towns, too, had its influence on other activities, such as protection, recreation, status creation, education, religion, and the other great classes of human activity.

It is possible that the economic functions in the time of the household economy based on the use of the plow and domesticated animals made the family the greatest social institution in power and influence that it has ever been, greater than in earlier hunting and hoe cultures and greater than in later cities of the age of mechanical power.

With the coming of factories and transport run by mechanical power and the great multiplication of communities of very large size, relative diminution of the economic function of the family and of other correlated functions is an often-told story.

The Role of Technology

Two great influences shaping the structure of the family have been signalized: these are the size of the community and the performance of economic functions. While economic production and community size are causes, they are also results of preceding causes. We think that an important cause of changes in community size and of economic production is technology, which is used here as a general term to include the knowledge and use of inventions and of material culture, as well as the application of science.

For instance, it was the discovery that seeds could be planted and cultivated by human beings and the invention of the digging stick or hoe that changed the hunting cultures, with their wandering bands, into larger, settled agricultural communities. It was the plow and the domestication of animals that led to still larger communities, which became still larger if they were on water where boats could be used. Finally, the many big cities of today are the result of factories and railroads and have expanded into large metropolitan areas with the invention of automotive transportation.

Similarly it may be argued that the economic organization is changed from time to time by invention and discovery. We think the large household, which sometimes included kin, both vertical and lateral, as well as parents and children, was more prevalent in the plow culture than in the hoe culture or the hunting culture. The skills of the handicraftsmen in making stone tools and boats, working with metals and in household construction, in preparing skins for use, in making wheels, in making furniture, and in creating fine fabrics expanded with technological development leading to division of labor, exchange, trade, and transportation, even when production remained in the household. With mechanical power applied to moving metals, there came mass production and many cities with a galaxy of institutions.

Technology, then, by affecting community size and by developing and transferring the economic functions of the family, is an indirect once-removed factor of great importance affecting the family.

Social Control

A useful institution becomes socially valued. Such is the case with the family. If there be disruption or disorganizing tendencies connected with such an institution there will be agencies of regulation and control. One of the disruptive forces in the family is the sex appeal to one or both of the mates by individuals outside the family. There is thus a tendency for society to channelize sex activity, particularly for mates in families. Without such controls not all mates would confine their sexual relations to each other, which might result in an unstable family organization. Family stability is considered to be especially important where there are young children to rear. Otherwise they might not be reared so well. Hence there are laws regarding divorce and adultery and codes approving chastity and moral disapproval of deviant sex practices. To the support of these controls there are marshaled the forces of religious sanction. So powerful an urge as sex is difficult to keep in the authorized and ideal bounds, so various societies have provided for various outlets or escapes from the approved regimen, where they do not prove too disruptive.

Controls are also needed for the family not only as a procreative institution but also as an institution of economic production.

The members of the family must be held to their various duties, which should be performed regularly and frequently even though arduous, monotonous, and fatiguing. Goods must be produced on schedule. Hence an economic institution needs a head, a boss, with the authority to compel obedience on the part of the labor.

Then, too, families have property that must be guarded, divided, transmitted, or otherwise disposed of. So there are laws regarding property, often a family as well as an individual matter. Property, especially landed property, has had a good deal to do with the continuity of families over generations and with the residence of brides and grooms.

Property, production, and sex are important to society and hence are subject to controls taking the form of laws, morals, religious sanctions, and informal customs, the infraction of which is accompanied by some form of punishment.

Cultural Lags

When a complex institution of interrelated parts is changing, not all parts change at the same time or at the same rate. Thus the family in one locality may lose many of its economic functions, but legal controls of production and property may remain unchanged or change more slowly. Similarly, if cities cover the land rapidly, say within a century, families therein have a different daily life from what they had in the rural areas from which they came. This daily life may differ as to where the members of the family work or spend their time, or as to the times of going to work, or their methods of recreation. Yet the social codes suited to rural life may persist with little change into the new urban setting. Thus it may be considered that "woman's place is in the home." Or still valued may be the old adage "early to bed and early to rise makes a man healthy, wealthy, and wise," which was very well suited to a rural family life that dealt with domesticated animals. Or, again, man is still considered the head, the boss, as he was in reality when production was in the home.

In cities the family bonds weaken, and the members of the families emerge as individuals with rights as independent persons. Yet the laws regarding property rights for women are changed very slowly.

In general the social valuations that take the form of laws, sanctions, moral codes, and ideologies are singularly resistant to change. The economic or technological aspects of families often change first, and the ideational aspects change later, thus remaining for a time out of harmony. This fact that the structural parts of a family do not fit well during a period of rapid change makes understanding difficult unless this phenomenon of cultural lag is recognized and worked into the analysis.

Five Factors

We have reviewed five factors that influence the structure and functions of the family. The size of a community and the location of economic functions are seen to influence the family greatly. Where the size of the community increases much, the family is expected to change particularly in its functions. The change, however, is not immediate. For the family is likely to try to maintain for a time its old ways. So, too, when the family loses or gains a large proportion of the economic functions in a society or community, its structure changes as do also various other functions correlated with economic functions. Particularly are its power and prestige affected. The prime mover of these changes is frequently technological development, operating on community size and economic activity.

This process is complicated by the sanctions and controls which society places on a family and which have so much to do with conduct, since they affect ideas of right and wrong and evaluations based upon emotions and sentiments. And back of these are often law and punishment.

These sanctions and controls change often more slowly than the other factors affecting the family as an institution, such as material culture, population density, and economic production.

The foregoing represents an attempt to generalize over a very large and complex field. As generalizations for which little evidence has been given and for which satisfactory evidence does not exist, especially of families in the prehistorical eras and areas, they should be taken as theory, family theory.

Looking at this theory critically, it could be true only in general. In the first place there are more than five factors affecting the family. For instance, the sex ratio of adults has an influence, and the widely spread polygamy among preliterate people is probably related to the hazards of life to the men, who follow the more dangerous activities, which thus lead to an excess of women. But here again polygamy and monogamy change slowly and would not quickly be adapted to a fluctuating sex ratio. The existence of polygamy is also the result of other factors than the sex ratio.

Then again the sequence may not always be as set forth in the preceding paragraphs, that is, from technology to economics to the structure of the family with ideational lags. It may be that ideas—as, for instance, in the Western urban world on the position of women, their freedom, and rights—may be imported and adopted into rural areas of the Orient by the carriers of some ideology of a semireligious nature or otherwise and adopted first before the economic structure is harmoniously suited to the change. Such may be the case for instance of the revision of the Hindu code proposed by Ambedkar in the Indian parliament, but not as yet adopted.

There are types of minds that dislike averages and even refuse to use them. They insist on the presentation of the whole frequency distribution, of which the average is a most inadequate condensation. Such types of minds will renounce the foregoing generalizations.

But where theory has not been proven it still serves the useful purpose of being a tool of analysis and a source of hypothesis. We shall apply, then, some of these generalizations to the changing family of the modern Western world.

The Modern Family of the West

The urban families of the nations of western Europe and the United States have common features as well as differences.

Most important is the loss of functions to other social institutions, which have developed these functions much further than the family has. Thus production has been transferred to the factory, though consumption remains as an important family function, with men, women, and children spending much of their time away from home. With the shift of economic functions there have been transferred other functions. Protection has increasingly become less a family function in cities and more a function of police, courts, governmental insurance, private pension plans, old-age bureaus, and health regulations. Recreation has become commercial and hence outside the home. Religious worship is rare in homes, though religion is something of a barrier in formation of families for persons of different faiths. Marriage ceremonies are increasingly civil ones. Particularly in cities have the power and prestige of families as such declined. Power is in government and industry rather than in the family, as it was in feudal times. Women and children are less under family discipline.

The most vigorous functions remaining to the family are affectional and educational. The affectional function here includes procreation, as well as affection between parents and children. Educational functions in the family here are those that shape the personality of children before they are of school age. Affection may exist between members of different families, and schools share part of the educational function.

The family and household are becoming smaller[1] in size partly because of the diminution of economic production in the household and partly because of the costs of rearing children which must be paid to agencies outside the family. This reduction in size is made possible by discoveries in methods of avoiding conception other than abstinence. The invention of contraceptives is the particular technological development that is largely responsible for the reduction in size of the family.

In many countries there is a tendency to form families at earlier ages, which seems to be due in part to the possibility of marriage without necessarily having children to support and also possibly to the employment of young wives, without children, who add to the family income. Early marriage is also favored by prosperous phases of the business cycle. Thus earlier marriage is influenced by the invention of contraceptives and the technological

1   The evidence for this statement and others which follow are found in the book *Technology and the Changing Family*, by W. F. Ogburn and M. F. Nimkoff (Boston: Houghton Mifflin & Co., 1953).

and economic developments which furnish remunerative employ-ment to wives outside the home.

In the formation of families the choice of mates is based less and less on economic qualifications, such as good housekeeping skills and business capacities, and more and more on personality considerations characterized by romance and companionship. These trends are obviously due to the decrease of the economic functions of families.

The authoritarian family with powers of discipline and pun-ishment centered primarily in the male head is declining, with consequent freedom to wives and children and the granting of more legal rights and economic and social opportunities to women. This change is due to the inventions that moved produc-tion from the household to the factory and that built cities which furnished economic opportunities outside the home.

The restriction of sex activity to the family on the part of women and possibly men is becoming less. This increased sexual freedom seems to be due to the technological and scientific de-velopments that led to the use of contraceptives, to the conquest of venereal diseases, to opportunities of privacy and anonymity in cities, to the decrease of religious authority over sex control, and to the naturalistic conceptions of biological functions.

The instability of families is increasing in that there are more permanent separations of mates and more marriages among those who have been previously married. This increased separation, di-vorce, and annulment occurs because there are fewer bonds that hold two persons together through life. If formerly there were seven ties, i.e., functions, that held the family together and now there are only one and a half, more disruption is to be expected. Permanent separation of mates is more common in cities, where there are fewer family functions than in rural areas; more com-mon among childless couples, where contraceptives have been effectively used; more common among the young, with more imperative demands of sex compatibility and affection; and less common among religious groups whose codes are less affected by modern science.

Family social status and family pride are decreasing, as would be expected when wealth is concentrated in industry and power in government and when families are becoming less stable with emphasis upon romance rather than upon social virtues and achievements.

The ideals, social controls, and valuations of the family are changing, too, but much less rapidly; and newer ideals are slow to arise. Thus the professed attitude toward divorce seems to be to make a husband and wife live together whether they want to or not. Compulsory habitation of husband and wife together seems to be a goal, though in practice the courts do not always act accordingly, even though the legal statutes remain unchanged. Compulsory habitation together in pre–Industrial Revolution days was not a goal but a means to a goal, which was to keep the production of the household going without too much labor turnover and to rear successfully a large family. But where there is no family production and there are many childless couples or families with few children living at home, the dangers and hazards of disruption, though existing, are much less. The social valuations of the family, as found in laws, moral codes, and religious rules, do not make distinctions between families without children and families with children. Under the new urban conditions there are many wives who have never had a child and many whose few children have been reared and left the nest. If the remaining functions of the family are largely those of producing happiness and companionship for mates and rearing children, then obviously these functions are quite different for families without children and families with them. But such differences are not yet formulated into social codes and widely recognized social valuations. The precedents of court action seem to be moving in the direction less slowly than legislative action.

The sloughing off of various functions of the family except the personality functions has meant a focusing of attention upon the happiness and companionship of mates and on the rearing of little children. An inventory of the researches of sociologists shows that their investigations are increasingly concerned with such topics as mate selection, courting procedures, sex aspects of marriage and family, sex education, education for marriage and family, happiness in marriage, personalities of children where there are only one or two in the family, factors affecting compatibility, the resolution of marital conflicts, and the success or failure of remarriage. These interests are quite in harmony with the analyses of the factors affecting the family as set forth in this paper and with the trends herein described. The welfare of the future families depends much upon the success of the researches and wide diffusion of the knowledge derived therefrom.

15

RACE RELATIONS AND SOCIAL

CHANGE   *1961*

Conceptions

RACE relations may be of various kinds. Some are antago-
nistic and may end in warfare. Others are oppressive or accom-
modative. Some are co-operative. When we work to improve social conditions, as we do in our era, we look at race relations as a
social problem, and it is seen largely as one of discrimination and
tension.

"Race relations" implies interaction between races, and so it
is. But the term is not adequately descriptive. One reason is that
race, a biological concept implying inherited biological structures, does not determine social behavior. In man, a single species, differences in the structures of peoples do not signify differences in functions, as is the case when one species is compared
with another. The differences in the behavior of races are social
and cultural, not biological.

For instance in the villages of India the discrimination against
the lowest caste is almost identical in details to the discrimina-

Reprinted from *Race Relations, Problems and Theory: Essays in Honor
of Robert Park*, ed. Jitsuichi Masuoka and Preston Valien (Chapel Hill,
N.C.: University of North Carolina Press, 1961), pp. 200–207. Read at the
dedication of the Robert E. Park Building, Fisk University, March, 1955.

tions against the Negroes in the villages of the southern United States in the latter half of the nineteenth century. Yet in these villages of India, the upper and lower classes are of the same race, without any visible inherited physical characteristics which indicate differences. From these observations on India and the southern states of the United States we should conclude, I think, that the discrimination is based on something other than race, though among some peoples race furnishes inherited insignia that differentiate one group from another and thus facilitate mass discrimination. Why is it that in Indian villages caste prejudice without race differences in a particular village is the same as so-called race prejudice in the United States? The answer will be found in the phenomena of rank and status involving privilege or servitude, connected with religion, occupation, or economic condition. Discrimination and prejudice exist, too, in the United States between social classes of the same race, between minority and majority groups, between men and women, and between workers in different occupations. In all these cases the focus is on status and rank. We therefore consider race prejudice as largely social, with race as a tag.

Social change is change in society, though not necessarily in every part of society. But if change is occurring in many parts of society, these changes are likely to produce changes in other parts because of the many interrelationships that exist between the different parts of society, though some parts of society are so little related that they are called "independent" rather than "interdependent." Yet I have found poetry to be affected by the airplane, though technology and poetry would seem to be independent of each other. We should expect in a culture where there is much social change that race relations would not remain unaffected.

Then, too, there are general principles and processes of social change that apply to changes in race relations. Social change may either increase discrimination or decrease it. For instance, when in the earlier stages of agriculture some landowners were increasing their holdings by war, marriage, or otherwise, and others were being deprived of their land, their social change must have increased the amount of discrimination. Such also was the case when the Assyrians, for instance, waged wars to capture slaves to increase their labor supply. In urban India, on the other hand, social change is lessening discrimination against the lower castes.

Changes in Income

The concern of this paper is with modern times. In our society in the United States social changes that promote changes in race relations occur notably in education, in occupations, and in changes in technology, though these in turn may effect technological developments. Occupation and income in the United States have also been affected recently by war and by the restriction of immigration from Europe. These brief statements are of topics that will be discussed in the remarks which follow.

The increase in income in the United States has doubled within the past fifty years in money of constant purchasing power per member of the labor force. Poverty has been reduced about four-fifths. The low income groups have thus been able to get more education, to maintain better health, to wear better clothes, to travel more. This lifting above the poverty line of low income groups has led to a somewhat different treatment of them by salespeople who want to tap this increased income and by politicians who want the votes of this more fully enfranchised class.

The rise in per capita income during the last fifty years in the United States has not been confined to the lowest income groups. It has occurred in all income groups but somewhat less in the highest brackets. Hence the members of a minority group who have had higher incomes have become richer, as well as those with lower incomes.

The cause of this rise in incomes can be attributed to an increase in productivity, and the increase in productivity is largely the product of technological and scientific development. Machines have greatly increased the production per worker using them.

There were, however, other causes of this increase in incomes of the low income groups. Thus the restriction in immigration from Europe to the United States in the middle 1920's raised the incomes of the farm and village workers who maintained the flow of labor to northern factories which had been reduced by the cessation of immigrants from Europe. Thus these minority groups who migrated experienced less economic discrimination.

The wages in minority groups of low income were also raised in the United States by the wars of 1917–18 and of 1941–45. The supply of labor to factories and farms was reduced by war, and wages were raised, aided by inflation and by internal migration that the war stimulated. So war, the restriction of immigration, and mechanical invention have been influential in reducing economic discrimination, probably much more than exhortatory or organized reform movements made without these influences.

The increase of higher incomes within a low-income minority group means that some members of the lower classes move upward into a standard of living characterized as that of the middle classes. Then a minority group which was in the low income class becomes differentiated into a lower and middle class. This expansion of a racial or ethnic group to include a middle class and even an upper class is accompanied by differentiation in occupations, in manners, in tastes, in education, in dress, in speech, and in various other ways. The effect of such a differentiation means that the former uniformity in discrimination cannot longer be maintained. In short, the individuals in the upper classes in an ethnic group must be treated differently from the individuals in the lower classes, although it may take some time for this differential treatment to occur as the old custom lags on for a while. Thus the tendency to treat all individuals in an ethnic group as if they were the same is weakened.

Discrimination by the majority against the minority is practiced more easily and effectively if the distribution curves of certain personality traits overlap little or not at all. The differentiation of a one-class ethnic group into several increases the overlap and brings the averages of a personality trait of that ethnic group and the remaining population closer together, hence lessening the opportunities of discrimination.

Social Mobility

We have spoken of increases in income aiding in the creation of middle and upper classes out of a one-class group. There are other forces than income. These are in general the forces that create social mobility. One such force comes from free public education, particularly at the secondary and college levels.

Another such force affecting social mobility is the proliferation of occupations based upon skills requiring training rather than ownership of property; for skills, in the amounts needed to characterize occupation, are more easily obtained than property. Diversification of occupation in a racial or ethnic group reduces the ease of discrimination against the group as a whole. Occupational differentiation also favors income differentiation.

Still another force of change that affects discrimination through social mobility is the mass production of consumer goods, particularly of wearing apparel, such as plastic jewelry, synthetic fibers, cosmetics, and also of such durable goods as television sets and automobiles. These all tend to render less distinguishable the various marks that set off one group from another. The overlap of these characteristics also is increased. Mass production, which results from technological development, seeks always larger markets. This it does by lowering prices. But the same result occurs when incomes are raised. So a rising standard of living increases mass production, with its consequent effect on race relations.

It should be noted, parenthetically, that social mobility is also affected by factors other than class barriers in the form of laws, regulations, and customs. Social mobility is also affected by the structure of the group. Thus we might have great fluidity for rise or fall in status, say, in the army. But this fluidity is limited in fact by the necessary ratios of generals to colonels, to captains, to lieutenants, to sergeants, to corporals, to privates. The shape is pyramidal. Hence, even though a private were free to become a general, only a small number could ever actually achieve such a mobility. Social mobility is also affected by population growth. Thus there are more generals in a big army than in a small one.

Though social mobility may decrease the amount of discrimination, it may increase the awareness of it and hence increase tension. Consider, for instance, a class society where there has been no social mobility for centuries, a society of castes. The class rela-

tions are routine and are, like habit, largely removed from awareness, unless there be some intermittent brutality, deprivation, or
physical pain. In such societies, outside observers, generally from
the upper classes, say that the lower classes, who have no conception of social mobility, do not want to improve their lot. Such
societies are generally stationary and hence are not a favorable
milieu for developing the idea of progress.

Custom

Societies that change break down customs. If the change
is widespread, as it tends to be because of the principle of related
parts, these class and caste barriers are weakened. As social mobility occurs within a minority group or across class barriers, this
weakening is seen as an opportunity. A desire to improve one's
lot is created or, if existing, is stimulated. Discontent is encouraged by an "agitator," as he is called by the members of the
upper classes. This discontent is accompanied by envy, which
likewise is stimulated by opportunity. Thus democracy encourages envy.

A social change that tends to break habit, custom, and class
barriers often increases spatial mobility because it presents new
opportunities in other localities. Migration also is encouraged by
the transportation inventions as well as by economic opportunity.
The movement of an oppressed ethnic group long resident in a
rural region to urban areas in a distant area, where the ethnic
group is little known, presents opportunities for social mobility.
If, however, the numbers are large, the competitive struggle intense, and distinguishing insignia in evidence, there may be more
tension than in areas of less change and hence of more routine.
Eventually the tension gives way as accommodation or assimilation succeeds, unless other changes precipitate new tensions.

Ethnocentrism

Changes in race relations are affected by pride, *esprit
de corps*, loyalty, and especially by ethnocentrism. This belief in
the superiority of one's society or class, in some if not all attri-

butes, over other societies or classes is extraordinarily widely spread, even to classes that have a very low ranking in the possession of the good things of life. This observation is quite surprising and contrary to the appeal of socialist organizers: "Workers of the world unite! You have nothing to lose but your chains." The prospect of advancement is greater because of discontent. With such a prospect as change brings, ethnocentrism is less likely to exist in low income classes than in a stationary society with rigid class barriers or with little prospect of economic improvement. Ethnocentrism has been observed among the untouchables in India, strange as it may seem, and among poor isolated mountaineers in the southern Appalachians.

An interesting question concerns the degree of possible development of ethnocentrism in a minority group where some hereditary trait makes assimilation, or barrier-crossing, difficult as compared with its development in a different group. It would appear that ethnocentrism would be more probable in the former.

There are many factors that affect ethnocentrism. War, for instance, tends to diminish it among the subsocieties within the nation at war but not to diminish the ethnocentrism of the nation itself. Against ethnocentrism appear to be the democratic ethos and the Christian doctrine of the brotherhood of man. However, if social and hereditary traits be distinguished, this need not be so. For instance, in our society we have a pride in nationality, a pride of university, a pride of fraternity, a pride of profession, but we do not approve the expression of pride of family and of racial pride based on heredity.

Should ethnocentrism develop in a minority racial group, what effect will it have on race relations? Would it act as a further deterrent to assimilation? Would it increase tension and the possibility of conflict? There appears to be some evidence for whatever answer be given. These questions deserve further study. Class pride is a stimulus to achievement. The envy which democracy and social mobility foster would appear to be lessened by ethnocentrism.

Cultural Lag

Change in race relations may be caused by innovation, or social invention originating directly within the area of race contacts, or it may come from inventions occurring outside this area but impinging upon it. In the latter case there is likely to be a lag in adjustment to the outside force. If this change tends to lessen discrimination, then the lag will appear among the members of the race who have done the discriminating. For instance, the members of a dominating race who take advantage of their preferred position to discriminate against a racial group with low incomes, little education, and homogeneous occupations of a servitude type are loath to give up their vested interests when social change has altered the rank of the oppressed class by raising incomes, increasing education, and diversifying occupations. They continue to act as if there has been no change, and their actions are quite out of harmony with the new status. I may say that little has been made of this cultural lag as an argument to improve race relations.

Ideologies

The discussion of social change and race relations has proceeded with little reference to leadership or to ideology. This avoidance has been deliberate. I like to consider first what will happen without any special leadership or without any unusual effort toward ideal goals.

As to the role of leadership, I recognize that nearly all social action takes place through leaders. Yet it is difficult to say whether the leader helps to create social forces or whether the leader is an agent through whom social forces work, that is, whether the change would have occurred if a particular leader had never lived. In any case, in class conflict there are leaders on both sides.

As to the role of ideas and those collective representations of ideas called ideologies, it is not always clear when the ideologies are responses to material stimuli and social conditions and when ideologies help to create the material and social conditions.

There are ideologies that are relatively independent of material conditions; they exist in a great variety of conditions without much change. These have influences on technology, on economic trends, and also on race relations. Some of them are the movements of humanitarianism and of democracy; the conception of the superorganic, or cultural environment; the appreciation of the individual in relation to the state and society; and the recognition of the relatively minor differences between races and between the hereditary bases of large groups of any people. Other contributions to these streams of ideas are the revival of the conception of the brotherhood of man and the visions of social justice.

These ideologies, as they are developing, operate along with economic and technological forces in the direction of lessening discrimination and in the reduction of tension particularly. Indeed it is difficult to find a widely accepted ideology that encourages discrimination, though the ideology based on eugenics and the biological inequality of races appears to be such. It has the aspects of lag, however.

These ideological movements are especially significant when the "cake of custom" (in the picturesque words of Walter Bagehot) which has hardened around race discrimination begins to crack. When social change breaks hard custom, the forces that were held become fluid, perhaps later to form a new custom. It is then that ideologies exercise exceptional influence. When recently customs of dress began to break, the ideologies regarding health and biological welfare led to dress reform in regard to temperature and pressure of clothing. Similarly, as the customs regarding race discrimination change, ideologies are important in lessening tensions and bringing reforms. They are particularly effective in a democracy in areas where the government operates, as in courts, voting, schooling, and employment.

Conclusion

The analysis indicates that the social forces of our time—technological, economic, and ideological—are operating to lessen discrimination in the relations of one race and one class to another and possibly to reduce tensions in some areas, but not in the relations of one nation to another. They operate against resistances, many in the form of lags. These resistances crumble, sometimes rapidly but generally slowly. The crumbling can be speeded. In closing I am reminded of the title of a pamphlet published in 1954 in England by a committee of intellectual leaders of the Conservative party—the title was "Social Change Is Our Ally."

16

SOUTHERN REGIONAL FOLKWAYS

REGARDING MONEY   *1943*

WHEN an important invention is widely adopted, it usually produces changes in customs and institutions. Thus the radio
has affected styles of oratory and changed the nature of political
campaigning.

It is possible to view money as a mechanical invention. Consequently, since it is an important invention, its wide use would be
expected to produce changes in our habits and institutions. We
know, of course, that money thus affects trade and creates banks.
Some of its less obvious influences on our habits also have
occurred. These less obvious influences are usually called "secondary" or "derivative" effects of an invention. Thus money makes
human relations less personal and friendly and more commercial
and formal. It is toward some of these derivative effects of the
wide use of money in society that attention is directed.

In order to see what effects money has on us, it is desirable to
observe first the customs of a people who do not have a very wide
use of money. One of many such societies was the Old South, the
southern states of the United States prior to the Civil War. Of
course, money was invented a long time ago, even before the

Reprinted from *Social Forces*, XXI (March, 1943).

alphabet, and the South had some money. But the economy of the Old South was clearly not a highly developed money economy, since the farmers were in large part self-sufficient. There were cash crops, of course, and the money from cotton and tobacco was used to buy silks, jewelry, metal products, books, and such objects as could not be produced on the farms.

A completely moneyless society is one where the farms are much more nearly self-sufficing. Under such conditions trade can be carried on by barter. There are no wages, since members of the family or slaves are the laborers. Some few payments may be made in kind. Exchange of a rudimentary kind is achieved by gifts, and giving is usually an important practice in such societies. Instead of hiring labor when extra services are needed, as in harvest time, labor is volunteered.

The economy of the Old South was, of course, not a completely moneyless one. There were cities, a high development of culture, and much trade. Still, there were many farms that raised most of the food eaten. These farms also had rooms for spinning and weaving. A few of them had blacksmith shops attached. Some tanned leather, made furniture, prepared what medicines were needed. So that many articles, bought now with money, were not bought in those days but were made in the homestead. I once saw an old plantation house with forty-three rooms in it, one of which was a jail. There had been five hundred slaves on the place. Out of so large a population an occasional recalcitrant would appear. Such an establishment naturally made much of what the members consumed. Hence not much money was needed in daily use.

This fact is illustrated for instance in the letters of a young Mr. Lovell, who left his father's plantation on Sapelo Island, off the coast of Georgia, in 1820, to go to college at Yale in New Haven. In his letters he is impressed with the frequent use of money and shows his astonishment at the fact that there is little you can do and few places to go in New Haven without spending money. As a youth he had seen very little money. He lived on a plantation, not near town. There was nothing to spend money for in his daily life on the farm. Purchases for the plantation were made by the father in large amounts when he went to Savannah or London. Consequently money was something with which the son was not well acquainted.

There have been, of course, many other relatively moneyless societies. But in the United States, the South was more rural than the New England states, and there were slaves, which slowed the adoption of the use of money as wages. The rural West was developed later, when there was more money in use. So the South may be taken as an illustration. While there was indeed a good deal of use of money in the South before the Civil War, still there are to be found many of the characteristics of the moneyless cultures.

The South has changed greatly since the Civil War. Railroads, factories, and cities have come, together with the wide use of money. But some ideas, characteristic of the days of the self-sufficing plantation economy, have persisted into the industrial civilization of the twentieth century. It is well known that ideologies continue long after the conditions that brought them into existence have changed. Thus the adage still persists that "woman's place is in the home," an aphorism more appropriate to a time when spinning and weaving were women's occupations in the home than it is now, when one out of four women work outside the home and when about fifty per cent of the urban homes have no small children in them.

Such a survival of an attitude of a moneyless economy is indicated by the phrase "almighty dollar," which is often heard in the South. The dollar can buy so many things, can do so much, that it is like the Almighty himself. Such an observation, it seems to me, would more probably be made in a society to which the dollar was a recent acquisition. The expression would hardly be used in a city that has had money for two hundred years. The power of money to buy is taken for granted there and needs no signalizing. The frequent use of this expression, "the almighty dollar," represents an attitude toward money in the South that traces back to a society without much money.

Another expression I used to hear in my boyhood in the South and haven't heard elsewhere is, "This is something money cannot buy." Indeed in the Old South there were many things that money could not buy, especially those involving sentiment. The fore-going remark was made usually with a sense of pride and with a contempt for money, with all its powers.

The explanation of these observations, lies, I think, in the fact that in the Old South there was little money in circulation. Its use was restricted to definite formalized channels. Money was used to purchase from recognized institutions such as stores and markets. In purchasing from stores, a large number of these transactions would be with mere acquaintances rather than with friends. Such transactions involved no obligations, no gestures of friendliness. It was business. The passage of money marked the commercial. Money, however, was not used in those days to make small transactions between friends, though it was proper to do business with friends when large sums of money were involved, as in the purchase of real estate or slaves.

The introduction of any invention has a limited use at first. But as money became used more, it naturally was applied to a wider and wider range of types of transactions, until today its conquest is almost complete. There are few transactions that cannot be made with money today. As this conquest was getting under way, it is natural that the dollar would appear to be almighty and that in the heroic defense there would be some things that money could not buy.

One of my playmates as a child picked flowers at the request of his mother and sold them to help raise funds for the church. Later, when the enterprising youngster conceived the idea of selling the flowers he picked to make money for himself, he was reprimanded and not allowed to do so. It was not proper to sell for oneself but all right to sell for the church. This idea in regard to selling is a survival from the time when those who lived in the châteaux and on the plantations considered those engaged in trade as in a class beneath them. Those who lived on country estates had a prestige not possessed by those who lived in town houses. Something of this attitude, characteristic of several hundred years ago, still persists in spots at the present time in highly industrialized England, where the social status of the country house is still very high. For a time in the Old South, occupations concerned with cotton and the professions held a superior social status to merchandising. Merchants dealt with money; planters did not.

I had a neighbor, a relatively poor man, who plowed for himself, who would plow without charge to help a neighbor, but who would not plow for money for anyone. It was "beneath him" to do so. The payment of money for labor had not yet become a wide practice. There was a time when wages did not exist. There were slaves, or labor was freely given when it was needed, as in clearing land for a barn-raising. This volunteer service was, of course, remembered and would be reciprocated at some future time, no doubt, in one way or another. In the face-to-face groups of the moneyless society, there went with this exchange of services a friendliness and sometimes a sentiment not found in the modern money transactions for wages. Since money transactions were often impersonal, cold, and formal, there would naturally be a resentment against being paid money for services that were usually, in earlier times, the gesture of friendliness.

Another illustration is quite recent. In the winter of 1940, I was driving through a locality in the mountains of east Tennessee, in search of a family cemetery. A poor farm laborer, scantily clothed, helped me locate it. It took about two hours of his time, for which, after some debate with myself, I decided to offer him a dollar. He declined, with dignity.

During the same trip I also observed an illustration of the survival of the practice of the volunteer exchange of service. In an old southern city a party was given me one evening. In making preparations, my hostess was aided by two of her closest friends, though she was quite able financially to hire a cateress and belonged to the social class that would have done so in a northern city. Undoubtedly, when one of these friends entertained some time in the future, my hostess would likewise help her in the arrangements. Thus a practice, labor exchange, that was characteristic of a moneyless society persisted into a time when it was the usual practice to hire assistance with money. So also the custom of friends and neighbors, in the case of a death, offering to sit up with the remains of the deceased persists in various localities despite the fact that the presence of a local funeral director makes such volunteer service unnecessary.

The establishment of the payment of wages in money was extended unusually slowly in the South, perhaps because of slavery, and even met with some opposition. Such may be the interpretation of the late development there of tipping. It is not even now as widely spread a custom in the southern cities as in the northern, where one does not easily go wrong in offering a gratuity. But in the South it is not readily clear that a tip will not offend or even insult. I recall as a lad of fourteen being offered a tip for delivering a telegram by a northern visitor to our small town. I handed the money back. The South is a land of kindnesses expressed in many ways but not in small sums of money.

The resistance to tipping in the South may be attributed to slavery rather than to absence of money. But in this case, they both trace back to a common source, the absence of the custom of paying money for wages. Slavery intensified and prolonged the custom.

The intrusion of money in settling personal differences is resisted in the South. In certain types of behavior the approved method in a moneyless society is to fight or merely break off relations and not sue for damages. It is natural then that the application of money to settle a "breach of promise" to marry would seldom be found in the South. The idea seems quite incongruous that the payment of money would heal a broken heart. Indeed it required some time for the courts in general to extend their rule in the moneyless societies over many personal affairs. The custom was to have all such personal difficulties or arrangements handled by individuals or by families. It was more appropriate to settle them by the duel, the feud, or by lynching. To take to the courts to settle certain matters for money officially was a confession of individual or family failure. In the southern states the percentage of divorces where alimony is sought is about one-third the percentage in the agricultural states of the West. The southerners' reputation for resorting to the fight rather easily probably stems from this same background, when it was better to settle such matters personally than to have them settled by the police or by monetary fines. Thus Judge Lumpkin (30th Ga. Rep. p. 891) makes the following comment in a decision on adultery:

This is the first action of *crim. con.* that has been before us. We trust it will be the last especially when the *factum* of the adultery is proven by one witness only, and that witness the son of the fallen woman; and thus instead of keeping the discovery he made, locked up in the secret chambers of his bosom, thus covering the shame and nakedness of his erring parent, or seizing the first weapon at his command and rushing upon the guilty paramour and wiping out with his heart's blood the dishonor inflicted upon the family, for which prompt and manly vindication of the household altar and the marriage bed, earth would have proclaimed, "Well done" (Penal Code, 4th Div. XVI. sec) and Heaven would have echoed back the plaudit (Lev. 20:10). Instead of all this, Ransome Wood, from the witness stand, in maintenance of his father's suit for pecuniary damages, publishes and perpetuates to all coming time the sin and degradation of the mother that bore him.

Changes in customs regarding courts, divorce, breach of promise, alimony, duels, and feuds are of course not directly traceable solely to the one cause of the degree of use of money. Such customs are the result of many factors, such as religion, the family, tradition, etc. It is here argued that money is one factor of many, though at times important. Money is making an inroad into such personal transactions, but slowly and with resentment.

Customs on such large matters are often a part of an integrated code of behavior. Thus some of the customs of the "southern gentleman" appear to come from the aristocratic code of two or three hundred years earlier in Europe. But eighteenth- and seventeenth-century Europe was not yet a monetary economy. The attitudes of the aristocrats were like the attitudes of a moneyless economy. They high-hatted tradesmen and people who worked for money. The code of the gentleman, like the code of the aristocrats, is held by the gentleman and the aristocrat, who have not read Sumner's *Folkways*, to be an eternal verity, a set of rules that are good at all times everywhere, like the virtues set forth in the Bible. The point here made is that these codes, however acquired and irrespective of how many factors bring them about, are modified here and there by the wider use of money, as is evidenced by folkways in the South.

These observations that the South has not yet become adjusted to money and resents its use in certain regards do not, of course, mean that the southerner is indifferent to wealth. Quite the contrary. He desires to be rich as much as a citizen from any other section of the country. He simply has not become accustomed to certain types of monetary transactions. In those pursuits where the use of money is the accepted practice, the southerner may prove to be as eager for money as anyone else. The point is that the range of activities involving the passage of money is somewhat more limited there than in the other sections of the United States, where the money economy is more fully developed. A student from a southern university was telling me recently that their library has just instituted for the first time money fines for the late return of borrowed books. But, it seems the library officials enforce the rule with reluctance. It is as though the entrance of money into a new area is resented.

A common observation regarding the adoption of an invention is that it meets resistance. The iron plow was opposed, for the iron would poison the soil. The four-wheeled carriage was forbidden by law in Hungary. The English fought the use of coal. Still, it seems strange that so desirable an object as money should be opposed. Yet these surviving southern folkways indicate an opposition.

Thus, from my youth, I recall an attitude of contempt for money more prevalent than I have noticed in the North. This attitude seemed particularly strong among the religious, who were often given to praising the pursuit of the virtues over the love of money. To be honorable was more important than to acquire money. A friend of mine from Kentucky recalls being advised by his grandfather in a serious conference on life's values not to worship money or go chasing after it, but to remember that he was a southern gentleman, and southern gentlemen put other values before money. Morals were not to be sacrificed for a mess of pottage, nor should one sell one's soul for thirty shekels of silver. These attitudes are an index of religious forces, but the point is that they were used to belittle money. To be "stingy" was bad becase it meant too great a love of money, which was a sin. The word "stingy" seems to be in greater use in the South than in other sections of the country. The expression "money-mad" also seems to be more frequently heard in the South. The commonness of both these expressions indicates a resistance to the spread or abuse of money. A very poor person in the South may with pride refuse to be niggardly with money. To quarrel over a small bit of money is, somehow, to lower oneself, indicating the resistance to the intrusion of money into the smaller exchanges of life.

Part of the training of a lady (and of a gentleman) in Scarlett O'Hara's time was never to appear to be curious or to inquire of others how much money an article cost, nor ever to be so bold as to speak of something in terms of its cost. This code is not, of course, confined to the Old South. There may be various reasons for such good manners, but one explanation may very well be the resentment against expressing values in money. It is better to show indifference toward cost outside the market place.

The Negroes of the South are not without their own attitudes toward money. They never had any money when first freed and hence did not know what to do with it. Their wages were low and they never learned much about saving. A friend recently reported his experiences in helping finance a Negro church. He reported that the Negroes were willing to save to pay a debt, for which they were trained; but they were not willing to accumulate in advance to make a purchase price. The saving of money seems to have come slowly with Negroes.

Another southern custom that may be interpreted as a resistance to the adoption of a monetary economy is the habit in a business appointment of not taking up business matters immediately. It is good manners to comment about the weather, to inquire about one's health or the welfare of one's family, or to talk about politics before taking up a business transaction. Some southern business men consider it decidedly rude for a person to rush right into a business matter without first "passing the time of the day." This custom almost surely follows from several sources, such as a slow tempo, early methods of trading, or a personal society where everyone knows everyone else. But it may also show a resentment against money. Why should it be *rude* to come quickly to money matters without any preliminaries? Does it not indicate an assumption that you have too great a concern for money and a willingness to make money for money's sake? You do not want to be so classified and resent it. There is thus a possible monetary explanation, though not a certain one.

Before concluding, it is again noted that the South is not the only area of the world where such folkways are found. Also it is again remarked that changes in southern customs are not solely due to the wider spread of the monetary economy, for there are many other factors. But it does appear that several of the manners and customs of the South become clearly understood when they are seen as survivals of attitudes of a moneyless society. Money appears first in a limited sphere of transactions in a society. But it gradually penetrates into wider and wider circles of exchanges and relationships. But in doing so, it is opposed. Many of these attitudes of the South after the Civil War are best understood as oppositions to this wider use of money. In the course of time, these survivals will disappear, and the adoption of money will be as complete in the South as elsewhere.

17

TRENDS IN SOCIAL SCIENCE *1934*

A COMPARISON of articles in the social science journals in the United States over the past third of a century reveals many differences. These differences are in both method and subject matter. Similar changes are shown by the books published, the programs of the annual social science association meetings, as well as the various periodic reports of research in progress. These changes have varied in the different social sciences—sociology, economics, political science, and statistics. A discussion of only a few of the changes will be presented in the brief space allotted this paper. It will not be possible to present changes systematically or to record here the considerable volume of evidence.

Differentiation

A very useful guide to follow in observing trends in the social sciences is the lines of their differentiation. Herbert Spencer used to describe this as a process from the simple to the complex, from the homogeneous to the heterogeneous. Without accepting the universality of the principle that Spencer claimed for it, it is certainly true that in all the various social sciences much differentiation has occurred in the past quarter of a century. It has pro-

Reprinted from *Science*, LXXIX, No. 2047 (March 23, 1934), 257–62. Address of the retiring vice-president and chairman of Section K—Social and Economic Sciences—American Association for the Advancement of Science, Boston, December, 1933.

ceeded so far indeed in statistics that one statistician now has difficulty in understanding the language of another. The eugenist and the monetary expert speak a different language. A zygote means little to the student of money, while the eugenist is not expected to understand the relation of devaluation and inflation. All this leads to such specialized publications as the *Journal of Juvenile Research,* or the *Bankers', Insurance Managers', and Agents' Magazine,* and (in all countries) to 4,500 social science journals and serials.

One of the consequences of this specialization is a smaller proportion of general articles and general works. Synthesis becomes more difficult. The recent death of Wilhelm Wundt removed the last social scientist who knew it all and who was able to synthesize on a large scale. And there will never be another, for the differentiation has since Wundt's time become too great. There seems to be just as great a demand for general works, but their production by scholars is more difficult. This decrease in the proportion of comprehensive works and articles is of course to be regretted. At times the demand becomes so great that the output is increased. Thus in history, shortly after the war, there was a demand for world histories to give a perspective. Also the orientation courses in the junior colleges in general science and in social science lead to more comprehensiveness, if not to synthesis. There seems to be at times an alternation between a more intensive specialization and a more comprehensive summation. To this decline in the proportion of general works at the present time some exceptions may be noted. The textbook, for instance, is a general work which has a steadily increasing demand. A textbook, however, is not a research work, but rather a compilation of materials set forth in a pedagogical form. Histories are another possible exception, because they all may be considered as general works.

Expansion

Another trend in social science has been its expansion. The scientific movement has been annexing territory to the already vast domain under its sway. Expansion and differentiation have gone along hand in hand. In fact, differentiation is a device which encourages expansion.

The wider extension of scientific activities is due to the great popularity today of science. This was not so true of the science of Galileo. But scientific medicine, applied chemistry, electricity, and scientific agriculture have brought such marvelous benefits to mankind that the word "science" has become magic. Everyone wants to be scientific, even when he should not be, even when he is trying to be ethical, educative, journalistic, or even poetic. Hence, the word "science" is applied today to the simplest of operations.

In the beginning of the social science movement the term "science" was one of grandeur and was applied to matters of great dignity, such as international trade, the wealth of nations, the origins of democracy, while subjects such as quarrels among married couples or the misbehavior of boys and girls were then hardly considered subjects worthy of science. Something like these conditions exist in Europe in sociology today, where juvenile court records, for instance, are not thought of as within the scope of science, although the conclusions drawn from these records are often quite scientific. A similar restricted use of the term "science" has been noted in regard to primitive peoples. Consideration of their scientific achievements are judged in the fields that convention has designated as science, such as astronomy and chemistry, fields in which they are not at all scientific. Their achievements, however, in toolmaking, in agriculture, in the domestication of animals, or in hunting are not considered as science, but it is here that their scientific achievements are considerable. Of course, science as a method of discovering reliable and enduring knowledge may be applied either to the most trivial or the most significant. The science is as good in either case.

In political science at the beginning of the century major interests were in the structure of governments, in juristic problems, and in the field of political doctrines. Later political parties grew as the object of scientific study. Still more recently in this discipline, the word "science" has been extended to cover the investigation of a whole range of non-governmental bodies, such as labor unions, farmers' organizations, women's clubs, and civic bodies, which in truth have much to do with the way governments operate. So, also, the newer study of public administration has extended the scope of science over a great mass of practices that were formerly given little serious scientific attention. Indeed, these newer trends in political science employ somewhat more scientific procedures than did the older studies of law and political doctrine.

In economics the great territorial expansion of the scientific movement took place before the beginning of the present century, for the practical questions of our economic life have always been considered among the most important, and hence worthy of the great name of science. Yet more recently new subjects, such as the business cycle, not formerly studied, have been taken up by the economic sciences. The period under consideration has seen the rise of the many schools of business. There the scientific method which has been used in studying the economic questions of society is used to study the economic questions of business.

In sociology the scope of science has extended to encompass the whole field of social work. At least the aid of scientific study of social work problems is being utilized for social service. Other fields in sociology in which social research has expanded are rural social life, urban communities, the family, juvenile delinquency, and organized religion. The evidence from the sociological journals also indicates a recent growth of interest in the phenomena of social change. Perhaps the greatest expansion of activity during the past two decades in sociology has been in the field of social psychology. In sociology the interest in psychology has been much more marked than in economics or in political science, though the social aspects of psychology have been incorporated to a greater or lesser degree in all the social sciences. An illustration of these processes of expansion, differentiation, and spread of the word "science" may be noted in social psychology in the study of child behavior. Batteries of trained observers have watched little children playing together for weeks, have recorded each type of movement thousands of times, and have expressed these relationships in mathematical formulas. That so much measurement should be given by trained scientists to the number of times one child snatches a toy away from another has seemed to some of the older group as a debasing of science. But the net of scientific inquiry has been thrown wider and wider to catch the process of personality formation.

Modern Social Problems

These processes of differentiation and expansion have led to a great shift of interest to the study of modern social, economic, and political problems. It was to have been expected that the expansion would lead in this direction, though such was by no means inevitable. Why has the trend been toward the solution of modern social problems?

The trend of science is a function of at least two factors. One is the demand for knowledge. The other is the presence of adequate scientific tools and materials. The demand for knowledge about our social problems is natural. The growth of this demand is due to the increasing volume and rapidity of social change. For social change brings problems because of the unequal rates of change of the different parts of society, and with change come greater possibilities for efforts toward their control and direction. In other words, there are more social problems and more possibilities for their solution. This shift of activity toward social problems is to be noted in anthropology and history, disciplines where it would be least expected. The anthropologists contribute to the present-day study of race and the relation of culture to personality. The historians are bringing history closer and closer to date, while some are even making contemporary investigations. A line of demarcation between history and the other social sciences based on time is becoming less easily ascertainable. This urgent need for guidance on the modern social questions of policy has been accompanied in this country by grants of funds for their scientific study on the part of private foundations and on the part of government. Such funds have had an extraordinarily stimulating effect. An illustration is the great volume of research activity among rural sociologists and agricultural economists fostered by grants of money from Congress.

Science grows not only because of the demand for knowledge but also because it has the equipment with which to make the pursuit. Cytology rests upon the use of the microscope. The technique of handling time series of economic data has made possible a great deal of research activity on economic and business trends. The lack of capacity to deal scientifically with material has not, however, been so much of a hindrance to activity as it has to successful achievement. Thus primitive peoples were very active in studying and practicing medicine but accomplished little, and modern peoples have been greatly concerned with race relations, but their scientific accomplishments in this field have been few.

But certainly one of the reasons for the increasing research in contemporary problems is the greater facility for dealing with them. Records and measurements are in general better the more recent the phenomena are. For we have been improving the collection of data. Thus weekly index numbers of prices are very recent, and only in 1930 was there a census of the distribution of goods. On contemporary questions, it is also possible sometimes for an investigator to make his own collections of data, which cannot be done so well for the past.

Recessions

The discussion thus far has been largely concerned with the great expansion of social science, and one might well ask the question, Have there been no recessions? Unquestioned recessions are not easily found. There have been shifts of interest, but in these cases there may have been no actual decline, only a percentage decline. Thus, in the case of biological sociology, there seems to be a smaller percentage of sociologists with major interests in this field than formerly, despite a very appreciable interest in eugenics. The causes of this possible decline may be altogether special, namely, the natural ebb of an overexpanded interest in Darwinian biology and the very great rise of interest in culture, which has caused considerable modification in the claims of social biology. There are also special reasons why there has been a shift of emphasis in political science away from the legal approach. But the decline of emphasis in economic "theory," in systematic treatises in sociology and in the history of political doctrines is due to the same general cause, previously referred to. Changes in emphasis are occurring continuously in matters of contemporary social questions. Thus the World War brought renewed interest in international relations and in population questions, and as proportionately more attention is given to these, less is devoted to other problems, such as certain socioreligious questions, slavery or immigration.

Boundaries

The trend toward specialization and that toward the solution of practical problems are at times in conflict. The conflict lies in the fact that the fields of specialization do not synchronize with the circumference of social problems. Thus there is no field in economics that completely covers the labor problem, yet most of the research workers in this problem are trained in economics. The differentiation of a social science based wholly on the study of modern social problems would be different from the differentiation of a social science that was never concerned with practical questions. Attempts have been made at various times to organize a body of scientific knowledge in social science with little consideration of practical problems, and the result has been a set of abstract formulations, quite unrealistic. The actual development is a compromise between these trends. The influence of the reality of present issues is forcing revisions of so-called pure sociology. The concepts of "pure" and "applied" science were borrowed from natural science, where a body of "pure" science is worked out and "applied." The flow is from the "pure" to "applied," though there are some counter movements. But in social science the usefulness of this differentiation may be questioned. The flow is perhaps more from the "applied" to the "pure," that is, from those practical problems which are analogous to the field of "applied" science to the systematic body of knowledge which is analogous to the field of "pure" science.

But whatever may be the effect of practical problems on the growth of social science, during the past decade the study has tended to break down the barriers between the various social sciences. A student of crime must cross many boundary lines to search in the fields of biology, psychology, law, economics, psychiatry, and sociology for the answers to the questions he seeks. There is thus a trend toward fluidity in boundary lines, so much so sometimes as to almost undo the effects of previous differentiation. For instance, it has been said that in the future all economics will be political economy. This result is expected because of the increasing partnership between industry and government.

Tendencies in human affairs are often accompanied by countertendencies. It may be asked therefore whether boundary lines in the social sciences are tending to become less fluid. I think so, particularly between the scientific part of social science and the intellectual undertakings that are not especially concerned with scientific research, such as ethics, philosophy, and literature. In earlier times the social sciences and the humanities were not separated. Philosophy and sociology were undifferentiated. The literary essay was not distinct from political science. But soon this differentiation took place, yielding specialization in journals, in professorships, and in national associations. Nevertheless, much writing in social science, both in articles and in books, is still an undifferentiated mixture of attempts to persuade, to entertain, to interpret meanings, to be literary, to discuss ideas, and to express one's beliefs and prejudices, as well as to draw reliable conclusions from data. But a volume of writing known as social science research, which is concerned only with presenting the new knowledge and the method whereby it was discovered from data, has become very large in amount. This type of writing is sometimes slightingly called "fact-finding." It is becoming quite sharply distinguished from journalism, propaganda, ethics, philosophy, or essays. Between research and these other types of intellectual display the boundary lines are becoming more rigid.

The splitting-off of other types of writing from the presentation of research is resented by many, especially by those who like to influence others and to interpret meanings. But the further erection of barriers between the exposition of research and other types of writing in no way diminishes the activity of those who wish to discuss meanings and ideas. Nor is there any invidious comparison as to the value to society of scientific writing and of other types of intellectual writing. Who can say which is of more value?

We conclude, therefore, that the barriers between the different social sciences are becoming weakened, but the barriers between scientific writing and other kinds are becoming strengthened.

Method

This divorcing of other types of writing from social research is not so much a separation of subject matter as of method. The method of the essayist is different from that of the scientist. This divorcing of social science from other than the scientific suggests a possible restriction of method rather than an expansion and differentiation, as was the case with the subject matter. The long discussions of methodology in sociology have given way to consideration of techniques of investigation. It seems obvious that the methods of intellectual activity in general are more varied than those specifically concerned with science, at least that part of scientific work that draws conclusions from data, which is the portion that usually finds publication. Scientific verification restricts intellectual activities to the evidence and limits the mental associations that are dictated by emotion, which form such an attractive part of less restricted intellectual work. Of course the first phase of scientific work, namely, originating the idea, developing the "hunch," and formulating the hypothesis, is a much less restricted intellectual activity than the verification and permits of the greatest freedom of association of ideas, emotional or otherwise. But this phase does not become a part of the literature. So we say, then, the splitting-off of social research from other types of writing has meant a reduction in the variety of methodology.

Indeed, there has been increasing reliance upon the historical, descriptive, and statistical methods to the exclusion of others. It may be well to exemplify by reference to some of the social sciences. In ethnology the rise of the historical method since the beginning of the century has been quite phenomenal. This method in ethnology arose as a protest against the various attempts to explain cultural phenomena in terms of biology, race, instincts, and climate. Within more recent years there is said to have been something of a reaction away from the historical method in anthropology, as it was practiced, in favor of a functional approach. But indeed a functional account actually is, if done well, an extension of the historical or descriptive method into the new fields of meanings and functions.

In economics, the recent interest in institutionalism really means a use of the historical or descriptive method. The method is somewhat in contrast to the methodology of so-called economic theory, which was observational analysis of complex relationships of the important concepts. These observations, however, did not rest on strictly inductive work but were based upon abstracted situations. It was a short-cut method of dealing with the *Gestalt* and got very good approximate results. More recently "economic theory" has been supplemented by the statistical technique.

In sociology the historical method has not been so extensively used as has the descriptive, the chief method of contemporary social investigations and surveys. The historical method in sociology is found particularly useful, as in anthropology, in explaining phenomena in terms of culture, as in contrast to supposed explanations in terms of psychology of races. It is also an aid in the determination of the psychological factors. The case-study method, when properly pursued, is an attempt to get at behavior by the historical method. Studies of social change rely also on the historical method.

The historical method in the social sciences is of course more than merely the history of single events. It is also the history of relationships; and, when these relationships are successive, of processes. To describe the events of the past, though difficult enough in some instances, is much more simple than to describe accurately processes and relationships. Early writers in social science were concerned a great deal with describing what they called social processes. But soon it was found that further detailed descriptive work was needed. So there followed this increase in the use of the historical method.

Techniques

The demand for more reality in the generalization of processes and relationships in the historical and descriptive methods has led to an increasing use of statistics. An illustration of this is the necessity for quite exact accounts of the process of business fluctuation. No description in loose terms will meet the requirements, which in this case are no less than the necessity of predicting the booms and depressions. All the evidence shows great extension of statistics during the period under review, particularly during and since the World War.

The increasing use of statistics has come about partly through the better provisions made for collecting them. The usefulness of statistics was very apparent during the war, when the production of industry had to be adapted very closely to the wartime needs felt both by the government and business. It is said that those countries that have dictators find a greater need for statistics because of the planning and control involved in these recent dictatorships. Thus Italy and Russia have surprisingly good statistics. In the United States the co-ordinated effort of the New Deal to pull out of the great depression of the early 1930's called for more statistics. Particularly has this been true of the National Recovery Administration and of the Agricultural Adjustment Act. The monetary program rests also on the more exact measurement of statistics and the frequent reporting of them.

The wealth of the nation has also been a factor in the growth of statistics. The collection of statistics and their manipulation are costly to government, to business, and to private bureaus and universities.

It should also be mentioned that invention within the field of statistics has produced new useful formulas that are especially adapted to the social sciences. This is true of index numbers, measurement of trends, correlation and contingency coefficients, scales for measuring social attitudes, equations of curvilinear relationships, methods of holding variables constant. These new developments have aided in the analysis of social phenomena.

Previously it was argued that the subject matter of social science had undergone expansion and differentiation but not its methodology. But there has undoubtedly been a multiplication of techniques, as has just been noted in the case of statistics. Similar expansion and differentiation also characterize the historical and descriptive methods.

The extension in the use of statistics has been most widespread in economics. There is of course much analysis and history in economics that is not very amenable to the statistical technique. But even in the field of economic theory there has recently been an increased use of statistics. One journal has been founded devoted solely to the application of this method to economic theory.

Less of the subject matter of sociology than of economics has been found suited to statistical techniques. About one-half of the social research in sociology uses the statistical method.

Of all the great social sciences, political science is the one where statistics has found least use. The descriptions of governments and their functions and laws call for few statistics. Some use has been made of the quantitative method in studying election returns, and no doubt as the role of quasi-governmental institutions of an economic or social nature become more and more the object of study, statistics will be needed.

At one time statisticians were a special group more or less apart from sociologists, political scientists, and economists and, along with these groups, were organized in a great national association. But now the economic association and the sociological society have large numbers of statisticians in them, and many of the articles in their journals deal with statistics. The original function of the American Statistical Association has thus in part been lost, and new ones developed. Statisticians therefore are becoming less differentiated from the other great social science groups, a reverse of the differentiating process.

Statistics as a method is important because it is the nearest parallel in the social sciences to the laboratory or experimental method. The essence of these methods is the holding of factors constant, so that the effect of the variation of a single factor may be seen. Statistics has a number of devices that do this very well, better by far than most of the other methods.

The Evolution of a Science

Finally, there remains one other way of looking at trends in social science. Oftentimes the process of development of a young science, as time goes on, is one from theory to verification, very much as is the development of a single piece of research. In the early stages a young science is supposed to be speculative, theoretical, concerned with concepts and exploration, and abundantly intellectual. A scientist looks over the field and busies himself with pointing out the significant, advising what ought to be done, and engages in the work of classification. He is looking for guiding principles around which to organize his material. There is a breadth and catholicity about his scientific endeavors and his vision.

Later, as some of this preliminary work reaches a point where there is much waste in dialectic or where diminishing returns set in, then verification is stressed. The emphasis then is on checking the speculations and hypotheses. The search is for more exactness and for greater reliability of the supposed knowledge. The checking is not so much by criticism and debate as by evidence and data. Intellectual processes are more disciplined by the restrictions called for in verification.

There are many individuals who regret such transitions in the growth of a science. They miss the discussion, the exploring, the debate about concepts, the apparent lack of appreciation of values, and particularly the unrestricted play of ideas which characterized the earlier phase. I doubt, however, whether there is much less of this type of intellectual work taking place. It is rather not so customary to print it. The demand is to restrict publication more and more, in scientific journals at any rate, to the presentation of research that has been tested by data and found to be reliable. The exploratory work, the discussion of concepts, and the building of theories seem to go on in the initiating of research; but these initiatory steps do not find publication until the verifying process has been done.

It is not at all clear that a science must inevitably develop over the years in such a sequence, that is, must go through this theoretical stage before reaching a verification stage. Presumably a science might profit from the mistakes of the past and proceed at once to the emphasis upon verification and reliability. But few of the social sciences have so profited from the pasts of other sciences, unless it be statistics. Certainly sociology, political science, anthropology, and economics went through something like the first phase of observation, classification, and theory. Perhaps economics pulled away first, followed by anthropology, political science, and sociology. At any rate, during the period being reviewed, there is everywhere increasing emphasis on reliability of knowledge. The greatest obstacles to the development of science in the social field are complexity of the factors and the distorting influence of bias. These are formidable, but certainly the trends of the present century are most encouraging, and we may look forward, because of social science, to a greater control by man of his social environment.

18

STATISTICAL TRENDS   *1940*

I

A VERY good starting point for discussing the trends of statistics is the year 1839, the date our association was founded. The year suggests the pre–Civil War and proslavery times. The excitement of Andrew Jackson had passed. No great event enlivened the mediocrity of the time. Martin Van Buren was President. Yet in the world of statistics the times were far from being mediocre. It was rather a period of awakening, the morning of statistics, growing out of a long dim twilight that dated back to the seventeenth century.

Let us note some statistical occurrences which took place in 1839. William Farr, the best claimant to the title of founder of vital statistics, was appointed in England as Compiler of Abstracts, which led to the superintendency of the Registrar General's office. He had already won fame as the author of a book on medical statistics and hygiene. At this time, a census of agriculture in France included questions in the production of corn per hectare and the number of livestock. In the same year, a committee of the Statistical Society of London, which in 1885 became the Royal Statistical Society, was appointed to report on the best method of taking the Census of 1841. Thus a hundred years ago

Reprinted from the *Journal of the American Statistical Association,* XXXV, Part 2 (March, 1940), 252–61.

the Statistical Society of London was co-operating with the organization of the Census, as the American Statistical Association is doing in the United States now.

The range of statistical interest at the time is shown by a survey completed in 1839 by Villermé, distinguished French statistician, on the health of workers in textile factories and by a piece of research published in 1839 by Benjamin Phillips in the *Journal of the Statistical Society of London* on the mortality from amputation. In the same year a method of improving a life table was presented by Demonferrand in France. Thus we see that research in vital statistics and in social surveys was under way, as well as economic statistics and census work.

There is a theory in sociology that great events do not occur in isolation but that they come in groups. Shakespeare's writings were only part of a cluster of great poems and dramas written by many other able literary men of the time. It is social forces that produce frequency distributions in achievement. Such forces were playing upon statistics in the years around 1839.

Statistical theory was also very much alive at this time. In 1839, readers were studying Poisson's *Research on Probability,* which had been published two years previously. Cournot was busy at his great treatise on the theory of probability, which was published four years later. The mathematical theory of correlation was also being developed in 1839, for the French astronomer Bravais was at work on a study of probability, published seven years later, which yielded a pretty good idea of correlated relationships, though he did not give birth to a coefficient of correlation.

The practical statisticians and the mathematical students of probability did not see much of one another in 1839. They seem to have dwelt in different lands. One man who was a citizen of both countries and spoke the two languages was Adolphe Quetelet, central statistical figure of the time, whose brilliant light was beginning then to shine over the various countries of northwestern Europe. For the year the American Statistical Association was founded saw the social scientists of Europe reading Quetelet's most famous work, *Sur l'homme et le développement de ses facul-*

tés, ou essai de physique sociale, published three years before. In Quetelet, writer on the mathematics of probability and practical statistician, we find the product of this cross-fertilization yielding studies on anthropometry, criminology, the behavior of man, social physics, and such particulars as the disproof of freedom of the will by statistics and the correlation of the writing of poetry with the age of the writers.

The shape of things to come in the statistical universe was taking form and was clearly visible to the discerning eye. The events occurring in the year our association was formed—which have just been passed in review—reveal the following factors in the development of statistics.

First was the practical work of statistics, promoted and used by the state in its problems, and second there were the mathematical studies of probability. The science of statistics was born out of the union of these two forces. These two streams of the practical and the theoretical continue down to the present day, and they are still widely separated, although there are many more researches based upon the union of the two than there were a hundred years ago.

From the field of practical statistical investigation, at least two main types have been common in the literature of the past hundred years. These are vital statistics and economic statistics. Both fields were a source of activity in 1839. The more active field then was vital statistics, but there were some statistical studies in agricultural economics and in commerce. The two interests found a common ground in sociological problems having to do with the welfare of the poorer classes. In the decade there were studies on costs of living of workers' families, on insanity, on crime, on strikes and combinations, and on medical experiences.

The organizational size of statistical work was clearly in evidence at the time our society was formed. In fact, it was organizational activity that was most characteristic of the period. Fact-finding was not only fashionable, it was a passion. There were at least ten statistical societies or statistical sections of scientific organizations formed in England alone in the 1830's. The governments were also very active at this time in statistical organizational work. They were making the registration of vital statistics compulsory, though the time was early for a new country like the United States. There was also much busyness with schedule-making for the Census, with educating the people on taking censuses, and with extending its scope to agriculture.

One final observation on these early years is to note the essentially practical nature of the origin of statistics. The concern was with tabulating the number of cattle, the value of imports, the number of births and deaths. Statistics was thus at the opposite pole from a great intellectual activity of the time, namely, philosophy of history, which was concerned only remotely with practical matters. The attitudes toward the two subjects still hold on the continent of Europe today. Statistics possesses resemblances to what today is called engineering. This point is well illustrated by the early nomenclature of statistics. In England it was first called political arithmetic in the seventeenth century. The Germans gave it the title *"Staatenkunde,"* from which came the word "statistics," meaning a collection of facts about the state of importance to statesmen. The burst of statistical activity around the 1830's was due to interest in the activities of the state in matters that concerned its welfare.

II

The outline of the science of statistics remains much the same today as in 1839. The field of vital statistics, if restricted to births and deaths, now plays a proportionately restricted role as compared with a hundred years ago, though many dominant figures in the American Statistical Association in recent times have been from this field. For years after the early days of fascism in Italy the populace read in the front pages of their newspapers the tables of births and deaths and population growth with keen interest, as we read the stock-market quotations on the back pages. If vital statistics be broadened to include the general subject of population, then there has indeed been a great growth. There are several thousand students taking courses each year in the statistics of population in American colleges today. The membership of the American Statistical Association has grown from 500 in 1900 to 2,500 today.

The popularity of population studies dates from Malthus, but the revival of interest has been greatest following the World War 1914–18. Since then the leading nations of the world have been very actively developing population policies, notably Italy, Germany, and Sweden. Formerly it was thought that the forces that made for quantity and quality of the population were in the hands of God or the instincts of man, but in either case they were not to be interfered with by the government. The growth of population policies of modern states, which must be based of course on statistical data, is a further indication that the original meaning of the word *statistics* is quite applicable to the science today. It is another indication also that the fertilizing influences that make the science of statistics flower come from the practical social questions of the time.

We have been speaking about the trend in vital statistics and population. More rapid has been the growth in economic statistics, which in 1839 was concerned with livestock, taxation, custom duties, and the cost of living. The growth has been particularly rapid in recent years, due in part to the fact that statistics has become an important department in many business organizations. A survey is now in progress from Washington to determine the number of statistical laboratories in connection with business organizations in the United States. As evidence of the interest in business statistics, in 1939 there were 4,875 students of business statistics in eighteen of the schools of business in the United States. The extension of statistics into economics is seen from such fields of study as income, business cycles, prices, production, foreign trade, taxation, money, finance, insurance, marketing, agricultural and land economics. In all these fields the data are largely statistical, and the conclusions would be of little use if there were no data of a statistical nature used. The questions asked by the Bureau of the Census on economic conditions in agriculture, business, wholesale and retail trade, and construction work outnumber those asked about population, births and deaths, health and population characteristics by twelve to one.

Statistics continue to be the facts useful for the state. Since economic activities are so large and so essential a part of modern man's activities, despite the many attempts to deflate economic man, it is natural that the statistics the state collects should be concerned with economics. But the state is expanding its activities. It reaches out also into other issues, such as the care of women and children, looking after the old people, health insurance, other forms of social security. The government is much interested in lessening crime; in improving the condition of the underclothed, the ill-fed, and the badly housed; in preventing industrial disputes. Hence, in these social fields it collects vast numbers of statistics. In the field of religion, it collects few, for the church and state are separated. The Constitution of the United States forbids governmental participation in particular religions, hence the statistics on churches and religion in the United States are inadequate. So as the years go by, the state comes to take more interest in sociological problems. Hence the rise of social statistics.

There are in the United States today [1940] eighty-eight different agencies of the federal government collecting statistics about economic and social conditions. This number appears to be very high to those who made out the one hundred and thirty-five million returns on 4,700 different forms in 1938, not a regular decennial census year. But a state cannot administer its affairs without knowledge of the conditions it deals with, any more than engineers can build the Grand Coulee Dam without expert knowledge about steel and concrete. The engineer learns about his materials in the laboratory, while the government obtains its knowledge from statistics. In both cases the knowledge needs to be precise, the result of measurement. What if the Census costs forty million dollars, it is necessary and worth it to the state, as well as to the uncounted users of census data.

The trends in statistics cannot be understood unless the correlation between statistical activity and governmental functions be recognized. As government in the United States increases its functions, as occurs under both Republicans and Democrats, it *ipso facto* increases its statistical activity. This fact is illustrated clearly by two events in the twentieth century in the United States. Two times the government's functions have had a tremendous expansion. One was during the World War in 1917–18 and the other during the depressions of the 1930's. In both crises the numerical growth of statistical work was meteoric. Statisticians were called to Washington in hordes, as were some who were not statisticians. The demand far exceeded the supply. From 1930 to 1938 the number of statisticians in government service in Washington is reported to have increased 700 per cent. Data are not available for the war period.

The reason for this growth in statistical work was the vast expansion of governmental functions during these two critical periods. The United States became, during 1917 and 1918, a totalitarian state, controlling prices, production, the press, labor, and exercising in general the functions found in the totalitarian states of Europe. These disappeared, however, during the return to normalcy after the war. During the great depression of the 1930's, the number of commissions and authorities created and popularly abbreviated to the letters of the alphabet, such as NRA, AAA, WPA, FERA, CCC, NRC, CWA, PWA, HOLC, TVA, are testimony of the great increase in the functions of the state. That the rise of the totalitarian state means the proliferation of statistics is shown by the impetus to statistical work manifested in Russia, Italy during the 1920's, and Germany in the late 1930's.

This discussion of the role of the state in the development of statistics throws light on the old question of how a science grows. Science is an organized body of knowledge. This body of knowledge takes a form with more or less system. The question is: How does the structure come to have the form it has? One theory coming in large part from the natural sciences with mathematical emphases is that the growth of a science comes from the activities of the inquiring mind, which seeks to find out the interrelationships between the different increments of knowledge as they are added to the existing stock. Thus a science comes to assume an architectural form. Such a conception is that of the growth of a pure science, so-called. This body of knowledge, such as mathematics or chemistry, is then applied to the solution of practical problems.

However, this division of science into "pure" and "applied" has never been a very successful description of the social sciences. Hence the history of the social sciences has strengthened the countertheory that the form assumed by a science is shaped by the practical problems of the time. Even geometry had its early origins in surveying and navigation, and the impetus to astronomy came from the practical problems concerned with the timing of crops and making of calendars. But later developments in mathematics and astronomy were little related to practical questions or even to the general *Zeitgeist*. The knowledge that the temperature of the sun is forty million degrees and that it is eight billion years old was not discovered as a result of any practical interest, nor does the information have any practical value. But in the case of the science of statistics, its growth is seen to be peculiarly the outgrowth of the study of the questions of the time, particularly those questions in which the state is interested. Many other social sciences are also tied closely to contemporary issues. Even history has to be rewritten from era to era. The dictatorship role which the contemporary social milieu holds over many social sciences is not especially conducive to symmetry of structure of the social sciences. More important is the nature of the knowledge and not its unity or form, which may be merely the demand of an aesthetic function of the mind.

III

Of course statistics was built upon mathematics, just as any invention is a combination of existing cultural elements. But the origin of the constituent elements is different from the origin of the resulting composition. The contribution of mathematics to statistics has led to a very great growth of a trend scarcely in evidence in 1839. I refer to statistics as a technique of measurement, to be applied quite generally, whether to issues of statecraft or not. Cournot, for instance, used some statistics, but more mathematics, most ingeniously in the measurement of economic phenomena and their interrelationships.

The use of statistics as a tool of scientific measurement is very well illustrated by psychology, where statistics has a wide use in the solution of psychological problems, rather than in the collection of information for the state. In the *Psychological Review* and the *American Journal of Psychology*, one-half the articles today are of a statistical nature. It is interesting to observe, however, that in the *Journal of Educational Psychology*, which deals with schools, an arm of the state, over 90 per cent of the articles are statistical. At the other end of the distribution is the *American Historical Review*, with only 10 per cent of its articles having any tables or charts. The *American Anthropologist* is not far removed from history, with 14 per cent statistical articles. The *Political Science Review* has slightly less, 12 per cent. The *American Journal of Sociology* carries 28 per cent. In the three economic journals, the *Economic Review*, the *Quarterly Journal of Economics*, and the *Journal of Political Economy*, 45 per cent of the articles include statistical tables and graphs. On the basis of the journal publications using statistics, the sciences are ordered as follows: psychology, economics, sociology, anthropology, political science, and history. That statistics is becoming a method of measurement in all these sciences is evidenced by the fact that during the past third of a century, the proportion of space used for formulas, tables, and charts in these particular journals has increased 115 per cent.

That statistics would find wide use in the social sciences as a scientific method might be inferred from the nature of science, which, as the facts show, progresses with measurement. "When you cannot express it in numbers" said the great physicist Kelvin, "your knowledge is of a meagre and unsatisfactory kind." In the physical sciences measurement is by weights and measures. In the social sciences we measure by counting.

In much science the measurement is one of relationships, be it of hydrogen and oxygen or temperature and volume. The laboratory is an invention to eliminate all influences except the one being measured. In this physical sense there are no laboratories in the social sciences, or very few. On the other hand, a statistical invention, partial correlation, in whose development statisticians in the United States have played a significant part, serves the same purpose as the laboratory does in the physical science. It eliminates the influence of extraneous factors, as do several other statistical devices. Aside from statistics there are few techniques in the social sciences which hold factors constant or eliminate them.

Equations with several variables, however, are as expensive as laboratories, if the costs of collecting the data be included. This fact recalls the fact that the wealthiest nations have the highest statistical development, for only the wealthy can afford statistics. Since the cost of collecting statistics is high, it is natural that this assignment falls to the government. Few individuals or businesses could make a cost-of-living survey that cost $7,000,000. Furthermore, government statistics are collected without bias and are available to conservative and radical alike. I recall a small cost-of-living survey made by labor unions that showed an increase in prices five times as great as the government showed a few weeks later. That wages were being raised in accordance with the rise in the cost of living may explain the vast discrepancy between the unions' survey and the government's. Let us hope that the statistical agencies of the state, as it becomes more and more an action agency, will continue to remain free from bias of political and social beliefs. Mechanical invention also favored statistical computation. These aids help. For the great assorting machine that goes by the name of the inventor, Hollerith, our own Census Bureau deserves the credit. Perhaps the Census may be first to use another machine, where the assorting will be done with an electric eye.

Another aid to the diffusion of statistics as a scientific method is the recent improvements in the methods of sampling and of measuring samples. The wider use of small samples tends to free us from the great cost of mass collection and also presents a useful tool to scientific bureaus with smaller budgets than the governmental agencies.

The diffusion of statistics as a scientific method throughout the social sciences means, of course, that statisticians are no longer a little esoteric band of government research workers and mathematicians. Statistics has become a part of economics, sociology, psychology, anthropology, and the other social sciences. Indeed in my address as president of the American Statistical Association some years ago I discussed the possibility of the association's disappearing, swallowed up by the economic, sociological, and other social science associations, or else the absorption—at some future date—of the American Economic Association, the American Sociological Society, and the other social science societies into the American Statistical Association, which would then be the one grand over-all social science.

This may be. But looking over the more immediate evidence, I see little statistical associations in process of being born in each social science. For instance, among the economists there are the econometrists, mathematical statisticians, who are organized and have a publication *Econometrica.* Among the anthropologists there is the *Journal of Physical Anthropology,* devoted largely to statistics. A statistical wing of the psychologists publishes the journal *Psychometrika.* Among biologists, *Biometrika* has been in existence a long time as a publication of statistical biologists. More recently in the United States there is the *Bulletin of Mathematical Biophysics.* Among sociologists there is the Population Association, with its quarterly, *Population Index.* Among historians and political scientists there is, so far as I know, no statistical publication nor any statistical organization.

In the early days, when statistical literacy was low, those who could read and write this strange new language were set apart from the others. They were labeled statisticians. But now most any social scientist can compute a correlation coefficient and can read and write the statistical language to some extent. Indeed, the arithmetics for the eighth grade in the public schools now have sections on statistics. So a degree of statistical literacy will be universal in the future, since now nearly 100 per cent of the children go to the elementary school and 65 per cent to the high schools. But, now, few are literate in mathematical statistics, and these groups in the different social sciences tend to organize statistical wings in these sciences.

This profusion of statistics as a method throughout the sciences is illustrated by the most unusual topics which have been investigated statistically. I mention a few.

The length of words in the writings of Horace and Dante.
The number and kinds of balls a pitcher pitches.
The height of statues in the Louvre.
The number of lines on the tip of the forefinger.
The rate of learning to play the piano.
The diameters of Italian shields in the Middle Ages.
The chances of a guest winning in a gambling house.
The relation of first to second prizes.
The flight of a bee.
On whether it is better to add up a column of figures or add them
   down.

In conclusion, these brief observations on statistical trends during the history of our association indicate rather clearly that statistics has been promoted greatly by the state and by the study of social phenomena of the present, since the more recent the phenomena the better and fuller the measurement. The structure of the science has been shaped largely by the practical contemporary problems. On the other hand the contribution from mathematics has done much to make it a nearly universal tool of research in all the social sciences, though not in all parts of them.

III. Short-Run Changes

19

THE FLUCTUATIONS OF BUSINESS

AS SOCIAL FORCES   *1923*

For a long time the phenomena of the financial panic and the business crisis have been a matter of common observation and memory. The Federal Reserve banking system is designed to prevent panics, but business crises we still have. Furthermore, additional study[1] has shown that it is erroneous to think of business as normally prosperous except for occasional severe business crises. It is fairer to think of our economic life as proceeding in a wavelike motion from prosperity to depression and from depression to prosperity and so on. These fluctuations of business conditions have come to be described as business cycles. The term "business cycle" is now widely used, though it is not strictly accurate as a descriptive term for the reason that it implies a regularity in length and amplitude not found in a business fluctuation. What is true is that business conditions fluctuate through a period of prosperity and then through a period of depression, remaining at the peak of prosperity or in the trough of depression for only a short part of the period.

Within recent times we can recall the very prosperous years

Reprinted from the *Journal of Social Forces*, January, 1923.

1   Wesley C. Mitchell, *Business Cycles.*

of 1916, 1917, 1918, and 1919, and the depression of 1920, 1921, and 1922. Sometimes we speak of such periods as "good times" and "hard times." These terms carry with them associations other than merely the balance of the accounting sheet. Indeed, it is not surprising that the status of trade, business, and manufacturing should have an influence on various conditions of social life. In the paragraphs which follow there will be shown the results of certain investigations into the influence of business conditions on the particular social conditions studied.

The way in which these investigations are usually made is to secure a numerical index of the social condition under investigation and to plot these indexes in a curve. Then it is observed whether the fluctuations of the curve of social conditions are synchronous with the fluctuations in the curve of business conditions. For instance, the marriage rate (the percentage of persons married during each year as compared to the total population for that year) for certain states can be shown by charting to be quite generally greater in periods of prosperity and lower in periods of business depression. The extent of similarity between the fluctuations of two such curves can be measured quite accurately by a coefficient of correlation which varies between .0 and 1. In the case of the two curves under discussion the coefficient of correlation is $+.87$ (omitting the year 1918).

BUSINESS FAILURES   It is to be expected that more commercial and business enterprises would go into bankruptcy during periods of depression than in periods of prosperity. This has of course long been known; after a panic, for instance, business failures spread like a contagion or an epidemic. Professor Persons has measured the relationship of these failures to wholesale prices and to pig-iron production and has found correlations of —.6 and —.7.[2] An interesting observation on this fact is that business failures tend to be seen in terms of personal ability. A man is said to be doing well if he succeeds in a business venture,

[2]   Warren M. Persons, "Construction of a Business Barometer," *American Economic Review*, December, 1916; also, *Indices of General Business Conditions*, p. 182.

whereas the particular success is due in part to the prosperous conditions, a social force. When a man fails in business, his failure is interpreted in terms of personal inability, whereas the business crisis and depression—a social force—may be the cause. Sometimes the process by which the business cycle causes failures is seen as a good thing, because it is said to weed out the inefficient and incompetent. On the other hand, to those dependent on the particular businesses failing, such an effect of business cycles is a disaster. If the course of business ran more smoothly there probably would be fewer unfit drawn into enterprises and less occasion for weeding them out.

UNEMPLOYMENT   When business enterprises fail some individuals naturally are out of employment. But in many instances when there is no bankruptcy the number of laborers employed is cut down. Therefore we should naturally expect unemployment to increase during a business depression. We can all remember what ravages unemployment, that great terror of the working man, made during the hard times of 1914 and 1921. In times of prosperity there is occasionally almost a shortage of labor. In 1909 Mr. Beveridge[3] showed that for England, the curve of trade-union figures for percentage unemployed from 1860 to 1907 fluctuated in close unison with the volume of foreign trade. In this country we have no unemployment statistics for the country as a whole. Only in a few states do we find statistics on unemployment, and they do not go back very far. Dr. Hart[4] has worked up estimates of unemployment as far back as 1902. These figures clearly indicate a high correlation with the business cycle for that period. Mr. Hurlin's[5] employment index numbers for Massachusetts, which are of course the other side of the picture of unem-

3   William H. Beveridge, *Unemployment: A Problem of Industry*, p. 42.

4   Hornell Hart, "Fluctuations of Unemployment in Cities of the United States, 1902 to 1907," *Studies from the Helen S. Trounstine Foundation*, I, 47–59.

5   Ralph G. Hurlin, "Three Decades of Employment Fluctuation," *Annalist*, October 24, 1921.

ployment, show a similar correlation. Dr. Berridge's[6] very careful indexes of employment and unemployment, estimated from the available sources, show a correlation with monthly pig-iron production for the period 1903–14 of +.89. Here, again, when an employee loses his job, as when a man loses his business, his loss is most frequently interpreted as a personal failure. A laborer without a job is often thought of as being lazy or unwilling to work. There is, as is seen from the foregoing correlations, another side to the picture. Social forces are responsible for a vast amount of unemployment. And here, again, is a very tragic effect of the fluctuations of business.

WAGES   Money wages tend to rise with expanding trade and to decrease or remain stationary in business depressions. This fact is indicated by a comparison of the series of annual figures for foreign trade and the series of wages for the same years, as listed by Mr. Beveridge[7] in his study of the English data for the period 1874–1907. On the other hand, real wages—that is, wages expressed in terms of the purchasing power of money, of what the wages will buy—seem to diminish in times of prosperity and to increase in times of depression. Dr. Davies[8] found a coefficient of correlation of —.7 between real wages and wholesale prices. The increase in unemployment, however, may mean that the average family budget of the wage-earning classes is less ample in times of depression.

POOR RELIEF   Unemployment and business depressions would, it is thought, be expected to increase the task of a large group of social workers. Charity and the bread lines appear more imperative in hard times. Mr. Beveridge's[9] figures for pauperism, indoor, for England and Wales, 1857–1907, correspond closely in

6   William A. Berridge, "Cycles of Employment and Unemployment in the United States, 1903–1914," *Journal of the American Statistical Association*, March and June, 1922.

7   *Op. cit.*

8   George P. Davies, "Social Aspects of the Business Cycle," *Quarterly Journal of the University of North Dakota*, January, 1922.

9   *Op. cit.*

their fluctuations with foreign trade. Miss Howland[10] has collected statistics of the numbers receiving poor relief in Massachusetts for the period 1892–1920. Using business failures as an index of the business cycle she found a correlation of $+.44$ and with wages she found the correlation to be $-.62$.

IMMIGRATION   The immigrants to our shores came in waves concurrent with cycles of prosperity, before immigration was cut off by war and legislative enactment. The volume of immigration is correlated with wholesale prices, 1879–1913, the coefficient as worked out by Professor Persons[11] being as high as $+.62$. The immigrant may come in search of liberty, to begin life anew, to escape religious oppression, or for other personal reasons; but he tends to come in periods of economic prosperity.

STRIKES   One would expect strikes to be related to prosperity and depression. If strikes were a spontaneous breaking-out of dissatisfaction and unrest due to hardship, grievances, and repressions within the walls of industry, we should look for more strikes in times of depression, when foremen rule with a harsher hand. But if policy dictates strikes, more strikes might be expected in times of prosperity, because of the greater chances of winning. During prosperity there are greater profits; labor is scarcer, and there is less fear of the strikers losing their jobs— that is, less unemployment. Furthermore, unions are somewhat stronger in prosperity than in depression. It should also be recalled that real wages are less in prosperity. Dr. Hansen[12] has investigated the number of strikes, 1881–1914, part of the record for the United States and part for Canada, and he concludes that in a period of long-run falling prices, 1881–97, there were more strikes in business depression, the coefficient being $-.34\pm.15$; while in a period of long-run rising prices, there were more strikes in business prosperity, the coefficient being $+.49\pm.12$. It should

10   Katherine E. Howland, "A Statistical Study of Poor Relief," *Journal of the American Statistical Association*, December, 1922.

11   *Op. cit.*

12   Alvin H. Hansen, "Cycles of Strikes," *American Economic Review*, December, 1921.

be observed, however, that his two periods comprise only a very few years each, and of course even fewer cycles. It is very probable also that strikes called by unions, non-union strikes, and the development of unionism in general may have something to do with the number of strikes in these two periods.

MARRIAGES   One of the earliest observations of the relations of social conditions to the business cycle was on the marriage rate. In 1901 Mr. Hooker[13] obtained a coefficient of correlation of +.86 between the marriage rate in England and Wales and the amount of foreign trade, 1861–95, foreign trade in England being used as representative of business fluctuations. In 1922 Dr. Davies[14] found for the United States a correlation between the marriage rate and wholesale prices, 1887–1906, of +.67, wholesale prices being taken as an index of the business cycle. Similar results were found by Miss Thomas and myself.[15] The data of this particular investigation were for only six states, but they extended from 1870 to 1920. The correlation coefficient was +.87. It is to be expected that more marriages would occur when business is good and fewer when business is bad, although the great size of the coefficient of correlation is surprising. Dr. Yule thinks that the very large degree of correlation is due to the fact that the non-occurrence of the event in business depression means in many cases only a postponement until prosperity returns. Mr. Hooker finds that the correlation is greatest when the marriage rates of about a third of a year later are correlated with foreign trade. There thus seems to be a slight lag in the correspondence.

DIVORCE   Professor Willcox,[16] as early as 1893, pointed out that in certain periods of trade depression the divorce rate

13   R. H. Hooker, "On the Correlation of the Marriage Rate with Foreign Trade," *Journal of the Royal Statistical Society*, LXIV, 485.

14   *Op. cit.*

15   William F. Ogburn and Dorothy S. Thomas, "The Influence of the Business Cycle on Certain Social Conditions," *Quarterly Publication of the American Statistical Association*, XVIII (September, 1922), 324–40.

16   Walter F. Willcox, "A Study in Vital Statistics," *Political Science Quarterly*, Vol. VIII, No. 1.

was so low that he thought there must be a causal connection. This relationship has been further investigated by Miss Mack[17] for the period 1867–1906, for the United States, and she finds the correlation with the business cycle to be +.70. There are thus more divorces in times of prosperity than in periods of business depression. The reasons for this fact are perhaps more plausible on the economic than on the psychological side. It seems that there would be, in general, more repression during depression and less substitutive and sublimational activity than in times of prosperity, hence, more incompatibility and more psychological unrest. Such psychological theories are of course highly speculative. The lag, if any, between the fluctuations of divorce and the fluctuations of business is not great. The size of the correlation coefficient is impressive.

BIRTHS   The birth rate does not seem to be very highly correlated with the business cycle. Birth statistics are not fully recorded in the United States. For several states,[18] however, there are birth rates for the period 1870–1920. When these rates are correlated with the figures of the business cycle for the preceding year, the coefficient of correlation is +.33±.07. These figures indicate, therefore, that with a one-year lag there are more births in prosperity than in depression, though of course this conclusion may be due to the fact that there are more marriages in prosperity and not necessarily to any direct influence of business conditions on fertility. These results have not been confirmed (or refuted) by the researches of other persons. The English data on births, studied by the same investigators, show a correlation with foreign trade, 1874–1910, of +.15±.11.

DEATHS   One would probably guess that there would be more deaths in business depression. Such a guess would be suggested by the known fact that the infant death rate is much greater in the lower-income groups and the common observation that tuberculosis is a disease of poverty. But it should be recalled that real wages are probably higher in business depression,

17   Ogburn and Thomas, *loc. cit.*

18   Ogburn and Thomas, *loc. cit.*

though unemployment is much greater. As to evidence, Professor Huntington[19] from his statistics of the death rate in certain regions of the United States, concludes that a high death rate regularly precedes hard times while a low death rate precedes prosperity, and he argues from these statements that health and ill health are causes of the business cycle, not results. His analysis and data seem not thoroughly convincing, however. The fact that for certain regions of the United States there are more deaths in prosperity and fewer in depression appears to be confirmed by the investigations of Miss Thomas and myself for the period 1870–1920, the correlation between the business cycle and the death rate being +.6. This conclusion is most surprising and striking, but the fact is not to be doubted, it is thought, unless the death-rate statistics are inaccurate. Although this relationship between deaths and the business cycle for the United States areas, 1870–1920, seems to be established, it is probably not wise to conclude without further research that prosperity causes an increase in the death rate and depression causes a decrease in the death rate. Before drawing such a conclusion of causal relationship, certain other factors known to be powerful in influence on the death rate should be reckoned in, namely, climate, epidemics, and health programs. These factors might be so powerful as to prove for so short a period an altogether spurious relationship. Still, we do not know that they would. The whole matter is one of doubt.

SUICIDES   The statistics of suicides for one hundred cities in the United States, 1900–20, as published by Mr. Hoffman, have been studied[20] and found to vary in cycles. These suicide cycles were found to be correlated with the business cycles of the same period, the coefficient being —.74. One would probably have guessed that the suicide rate was greater in hard times than in good times, but it is doubted whether one would have guessed such a high relationship as has been found to exist. Apparently,

19   Ellsworth Huntington, *World Power and Evolution*, p. 29.

20   Ogburn and Thomas, *loc. cit.*

the conditions of business have a tremendous influence on one's morale. Morale may be a matter of degree, suicide being an index of the extreme cases.

CRIME   In 1909 Mr. Beveridge compared with his curve showing fluctuations in foreign trade and the bank rate certain statistics of crime. He noted that there was some correspondence in the cyclical movement and thought that this was due to the fact that such a large percentage of the crimes recorded were larcenies. Dr. Davies[21] found that the annual admissions to New York state prisons, 1896–1915, were correlated with the price cycle for the same period, the coefficient being —.41. Miss Thomas and I correlated the total convictions in courts of record for New York State, 1870–1920, with the business cycle and found a correlation of —.35. There seems to be little doubt, therefore, that the total volume of crime is greater in business depressions. Crime is, of course, quite complex; and while it is to be expected, perhaps, that crimes against property should increase in hard times, it is not necessarily to be expected that this would be true of other types of crime. For instance, Mr. Beveridge's figures for convictions for drunkenness indicate just the opposite effect, namely, that there are more of these convictions in prosperous years.

The New York State figures for convictions for offenses against the person, exclusive of offenses against property with violence, show a correlation with the business cycle of —.12 ± .09. If there is any increase in offenses against the person in business depression, it appears to be slight.

CONSUMPTION OF ALCOHOLIC BEVERAGES   In general, the per capita consumption of beer is greater in prosperity and less in business depression, as is shown by Mr. Beveridge's figures for England and Wales. This seems to be true also for wines and spirits. For the United States, Dr. Davies found a correlation of +.78 between the per capita consumption of liquor and wholesale prices for the period 1895–1914. Also it is remembered that the convictions for drunkenness are greater in prosperous years.

[21]   *Op. cit.*

RELIGIOUS ACTIVITIES   It has been remarked that religious revivals are somewhat more frequent and more successful in periods of business depression. It has also been said that interest in spiritistic phenomena is greater at such times. Mr. Babson has commented frequently on the increase in church activities during periods of business depression. Dr. Davies has correlated the increase in membership in the Congregational and Methodist churches with wholesale prices (an index of the business cycle) for the period 1875–94, and he finds the very high correlation of —.67. The coefficient is high, and it seems probable that there is a causal relationship. It may not be that man turns away from God when prosperous, but it does seem that he seeks the Lord in hard times.

LABOR POLICIES AND LIBERAL PROGRAMS   Not the least interesting of the effects of the business cycle is the attitude toward labor, which is more or less at the heart of the liberal and radical movement. During 1915, '16, '17, '18, and '19, there was quite an impetus to this movement. Much was heard of industrial democracy, employee representation, works councils, efficiency, employment offices, personnel managers, welfare work, the creative impulse in industry, labor turnover, psychological tests, vestibule training schools, the bonus, the basic eight-hour day, etc. Many persons felt that all this heralded the dawn of a better day. But since 1920 these terms are seldom seen in print, and these issues are little discussed. They seem to have dropped out. Can it be that the business cycle is responsible? This point has been discussed by Professor Douglas[22] and by myself.[23]

One phase of the prosperity period is increased profits and a diminished labor supply. During the upward trend of the business cycle in the war period, 1917–19, profits were extraordinarily large, and the labor supply was so diminished as to be called a labor shortage. Labor turnover increased greatly, from 100 in

[22]   Paul H. Douglas, "Personnel Problems and the Business Cycle," *Administration*, July, 1922.

[23]   "The Effects of Business Conditions on Social Programs," *Association Monthly*, October, 1921.

1913–14 to 216 in 1917–18.[24] Labor usually turned over for
higher wages, and labor turnover also meant additional cost to
the employer incident to getting and breaking in a new force.
Public employment offices sprang up. The fear of losing his job
was removed from the laborer. Foremen could not boss or dismiss
so readily. The workmen tended to get a hearing before some
tribunal. Personnel managers took over the duties of the foremen.
They investigated grievances and tried to inculcate co-operation.
Welfare work increased. The workmen were in a much better
position to force permission to join the union and to win recognition for the union. Trade-union membership increased greatly,
by millions. To combat the unions and to interest the workmen,
employers started company unions, schemes of industrial democracy, works councils, and other forms of employee representation.
Production per capita fell. Professor Douglas cites data from
Chicago that indicates an average of 1,500–1,600 bricks laid per
eight-hour day in 1914–16, while in 1918–20 the average was
700–800, and during the depression of 1921 and 1922, in other
industries, production increased from 100 to 135. Dr. Davies has
found a correlation between per capita production and wholesale
prices, 1870–1920, of +.4. So there was a consistent propaganda
of increased production, accompanied by vestibule training
schools and psychological tests, during the war period. Absentee-
ism was met by the bonus. Most of these activities were highly
approved by the liberal. But with the surplus of labor and the
falling profits of 1921 and 1922, most of these structures have
crumbled. It seems, therefore, that for the last business cycle, at
least, labor policies and liberal programs have been profoundly
affected by business conditions.

CONCLUSIONS   It is seen, therefore, that fluctuations in
the state of business affect, in most cases strongly, business failures, wages, unemployment, destitution, immigration, strikes,
marriage, divorce, births, suicides, crime, liquor consumption,
religious activities, and liberal labor policies. I have cited only
the social conditions that have been subjected to rigorous scien-

24   Brissenden and Frankel, "The Mobility of Industrial Labor,"
Political Science Quarterly, December, 1920.

tific analysis. No doubt the social force of the business cycle is much more widespread. If so, probably further research will show it.

One conclusion to be drawn is that the quantitative determination of the influence of the business cycle on social conditions is the measurement of a social force of magnitude and importance. Frequently failure, wages, poverty, marriage, crime, etc., are seen as purely individual problems, in terms of personality, will power, and individual behavior, as though the subjective free will of the individual were responsible in a purely personal way. But there is another side to the picture. Here we have shown the objective determinism of a social force that profoundly affects social conditions. Since such a social force exists, there is value in seeing it as a social force and not trying to treat the situation in terms of individuals and personalities.

The thought at once arises, Can the violence of business fluctuations be lessened? The idea presents itself as a sort of new program for social reforms, the attainment of which would mean far-reaching and widespread effects. The elimination or modification of the business cycle, in general, appears highly desirable, particularly the elimination of business depressions. It is true that there are fewer divorces and more religion in periods of business depression. Of course, gains from a lessened business depression would be counterbalanced by a lessened prosperity. Still, stable conditions of business would mean less unemployment, less crime, and less destitution. But it is not at all clear that this social force can be controlled. Mr. Beveridge calls it "the pulse of the nation." He had in mind its effects, no doubt, rather than its necessity. Perhaps a stabilized dollar, or a regulated interest rate, or the dissemination of information regarding business forecasting would do much to lessen the fluctuations of business. This might be true even if weather be a cause. The matter of control or prevention has been little studied. We cannot predict what further research and human effort may accomplish. But one thing is certain: We should not act in ignorance of this social force, and our efforts should be timed in accordance with it.

20

BUSINESS CONDITIONS IN

PRESIDENTIAL ELECTION

YEARS   *1936*

With A. J. Jaffe

THE INFLUENCE of the business cycle on politics has been studied by Rice[1] and Tibbitts.[2] But the influence of politics on the business cycle has not been systematically investigated, although Ayres[3] has shown that prosperous times are about equally divided between the Republican and Democratic administrations, and Mitchell[4] has shown that the curve of business during presi-

---

Reprinted from the *American Political Science Review*, XXX, No. 2 (April, 1936).

1   Stuart Rice, "Some Applications of Statistical Methods in Political Research," *American Political Science Review*, May, 1926.

2   Clark Tibbitts, "Majority Votes and the Business Cycle," *American Journal of Sociology*, January, 1931.

3   Leonard Ayres, *Business Bulletin of the Cleveland Trust Co.*, October, 1924.

4   Wesley C. Mitchell, "Testing Business Cycles," *Bulletin No. 31*, National Bureau of Economic Research, March 1, 1929.

dential administrations is not at all like the business cycle. There is a popular impression that business is not as good during the year of a presidential election as in other years. It is the purpose of this paper to present the results of an investigation of this question.

I

As an index of business activity, the widely known index issued by the Cleveland Trust Company under the direction of Leonard Ayres was first studied and is referred to hereinafter as the Ayres index, or the index of business activity. A look at this curve (not here reproduced) with reference to presidential election years reveals no relationship. Comparison can be facilitated, however, by expressing the index of business activity during an election year in terms of the business indexes of other years of a presidential period. The results will be numbers above or below 100, indicating whether business was better or worse in the pre-election and postelection years, as compared with the year in which the presidential election occurred. Such comparisons are shown in Chart I for the thirty-six presidential elections. This chart shows, for instance, that in the election year 1932 business was worse than in either the preceding year or the following year. Business was 25 per cent better in the pre-election year and 20 per cent better in the following year. But in 1920, business was better in the election year than in either the preceding or the following year. In 1928, business was better in the election year than in the year before, but not so good as in the year following. The chart shows that there is a great deal of variation from one election period to another. One cannot say, therefore, from any one election period whether business is better or worse before or after an election.

After looking at the chart as a whole, it is clear that the patterns for election periods are very irregular. Out of the thirty-six election periods, only ten showed a V-shaped pattern, that is, a condition where business in the election year is worse than in either the pre-election year or in the postelection year; while there were nine election years when the V-shaped pattern was inverted, that is, when business was better in the election year than in either the year preceding or the year following.

Furthermore, in only nineteen of the thirty-six presidential election periods was business worse than in the preceding year; while in seventeen election periods business was better.

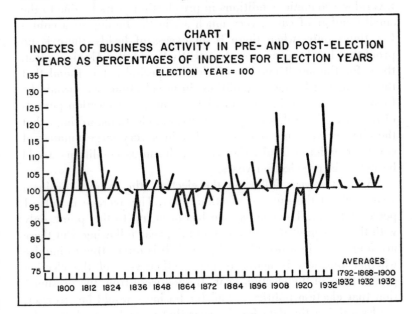

CHART I
INDEXES OF BUSINESS ACTIVITY IN PRE- AND POST-ELECTION YEARS AS PERCENTAGES OF INDEXES FOR ELECTION YEARS
ELECTION YEAR = 100

II

From this rough measure, we are not justified in saying that elections depress business. Obviously, if there is any effect, it is very slight, and a more refined measure is needed. Such a measure would be the extent of good or bad business in, say, pre-election years as compared with election years, rather than the mere enumeration of years when it was better or worse without noting how much.

The average distance of the line in each configuration in Chart I above or below the base line for the year preceding the election year would be a more refined measure, since it shows the extent of good business or bad times in the pre-election year as compared with the election year. This average for the thirty-six election periods shows business to have been 2.4 per cent better in pre-election years than in election years. Business is thus only a very little better, and this conclusion is based on only thirty-six cases. The question is, Might not this slight excess of favorable economic conditions in pre-election years be due to the small number of cases, very much as, in the tossing of a coin a few times only, when there is an excess of heads, there is no proof that heads occur more frequently than tails? Making a test, then, for the small number of election periods, it is found that the average of business conditions in pre-election years would be found to be worse in one out of ten samples of election periods of this size. From this sample of thirty-six elections, we infer that the chances are nine out of ten that in a very large number of similar election periods, the average business conditions would be better in pre-election years.

As to the year following the election, the average business year is about the same as election years. The average is only .1 per cent better. The comparison has been, up to this point, only with the year preceding election and the year following. But there are four years in a presidential period. It is interesting to inquire whether business is better in every other year of the election period than in the election year. If such were true, the presumption that election politics is bad for business would be stronger.

Examining the data for the year that precedes an election by two years, the average of business conditions is 1.2 per cent better. The average yearly status of business is then a small fraction worse in an election year than in any other year of the four-year election period. But the difference is so small that it may be due to chance, except perhaps in the case of the year immediately preceding the election; and even for this year the superiority of business is very slight.

In the early years of the United States, business conditions were largely affected by weather, since agriculture was by far the predominating economic activity, as compared with the present commercial and credit structure, which is affected by many other factors than the climatic. As the agitation of presidential candidates could not affect the weather, the business conditions of election years in these early days would hardly be different from other years. The country tended to become more industrialized shortly after the Civil War, but even more so after the turn of the century. When these earlier periods are excluded, the condition of business in election years, as compared with pre- and post-election years, is still lower, as shown by the following figures, which give the average percentages which the indexes of business in the pre- and postelection years were of the indexes of business in the election year, for the whole of our national history, for the post–Civil War period, and for the twentieth century.

	Since 1791	Since 1867	Since 1899
Average percentages for pre-election years.....	102.4	102.7	104.6
Average percentages for postelection years.....	100.1	101.5	104.0

Since the beginning of this century, there have been only nine election periods, which are of course very few; but the fact that business has been about twice as bad, relative to the pre- and postelection periods, as compared with the longer periods, means that the reliability of the conclusion that business since 1899 is worse in election years, on the average, is about as great as for the longer period. That is, the data show that the chances are about nine in ten that if a very large number of election periods under conditions existing as in the twentieth century were studied, there would be found worse business conditions in election years. Furthermore, for the second year preceding election (not shown in the preceding table) business has been better than in the election year, both for the period since the Civil War and for the period since the beginning of the century. Business conditions were then, on the average, a fraction worse in election years than in any of the three other years of the four-year election period.

III

The analysis can be further refined by making the comparison by months instead of by years. Chart II shows by months

(for the years since the Civil War) the average indexes of business as percentages of the index of October of the election year,
the month at the close of which the election takes place. From
this chart it is seen that business activity reaches its lowest point
during the four-year presidential cycle in the July preceding the
election date and not in the election month itself. This is not a

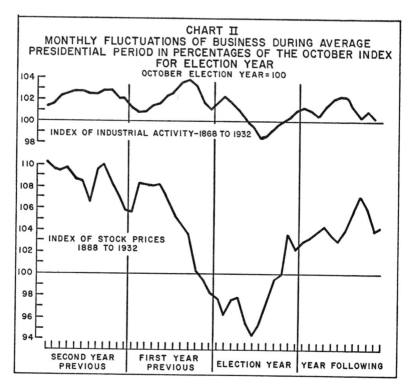

seasonal influence, for the seasonal fluctuations have been removed from the index, and furthermore, no such change occurs
in the other years. This monthly decline is from February of the
election year, and the drop is about 6 per cent, as compared with
a yearly decline of 3 per cent from pre-election to election year.
The highest point of business activity prior to election is in September of the preceding year, and the difference between this

high point and the low point preceding election is about 8 per cent. The pickup of business activity continues into the next year to the extent of some 6 or 8 per cent. The probability that a very large number of election periods would show business in July of an election year worse than in these peak months is between twenty to one and fifty to one. It is thus seen that comparing degrees of business activity by months shows best the low condition of business in an election year. It must be remembered, however, that this low condition of business in an election year is brought out only by averaging all of the election periods. Any one year will not conform to the pattern.

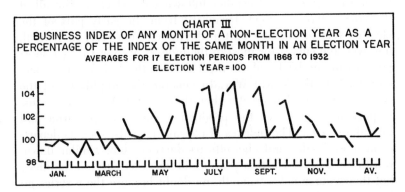

CHART III
BUSINESS INDEX OF ANY MONTH OF A NON-ELECTION YEAR AS A PERCENTAGE OF THE INDEX OF THE SAME MONTH IN AN ELECTION YEAR
AVERAGES FOR 17 ELECTION PERIODS FROM 1868 TO 1932
ELECTION YEAR = 100

These monthly comparisons can be shown in another manner. Each month of the average election year can be compared with the same month of the non-election years, as was done in previous paragraphs for the whole year. Thus, the average index of business activity for all the Augusts of the seventeen election years between 1868 and 1932 is less than the average index for all the Augusts of the pre-election years of this period by about five per cent and less than the Augusts of the postelection years by about 2.5 per cent. (For the period 1900–32, the per cents were 6 and 6 respectively.)

In Chart III are shown similar comparisons for all the months of the year. The summer months of the election year show the greatest contrast with summer months of the other years of the election period. Indeed, the pattern is not very consistent for the winter months. The effect of the election apparently makes its influence most felt in the summer months preceding the autumn election.

IV

A number of indexes of business other than Ayres were tried; but the results need not be presented here in detail, since they were much the same as those found with the Ayres index. Some have the low point in September preceding the election; others, in August; and still others, in July. Interest rates on sixty- to ninety-day commercial paper in New York City, however, reach a low point in December following the election. But all of the curves have a slope downward from the early part of the election year or the later part of the pre-election year. In general, however, the curves for most of the indexes are for a rather short period running back only to the 1880's or the 1870's; and some, only back to the World War. In general, the amplitudes of the swings are somewhat greater than those of the Ayres curve; this is particularly true of the production curves of pig iron and bituminous coal. The indexes of consumer goods, such as depart- ment stores' sales and cigarette production, show similar down- ward trends in the election year, as do the other curves examined; but their course is less smooth, no doubt because these series go back only a few years.

There is some interest in inquiring whether stock prices show depressed values during years of presidential elections in com- parison with indexes of industrial activity. These latter indexes are based largely on physical production and on volume of trade and are perhaps less susceptible to rumors and emotions than values of stocks traded on the exchanges, which are based to some extent on estimates of unknown future conditions.

In Chart II is presented a curve of the indexes of stock prices[5] from 1888 to 1932 in percentages of the October index, and it is similar to the curve of business activity shown above it, with which, however, it may be compared only with reservations. The

---

[5]   The stock prices are the Axe-Houghton index and are based upon ten to thirty-three stocks.

major fluctuation of the curve is the deep dip in the election year, as is true also of the curve of business activity. The other fluctuations in the stock-price curve are slight as compared in size with the one major dip. In the curve of business activity, the minor fluctuations are closer in size to the major fluctuation than in the case of the stock-market curve. It would thus appear that the election year is more of a major influence on stock prices than on business activity. It is probably not proper to compare the amplitude of the swings of stock prices and of business activity. The amplitude is affected somewhat by both the number and the nature of the items included. It is to be expected, of course, that the stock market will be more sensitive to campaign speeches than will production, and this the curves seem to show.

V

The conclusions of this inquiry as to whether business is worse in a presidential election year may be stated as follows:

1. The number of election years in which business is worse than in the preceding and in following years is not sufficiently greater than the number of years in which business is better to warrant a conclusion that there are more lean election years than fat ones.

2. If the degree to which business is good or bad is measured, instead of merely the number of years, then business in the years since modern industry has developed averages 2 to 4 per cent worse in election years; and the chances are about nine out of ten that if there were more presidential election years to be included in the sample, business would on the average be found to be worse in election years.

3. When comparisons are made by months, the lowest point of business in the four-year presidential cycle is found in the July preceding election, being some 8 per cent worse than in the peaks of the preceding September or of the following July. This conclusion is true only for the average, any individual election period being likely to differ quite widely.

4. The stock market seems to be more sensitive to the influences of an election year than do trade and production.

21

THE ECONOMIC FACTOR IN THE

ROOSEVELT ELECTIONS *1940*

With Lolagene C. Coombs

IT SEEMS to be generally agreed that Franklin D. Roosevelt is very unpopular with the wealthier groups in society and that he is held to be a very warm friend of the poor. Indeed, it is sometimes asserted that no president since Jefferson has so divided the voters along economic lines as has Roosevelt. Popular opinion on this subject, as on many others, is likely to be exaggerated. In any case, it is well to check by measurement the idea that the rich are against Roosevelt and the poor are for him. This has been done in some of the sample polls. For instance, *Fortune* finds that the prosperous present about 15 to 20 per cent more opposition to Roosevelt than is found among the poor. Similarly, the Gallup polls have found over twice as much opposition to Roosevelt among the upper third of the population as among the lower third. Where these surveys of opinion on Roosevelt have been presented by social classes, there has been shown, in accordance with popular opinion, this division between the

Reprinted from the *American Political Science Review*, XXXIV, No. 4 (August, 1940).

rich and the poor in their attitude toward Roosevelt. But the percentage difference is not quite so large as might be expected.

This difference between the rich and the poor in attitudes toward Roosevelt became accentuated around the middle of his first term. It is interesting to inquire into the extent to which those of the lower income groups voted for Roosevelt in 1932 and in 1936. For instance, in Chicago in 1932 it was shown that on the average Hoover did not get a majority of votes in a local area of the city unless the average rental value was over $80.[1] It would be interesting to see whether that critical rental value would have been less or greater in 1936 than in 1932 and how large the change would have been. It was not feasible to make this exact comparison for Chicago, for the information on median rentals was not available for 1936, but it was feasible to make a somewhat similar comparison, which will now be discussed.

An index of economic level was constructed for twenty-eight counties in Illinois.[2] This index was designed as a measure of income, much as the average rental by localities was used as an index of income. This index was composed of two parts, one representing the towns and the other representing the open country. For the towns, the index was based upon the average wages of those engaged in manufacturing and in retail and wholesale trade. For the open country, the index was based upon the average value of farm per person occupied in farming. These were combined after weighting them according to the proportion of the population living in towns and on farms.[3] This index was

[1]   W. F. Ogburn and Estelle Hill, "Income Classes and the Roosevelt Vote in 1932," *Political Science Quarterly*, L (June, 1935), 186–93.

[2]   The counties for all the states used in this study were selected on the basis of population (those used ranged between fifteen and thirty-five thousand) and on the basis of the per cent those occupied in business and industry were of the total occupied personnel of the county (for the counties used, this per cent was not less than 30 and not more than 65).

[3]   The index was constructed by the familiar method of combining the deviations from the mean of each series after it was divided by the standard deviation of the series. In constructing the wage index, each part was weighted by the proportion of the population occupied in each type of work.

correlated with the Roosevelt vote in 1932 to the extent of —.66. Thus more of those in the counties with the lower incomes voted for Roosevelt than in the counties with the higher incomes.

A new economic index for 1935 was constructed in the same manner as the one based on 1930 data. The correlation between this 1935 index and the Roosevelt vote in 1936 was exactly the same as was the correlation in 1932, i.e., —.66. Thus it is seen that the poor and the rich tended to vote for and against Roosevelt in 1936 in about the same proportion as they did in 1932. The evidence does not seem to indicate that by 1936, at least, there was any greater cleavage between the rich and the poor for these counties than existed in 1932.

Upon making further detailed inquiries, it seemed desirable to make some observations on other states. In Indiana, there was practically no change between 1932 and 1936, as indicated by the economic index constructed for forty-four Indiana counties on the same basis as was the Illinois index. The coefficients of correlation were —.35 and —.38 for 1932 and 1936, respectively. It may be noticed, however, that in Indiana the correlations were considerably lower than for the state of Illinois. In the neighboring state of Ohio, which is in the same general economic region as are Indiana and Illinois, the correlations were somewhat different, —.15 and +.04. In Ohio, for the thirty-two counties selected, the rich and the poor counties, as measured by our economic index, voted in just about the same degree for Roosevelt as for the Republican candidates. If there was any trend between the two periods, it was that the wealthier counties voted a little more for Roosevelt in 1936 than in 1932. What the explanation may be is not known, but it is possible that the political influences of some state party organizations may tend to overshadow the economic factor.

In Pennsylvania, which is further east and has quite a different political tradition from Indiana and Illinois, the wealthier counties of the twenty-eight selected for use in this study voted in both '32 and '36 somewhat more for Roosevelt than for the Republican candidates, the correlations being +.22 and +.19. This somewhat surprising fact calls for some discussion. It is recalled that the economic index for the counties is a combination of farm and urban elements and is based upon the value of farms and the average wages in the cities. It is quite possible, for instance, that this index does not separate out adequately the rich and the poor voters. It does not single out the wealthy business group on the one hand and the wage-earners on the other. Perhaps the percentage of the population who are income-tax payers might be a more successful index in singling out the wealthy. When the Roosevelt vote is correlated with the percentage paying income tax, the correlations for both years are negative, —.08 and —.14. These are based on only twenty-eight counties, and the correlations are so small as to be untrustworthy. In Ohio, the Roosevelt vote is correlated with the per cent paying income tax to the extent of —.14 and —.10, indicating possibly a slight tendency for the counties with the greatest number of well-to-do, as measured by the per cent paying income taxes, to vote against Roosevelt. But the shift between '32 and '36 is again negligible. In Illinois, the correlation of the Roosevelt vote with the income-tax payers is much less than that with the economic index based upon wages and farm values. The coefficients are —.19 and —.29 for 1932 and 1936, as compared with —.66 and —.66 for the economic index. The same general result is found for Indiana, where the correlation of the Roosevelt vote with the per cent of income-tax payers is around one-half or one-third of what it is when correlated with the economic index. In both Illinois and Indiana, a slightly greater cleavage between the rich and the poor was found in 1936 as compared with 1932, when the per cent of income-tax payers is used to separate the two groups. Perhaps we are justified in concluding, then, that with the exception of Illinois, the economic index does not show a very great cleavage in the Roosevelt vote along economic lines and very little shift between 1932 and 1936.

One other economic index is available, commonly known as the Goodrich index.[4] This index is based on data for 1928–30,

---

[4]   This index is based on the proportion of the population having telephones, radios, and paying income taxes, each county being expressed as a proportion of the total for the nation.

and since there was probably considerable change by 1936 it may not inspire much confidence. But it must be remembered that although the economic conditions in any county may have changed considerably from 1928 to 1936, it is not necessary that the relative position of one county to another in economic level would have shifted so much. The correlations of the Roosevelt vote and the Goodrich index are not very greatly different from those of the previous indexes discussed. In Pennsylvania, the correlation with the Roosevelt vote was —.09 and —.15, which is very much like the correlations with income-tax payers. In Ohio, they were +.03 and —.19, small and with a negligible shift. In Illinois, they were —.63 and —.42, showing slightly less cleavage in 1936 than in 1932. In Indiana, they were —.32 and —.29, lower correlations than with the economic index and showing less cleavage. In these four states it is also noted that the correlations of the Roosevelt vote and the economic index vary greatly from state to state. This conclusion suggested the desirability of making some inquiries for some of the agricultural states in the Middle West.

For this purpose, Kansas (thirty-three counties), Iowa (sixty-five counties), and Nebraska (thirty counties) were chosen. In all three of these agricultural states of the Middle West, the correlations of the Roosevelt vote and the economic index were positive. In other words, the counties with the higher incomes voted more for Roosevelt, and the counties with the lower incomes voted less for Roosevelt. This result is quite contrary to expectations. The coefficients of correlation in Kansas were +.01 and +.37 for 1932 and 1936, respectively. In Iowa, they were +.11 and +.31; and in Nebraska, +.19 and +.51. In all cases there was a tendency for the richer agricultural counties to vote more for Roosevelt in 1936 than in 1932. It is seen, therefore, that the farms and cities of the Middle West do not react according to popular opinion of the situation throughout the country. The difference may be due, of course, to the fact that these are predominantly farming states. It was therefore desirable to correlate the index of farm value and the Roosevelt vote for the counties (this would, of course, include the town votes, too). The

correlations were found to be as follows: Kansas, —.26 and
+.13; Iowa, +.25 and +.39; Nebraska, +.34 and +.37. It
would seem, then, that the well-to-do farmers of the middle western states tended to vote more strongly for Roosevelt in 1936
than in 1932.

Realizing the possible inadequacy of the economic index in
marking the cleavage between the rich and the poor, we may
again have recourse to the per cent of the population paying income tax. When the Roosevelt vote is correlated with the income-
tax payers, there seems to be a tendency from 1932 to 1936 for
the counties with more income-tax payers to vote more in favor of
Roosevelt. In Kansas, the correlations were —.16 and +.29; in
Nebraska, +.21 and +.40; and for the sixty-five counties in
Iowa, —.13 and —.16. Thus there was not very much change.
But if all the counties in Iowa are included in the correlation, it
becomes —.14 and +.16, which puts Iowa in line with Kansas
and Nebraska in the tendency for the counties with the larger
number of income-tax payers to vote more for Roosevelt in
1936 than they did in 1932.

The indications so far show that for these farming states of
the Middle West the well-to-do farmers voted increasingly for
Roosevelt. This is somewhat supported by the correlations between the Roosevelt vote and the AAA payments per farm, which
are +.47 for Kansas, +.22 for Iowa, and +.18 for Nebraska, in
1936. For these three agricultural states, the conclusions seem to
be, first, that the economic index which we have used does not
present a sharp cleavage between the rich and the poor; and second, that there is no great difference among these three states,
but that there is quite a bit of difference between this group and
that of Indiana, Illinois, Ohio, and Pennsylvania. Furthermore,
the well-to-do counties in these agricultural states seem to have
voted more strongly for Roosevelt in 1936 than in 1932.

Still another state may be mentioned. We have chosen California from the Pacific coast. For the twenty-eight counties used
in this study, the economic index was correlated with the Roosevelt vote to the extent of —.18 in 1932 and +.18 in 1936. Again
the differences in the correlations are rather low. The indications

are, however, that the wealthy counties tended to vote more for Roosevelt in 1936 than in 1932. The correlation of the Roosevelt vote with the per cent paying income tax did not change these conclusions significantly, the correlations being —.19 and +.02. (For all counties in California, the correlations are —.26 and +.11.) These figures are also supported by the correlation between AAA payments per farm and the Roosevelt vote, which was +.35. California, then, reacted in its voting behavior very much like the agricultural states of Iowa, Kansas, and Nebraska. California is, of course, largely an agricultural state, though the political organization of the Democratic party in this state is no doubt considerably different from that in the middle western states.

The analysis so far has been made on differentials between the counties in existing economic status. It is possible to approach the economic influence on the Roosevelt vote not by differentials in the economic status, but by differentials in change in status. For instance, from 1932 to 1936 the average earnings in wages in some Illinois counties declined, while in others it increased. What we would want to know is whether those counties where the wages increased most, or declined least, gave a smaller or a larger vote for Roosevelt. For Illinois, on the average, an increase in wages was accompanied by a decline in the Roosevelt vote; or, in other words, a decline in wages was accompanied by an increase in the Roosevelt vote. The coefficient of correlation between the shift in votes, and the shift in wages was —.23, negative, but small. This result, that a decline in wages was accompanied by an increase in the Roosevelt vote, as shown by the negative correlation, is found to be true in all of the states that we have studied, except for Kansas, where the correlation was +.26, and California, where it was +.41. All the correlations were small, however. In two states, Kentucky and Tennessee, from another political area, namely the borderline South, the correlation between the shift in votes and the shift in wages was —.10 and +.24, respectively. Thus in seven states the correlation of the shift in wages and the shift in votes was negative, and in three states it was positive. The negative correlation is, of course, in agreement with popular opinion on the subject. Why in three of the states an increase in wages should be accompanied by an increase in the Roosevelt vote is not clear. It is quite possible that political changes based upon other factors than economic ones may have been important in California, Kansas, and Tennessee. It is quite possible that the shift in wages, being different from an increase in income in the high income brackets, may be quite truly correlated with an increase in the Roosevelt vote, especially if the Roosevelt policies were successful in getting the higher wages. It is recalled, of course, that the shift in votes is for all of the voting population in the counties, while the shift in wages is for the areas outside of the farming areas, that is, for the towns and cities.

In two states, Kansas and Iowa, an increase in farm value was accompanied by a decrease in the Roosevelt vote, the correlations being —.18 and —.32. In Nebraska, however, an increase in farm values was positively correlated with an increase in the Roosevelt vote. In California and Tennessee, the correlations of the change in farm values with the change in the Roosevelt vote were negative, —.20 and —.60, while in Kentucky the correlation was +.13. The signs of the correlations were not changed when various secondary variables, such as age of the population, per cent non-farm, per cent of adult population on WPA, amount of AAA payments per farm, were held constant.

Another index of this shift of economic level, which would include both town and country, was computed by combining the percentage increase or decrease in wages with the percentage shift in farm value. When this index was correlated with the percentage shift in the Roosevelt vote, it was found that Illinois, Indiana, Ohio, and Pennsylvania had negative correlations (—.15, —.23, —.03, and —.04, respectively) and that the more distinctly agricultural states, Kansas, Iowa, Nebraska, and California, showed positive correlations (+.39, +.01, +.32, and +.24, respectively). Thus it is concluded that in the more industrial states of the Middle West and East, an increase in economic level, as measured by this combined index of wage and farm-value shift, was accompanied by a slight decrease in the Roosevelt vote, while the opposite was true for the western agricultural states.

In the course of the study, one or two other factors relating to the Roosevelt vote have been observed. Somewhat interesting is the per cent of the population on WPA in 1936. It is sometimes said that we do not bite the hand that feeds us or that we do not vote against Santa Claus. Hence it would be interesting to see whether the counties that had the largest per cent on WPA gave the greatest vote for Roosevelt. Such seems to be the case in Pennsylvania, where the correlation is +.30; in Illinois, +.63; in Indiana, +.37; in Kansas, +.15; in Nebraska, +.01; and in California, +.20. In Iowa and Ohio, however, the correlations were negative, —.10 and —.09. The trend of these correlations is according to expectations, but it should be observed again that the correlations are fairly small, with the exception of Illinois and possibly Indiana, where the correlations are +.63 and +.37.

Another factor that was interesting in its correlation with the Roosevelt vote was the age of the population. The index used was the per cent of the voting population that was over forty-five years of age. In the counties where the age of the population was greater, as measured by this index, there was a higher vote against Roosevelt. This was true in all the states in the study except Illinois, where the correlation was 0, and California, where it was +.01 in 1932. Furthermore, the correlations were higher for age than for the economic index and the Roosevelt vote.[5] The correlations of age and the Roosevelt vote were consistently higher for 1936 than for 1932. Perhaps the agitation by Mr. Townsend had become more acute at that time.

Other studies, particularly those by Mr. Gallup,[6] show that the older persons in the population tend to be less in favor of Roosevelt than is the younger element. The age factor, however, has not so far, we believe, been studied from the point of view of the

[5]   The correlations between age and the Roosevelt vote for 1932 and 1936, respectively, were: Pennsylvania, .—30 and —.54; Ohio, —.32 and —.56; Illinois, +.04 and +.06; Indiana, —.44 and —.53; Kansas, —.25 and —.74; Iowa, —.40 and —.57; Nebraska, —.19 and —.49; California, +.01 and —.04.

[6]   American Institute of Public Opinion, December 5, 1939.

economic conditions. In general, we know that the cities which have a higher economic level tend to have smaller numbers of old people in them. Some interest, therefore, attaches to the correlation of our economic index with the age index, namely, the per cent of the voting population which is over forty-five years of age. These correlations are, with the exception of Indiana, negative. For the various states in 1932 and 1936, respectively, they are: Pennsylvania, —.40 and —.20; Ohio, —.22 and —.23; Illinois, —.15 and —.25; Indiana, +.10 and +.24; Kansas, —.57 and —.66; Iowa, —.40 and —.57; Nebraska, —.19 and —.49; California, —.12 and —.22. It would thus appear that the counties which have the largest per cent of old people are in general of slightly lower economic status. It is therefore of interest to inquire whether the influence of age against the Roosevelt vote is to be explained by the fact that the old people seem to be in the poorer counties. When the economic factor is held constant, the correlation of the age factor with the Roosevelt vote is reduced slightly, but the negative signs are not changed.[7]

Similarly, we want to inquire whether the reason for the counties with the lower incomes voting for Roosevelt may not be the fact that the counties with the lower incomes have more old people in them. It may be found that age, rather than income, is responsible for the counties with the lower incomes voting for Roosevelt. Such seems to be the case in Kansas and Iowa. In these two states, it is recalled, the counties with the higher economic indexes voted more for Roosevelt in both 1932 and 1936. But the correlations were almost negligible in 1932 (+.01 and +.11) and about +.37 and +.31 in 1936. When the age factor is held constant, the correlations between economic status and the Roosevelt vote become negative, though small: —.16 and —.22 for Kansas in 1932 and 1936, respectively, and —.21 and —.03 for Iowa. In other states, the change in the signs of the correlations did not occur, nor were there any significant changes in the size

[7]   The partial correlations for the various states are: Pennsylvania, —.52; Ohio, —.57; Illinois, —.14; Indiana, —.49; Kansas, —.71; Iowa, —.50; Nebraska, —.36; California, .00 (figures for 1936).

of the correlations. In Illinois, for instance, the correlations remained almost the same, as they did also in Indiana.[8]

We concluded, therefore, on the question of age, that the reason the old people tended to vote against Roosevelt was very slightly influenced by the economic factor and that similarly the tendency for the poorer counties to vote for Roosevelt is very slightly affected by the fact that the poor counties have more old people.

An incidental comment may be of some interest. In a few of the states, we correlated the Roosevelt vote with the Democratic vote for governor by counties. The correlations were higher in 1936 than in 1932. In Pennsylvania, for instance, the correlation in 1932 was +.63 and +.91 in 1936. In Ohio it was +.76 in 1932, but +.96 in 1936. Similarly, in Indiana and Illinois the correlations were +.91 and +.84 in 1932 and +.95 and +.97 in 1936. This may mean that the Democratic party was more closely knit in these states in 1936 than in 1932. Since in general the Roosevelt vote was larger than the governor vote, it may indicate that the Roosevelt influence was important in the governor vote.

Conclusions

The economic index, designed to show differentials in certain average counties (selected according to population and the per cent of the working population engaged in industry and business) in economic levels, indicated a very slight relationship with the Roosevelt vote, but in general the poorer counties tended to vote more for Roosevelt. In interpreting this conclusion, it is important to realize that this economic index does not segregate out very satisfactorily the very small fraction of the population that received over $5,000 or $10,000 income. It is possible that if the population could have been divided into two groups, that receiv-

8   The partial correlations for 1932 and 1936, respectively, are: Pennsylvania, +.15 and +.10; Ohio, +.23 and −.11; Illinois, −.67 and −.67; Indiana, −.34 and −.30; Kansas, −.16 and −.22; Iowa, −.21 and −.03; Nebraska, +.12 and +.38; California, −.18 and −.17.

ing over $10,000 income and that receiving under $10,000 income, the correlations might have been higher. When the correlations were made not on the basis of economic level but on that of the per cent of the population paying income tax, the results were not very different from those observed when the correlations were made between the Roosevelt vote and the economic index. This result may be compared with that of the Gallup poll for 1936, when the voting population was divided into three groups on the basis of income. In the upper third of the population, 47 per cent were for Roosevelt, while in the lower third 75 per cent were for him. Thus nearly twice as large a per cent of the population in the lower third voted for Roosevelt as did so in the upper third. The correlation, however, was —.21, quite in line with those found in this study.

The statistics in this article and those of Gallup support the popular opinion that the poor tended to vote for Roosevelt and the well-to-do against him, but they provide a very valuable check in numerical measurement. The actual measurement seems to indicate that the differentials between the social classes may not be so great as might be inferred from talking with a member of either the extreme upper or the extreme lower income groups.

This study was undertaken also to see whether there was very much of a shift of voters along economic lines between 1932 and 1936. The correlations indicate a very slight, almost negligible, shift. That it was so slight was somewhat unexpected. It may have been due to the fact that the economic cleavage precipitated by Roosevelt might not have been felt by the population in 1936. After all, Roosevelt carried all the states but two, so he must have been quite popular. The Gallup poll has measured the shift of the economic classes in regard to Roosevelt since 1936, as reported a year later. The shift was practically negligible. For instance, in 1936, in the Gallup poll 47 per cent of the upper third of the population voted for Roosevelt, and in 1937, 46 per cent of this same group said they would vote for him. In the lower third of the population, 25 per cent voted against Roosevelt in 1936, and 23 per cent said they would have voted against him in 1937.

Neither Mr. Gallup's method of measuring the population differentials nor that used in this study indicates any tremendous shift in economic cleavage regarding Roosevelt. It is possible that if only groups receiving over $10,000 and those receiving under $10,000 a year had been studied, a greater shift would have been observed. In any case, both the Gallup poll and this study showed no great cleavage along economic lines which Roosevelt may have precipitated.

22

ARE OUR WARS GOOD TIMES? *1948*

With Jean L. Adams

THE EFFECT of war is generally considered to be destruction. Certainly, such it is in battle and in a country that is bombed
or invaded. Otherwise, the destruction is limited to materials and
lives lost outside the home country. But there are also construc-
tive effects of war, as will be noted in this article.

First, we observe that the consequences of war are much more
than loss of life and property. Industry, agriculture, government,
and schools are affected, for illustration. In modern wars there is
hardly a social institution that escapes its influence, and this influence is not always bad. The purpose of this article, however, is
not to be so comprehensive as to survey the influence of war on
the various social institutions. We wish rather to compare the
conditions in the United States during recent wars with the conditions of the business cycle in peacetime.

For such comparison, we shall be restricted to statistical
records, such as those of production, unemployment, divorces,
and births. By observing the movement of curves from such
annual statistical records in peace and in war years, we shall make
some deductions regarding the influence of war. For instance, the

Reprinted from the *Scientific Monthly*, LXVII, No. 1 (July, 1948).

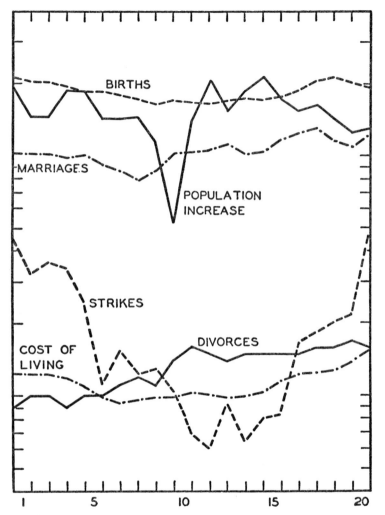

Fig. 1. War years and peace years almost indistinguishable. The six records cover twenty-year periods, but the periods (dates follow) are not the same; hence, the figures on the base line of the chart are not dates but numbers of years. Each series includes the years of either World War I or World War II. Without knowing the dates, it is rather difficult to locate the war years on the curves. The variations in the war years, then, are not significantly different from the variations that might be expected in

annual number of failures of industrial and commercial firms per 10,000 firms in the 1920's and 1930's was 90. In the war year 1944, the number was only 7 per 10,000 firms. We therefore conclude that one influence of the war upon business in the United States was to reduce greatly the number of business failures.

WAR YEARS NOT EASILY DISCERNIBLE IN SOME RECORDS Not all social conditions are so markedly affected by war as are business failures. The hours worked per week in wartime, for instance, are not greatly different from the number worked during peace. In the war years of 1942–44 the average number of hours worked per week in the manufacturing industries in the United States was 44; in the depression years of the 1930's the average was 38 hours. But in the prosperous years of the 1920's, from 1923 to 1929, the weekly working time in factories was 44.6 hours, or slightly more than in World War II. Whatever the influence of the war on hours worked per week, it was not profound.

For some statistical records during peace and war years it is difficult to tell from the curves alone which section of the curve is in the war period. This difficulty is illustrated by Figure 1, which sets forth undated curves of six annual statistical series. Each of these curves is for a twenty-year period, but not for the same twenty years. Each curve, however, does cover the period of either World War I or World War II. Looking at this undated chart, the reader will not find it easy, on the basis of the fluctuations of the curves alone, to locate the war years on each curve of the chart. In the series depicted in Figure 1, what occurred in war years could have happened in peacetime, and vice versa.

For curves of other statistical series, the war period may be recognized approximately. Yet in such curves, undated, it is difficult to determine from them alone exactly when the war began.

---

peacetime. Strikes and lockouts, 1917–37, total number of stoppages in thousands; marriages, 1925–45, rate per 1,000 population; divorces, 1910–30, rate per 1,000 population; births, 1925–45, rate per 1,000 population; population increase, 1910–30, in millions, calculated from estimates of Bureau of the Census; cost of living, 1927–47, index number of the Bureau of Labor Statistics. All series taken from *Statistical Abstracts*.

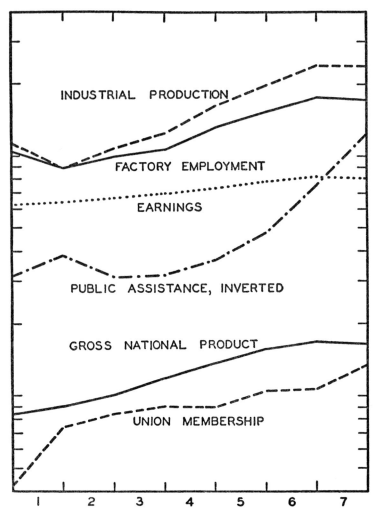

Fig. 2. When did the war begin? The curves include part or all of the war years of World War II, but all curves do not cover the same seven-year period. We cannot tell from these undated curves, though, exactly when the war began. Labor-union membership, 1936–43, in millions of members, from *Labor Information Bulletin*, August, 1947, p. 4; industrial production, 1937–44, index number from *Federal Reserve Bulletins*, 1935–39 = 100; real hourly earnings of production workers in manufacturing, 1938–45,

Six such curves are shown in Figure 2. Each of these curves is for a different seven-year period covering part or all of World War II. The reader will be interested in trying to find from the curves in this chart the exact year that the United States entered the war. Although the bombing of the fleet at Pearl Harbor came with suddenness, the day is not so dramatically registered on these time series. Most of the undated curves in Figures 1 and 2 are found dated in Figures 3, 4, or 5.

Figures 1 and 2 indicate that in some statistical records the recent wars of the United States have not produced enough of a change to be easily recognizable or the change produced has not been very greatly different from what has occurred in peacetime.

THE INDEXES OF PROSPERITY MEASURED OUR WAR YEARS Statistical series, presented like those in Figures 1 and 2, are used by economists to represent the fluctuations of business conditions. These fluctuations alternate between prosperity and depression. Such a course of business is often called a "business cycle," although the alterations of business are not as smooth as the cycle of the tides. Five statistical series are commonly used to describe the course of business. These are industrial production; bank clearings outside New York City; wholesale commodity prices; freight-car tonnage, representing production, trade, marketing, and transportation; and the percentage of all firms failing.

These five curves are shown in Figure 3. The depression years of the 1930's are clearly indicated, as is the prosperity of 1919–20 and the late 1920's. But the curves that are high in the prosperous business years of peacetime are also high in the years of World Wars I and II. This observation, we think, is important.

---

cents per hour, deflated by cost of living index, from *Statistical Abstracts*; factory employment, 1937–44, index number, *Federal Reserve Bulletins*, 1939 = 100; gross national product, 1938–45, in billions, deflated by cost of living index, from U.S. Department of Commerce, *National Income, Supplement to Survey of Current Business*, July, 1947, p. 19; public assistance, 1936–43, inverted, millions of dollars, deflated by cost of living index, Federal Security Agency, Social Security Administration, *Social Security Yearbooks*.

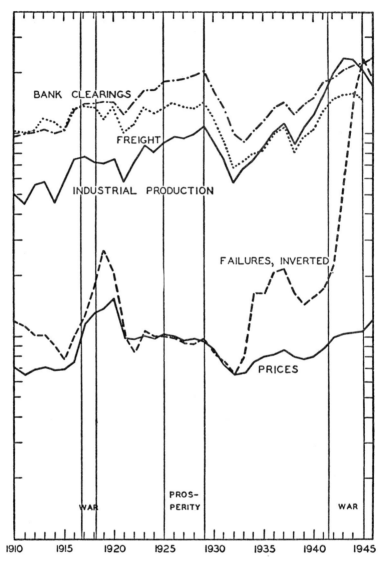

Fig. 3. Curves used to measure business cycles. The curves ordinarily
used to measure business cycles, when traced through the period
of World War I and World War II, show the war years to be
like the prosperity phase of the business cycle, as seen in the years
of the late 1920's. If the war years were unknown, the curves

The curves used to show the business cycle have the same behavior during the two world wars as during periods of peacetime prosperity. This behavior suggests that business was prosperous during war periods. This startling statistical inference is in sharp contrast to the idea that war consists only of horror and destruction, which it did in many countries.

The observation that war was a period of prosperity in the United States, as indicated by the time series in Figure 3, may be explained by those to whom the idea is unwelcome by stating that the curves in Figure 3 (except the one on business failures) show only business activity and not necessarily prosperity. Prosperity, it might be argued, is shown by profits, and although profits normally go with large production in peacetime, such need not be the case in wartime. In other words, industry could be very active in war years from patriotic motives only, without making any profit at all. Such might be the case, but the curve of profits in Figure 5 shows that profits, like production, were greater than usual in the war year 1917, and again in the years of World War II, 1942–45. Since the number of plants in operation was only a few more in 1917 than in pre- and postwar years, and was fewer than usual in 1942–45, we infer that the profits per firm were higher than normal.

The curves, then, which are used to measure the business cycle make the war years in the United States look a great deal like the prosperity phase of the business cycle.

GOOD TIMES ACCOMPANIED OUR WAR YEARS The years when business is prosperous are called "good times," that is, good

---

alone would seem to indicate these war years merely as periods of business prosperity, which are higher on the chart than the preceding and following depression phases. Freight, billions of tons of revenue freight originated, from *Statistical Abstracts*; commodity prices, wholesale, index number from *Federal Reserve Bulletin*, 1926 = 100, unadjusted; industrial production, index number from *Federal Reserve Bulletin*, 1935–39 = 100; bank clearings outside New York, in billions of dollars, deflated by cost of living index, from *Commercial and Financial Chronicle*; failures, industrial and commercial, inverted, number per 10,000 enterprises, from *Statistical Abstracts*.

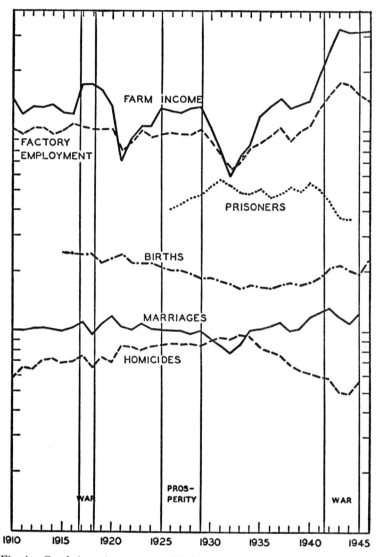

Fig. 4.   Good times in war years. With business prosperity are associated
          good times in other areas of life's activities. In Figs. 4 and 5,
          curves are drawn that have been found correlated with the busi-
          ness cycle and are used as evidence of good times. These indexes
          of good times generally show the same characteristics in war years

times in general, not merely good times for business. There is more money to spend for clothing, for recreation, for travel, and for food. Institutions other than business—for instance, the family and the church—experience good times, too, when business is prosperous. There are more marriages, more births, a better standard of living for farmers, fewer suicides, fewer murders, fewer admissions to prisons, an increase in the membership of labor unions, less public assistance for the needy, and a higher income for the nation.

There are, though, some conditions of life in periods of prosperity that might not be properly called "good times," but rather "bad times." For example, there are more divorces granted in years of prosperity than in years of depression; and, strangely, there are more deaths in so-called good times than in bad. That we call periods of business prosperity "good times" rather than "bad times" indicates that there are more desirable than undesirable conditions accompanying prosperity.

It is interesting to see how the thirteen indexes of good times listed in a preceding paragraph fare during wars. This has been done in Figures 4 and 5. These indexes indicate both world wars as good times as measured by these thirteen series. In wartime, there was more marrying, fewer murders, more money to spend or save, etc. The associations of the war years were, then, in many activities of life in the United States, pleasant ones.

DISTRESSING CONDITIONS FOUND IN WAR YEARS, TOO   That there were unpleasant associations with wartime is also true.

---

as in periods of prosperity in peacetime; that is, the curves are higher (or lower) in both war years and years of prosperity than they are in business depression. Marriages, rate per 1,000 population; births, rate per 1,000 population, both from *Statistical Abstracts*; factory employment, index number, *Federal Reserve Bulletins*, 1939 = 100; farm income, net income from farming to all persons on farms, per capita in hundreds of dollars, deflated by prices paid by farmers, including interest and takes, 1910–14 = 100; homicide deaths, rate per 100,000 population, from *Statistical Abstracts*; prisoners received from courts during the year, federal and state prisons and reformatories, rate per 100,000 population, from *Statistical Abstracts*.

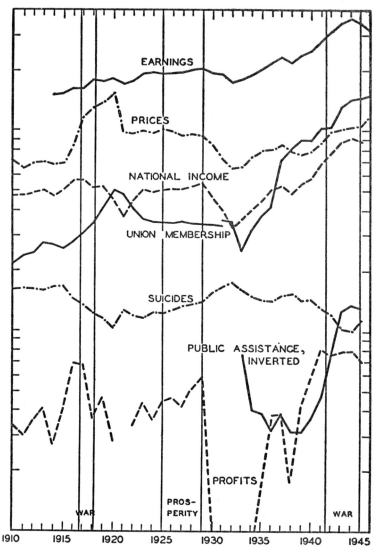

Fig. 5. Good times in war years (continued). Weekly earnings of production workers in manufacturing, deflated by cost of living index,
in dollars, from *Statistical Abstracts*; commodity prices, wholesale, index number from *Federal Reserve Bulletins*, 1926 = 100,
unadjusted; suicides, rate per 100,000 population, from *Statistical*

There were fear, sorrow, and separation from loved ones. Unfortunately, there are no index numbers for fear and sorrow; though the 14,000,000 in the armed services is an indication of the extent of separated families and lovers. From the reservoir of time series in the statistical yearbooks, a few annual series representing regrettable conditions are found (Fig. 6).

Looking at these curves, we may reflect on the degrees of distress they indicate for the war years. The curve for highway construction was low during the war, and discomfort was caused by the bad state of repair of the roads of our states and the streets of our cities. Taxes were higher during the wars, but increments of national income added were larger than the increments of taxes. The vast accumulation of the war debt was frightening, but its burden will be felt more in the years following the war than it was during the war. Rather, during the war, the debt added an inflationary buoyancy. It has been claimed that a smaller percentage of the eligible population voted in local elections during war years and that there was less interest in local affairs, but there are no published statistics available.

Divorces and deaths are tragic, but their wartime increase actually touches only a small proportion of the families. Divorces numbered 1,400,000 during World War II, but without war there would have been about 940,000 divorces, assuming the same divorce rate as from 1937 to 1939. Thus, the added contribution

---

Abstracts; labor-union membership, in millions of members, 1910–31, from Leo Wolman, *Ebb and Flow in Trade Unionism*, p. 16, average annual membership, 1931–46, from *Labor Information Bulletin*, August, 1947, estimated from graph; public assistance, inverted, millions of dollars, deflated by cost of living index, from Federal Security Agency, Social Security Administration, *Social Security Yearbooks;* net corporate profits, in billions of dollars, deflated by cost of living index (below the bottom line of the graph is a loss, except for 1934, which had a profit of .5 billion dollars but is not shown—no figure is available for 1921), from *Economic Almanac, 1946–1947*, p. 44; national income, in hundreds of dollars per capita, deflated by cost of living index, from *Economic Almanac, 1946–1947*, National Industrial Conference Board figures.

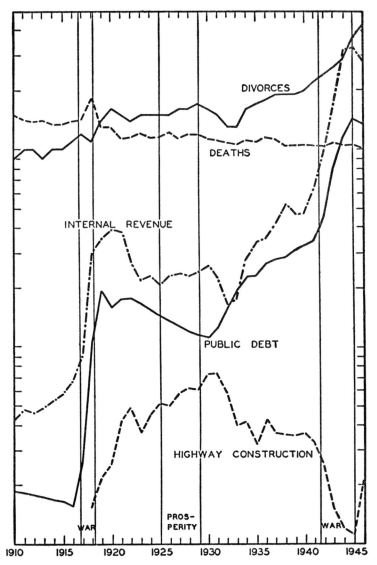

DIVORCES

DEATHS

INTERNAL REVENUE

PUBLIC DEBT

HIGHWAY CONSTRUCTION

PROS-
PERITY

WAR

WAR

1910 1915 1920 1925 1930 1935 1940 1945

Fig. 6.   Some distressful conditions of war years. Not all the activities of war years can be called prosperity and good times. Statistical records reveal some unfortunate conditions, such as those shown by the five curves of time series found in the statistical yearbooks. There are other distressing conditions in war years, such as fear,

to the number of divorces during World War II was 460,000, whereas the number of married couples was 32,000,000.

The war deaths were about 350,000; in three and a half years of peace at that time there would have been around 5,000,000 deaths. Thus, the war added 7 per cent to the number of deaths. Of course, not one of the families that furnished the 14,000,000 men to the armed forces knew that death would not strike. So there was fear, the memory of which remains as a terrible association of wartime, for which there are no statistics. To these distressing associations with war should be added the hard and fearful conditions of life for men at the front. One-third of the medical discharges during World War II were for neuropsychiatric reasons.

We do not think it possible to strike a net balance between the good and the bad associations of war years in the United States. To many, the utter horror of war overshadows all else. Nevertheless, the data of this article do show that the indexes we use to measure good times characterize the periods of our activity in the past two world wars. These observations are made on the United States and not on France, Japan, or Russia, where the sufferings of war were much more evident.

WAR AND PREPARATION FOR WAR   Our analysis has concerned the movement of certain indexes of social conditions during war years, but in the United States the years of war were not all spent in fighting. During the first parts of World War I and

---

for which there are no statistical records. Deaths, rate per 1,000 population; divorces, rate per 1,000 population; public debt, dollars per capita, deflated by cost of living index; internal revenue, income and profit taxes plus other revenue, in billions of dollars, deflated by cost of living index. All from *Statistical Abstracts*. Highway construction, in millions of dollars, 1918–29, from *Economic Almanac, 1946–1947*, p. 235, 1929–46 from *Statistical Abstracts, 1947*, p. 968, deflated by *Engineering News Record* construction-cost index, which measures the movement in construction costs in general, from *Statistical Abstracts, 1947*, p. 778.

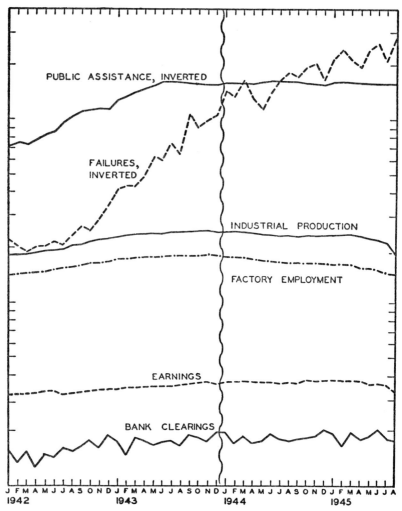

Fig. 7. Preparation for war and combat war. In the first part of the years
in which the United States was officially at war, in 1941–45,
activities were largely preparatory. In the latter part of the period,
combat fighting was much more extensive. The wavy line indicates, approximately, the division between these two periods—
more accurately for some of the curves than others. These curves,
which have been used to indicate good times and prosperity in
peace years, are high both in the preparatory and in the fighting

World War II we did little or no actual fighting, for we were not prepared to fight. We entered both world wars suddenly, with our soldiers inadequately trained and equipped. So the war periods were divided into two parts. The first part was characterized by preparation, which might have been done in peace years; in the second part we were engaged in actual fighting. We were able to be at war without much fighting because our allies held back the enemy.

The question arises, then, as to whether the prosperity and good times that characterized the war years of the United States were due to the preparation for war or to the conditions of a fighting war.

It is easy to see how preparations for war would bring great business activity and profits and, of course, the good times that accompany industrial prosperity. But how about the fighting years of war, after the initial period of preparation was over? In order to compare these two parts of our war years we have prepared Figure 7, in which are drawn some statistical indexes of business conditions, by months, during the period between the declaration of war and the collapse of the enemy. The first year of this period and most of the second year were months of preparation, with little fighting. During the last year and a half of the war period, the participation of armed forces in battles and bombings increased.

---

phases of the war years. Industrial production, index number from *Federal Reserve Bulletins*, 1935–39 = 100; bank clearings outside New York, in billions of dollars, deflated by cost of living index, from *Commercial and Financial Chronicle*; weekly earnings of production workers in manufacturing, deflated by cost of living index, in dollars, from *Statistical Abstracts*; public assistance, inverted, in millions of dollars, deflated by cost of living index, from Federal Security Agency, Social Security Administration, *Social Security Yearbooks*; failures, industrial and commercial, inverted, number per 10,000 enterprises, from *Statistical Abstracts*; factory employment, 1919–46, index number, *Federal Reserve Bulletins*, 1939 = 100, 1910–18 from Paul F. Brissenden, *Earnings of Factory Workers, 1899–1927*, p. 61, decreased by average percentage of difference in 1919–20.

The curves in Figure 7 were rising in the first part of the war, generally, until around the close of 1943 or the beginning of 1944, as they do in the business cycle with the recovery of industry from a depression. Such was expected. The question is: How did these curves behave after the period of preparation was over? The chart shows that they generally ceased rising and flattened out. In no case was there a significant recession, during the fighting years of World War II, from the peak or plateau of business prosperity. In other words, the short period of the actual fighting war was characterized by the same industrial boomtimes that signalized the period of preparation for fighting. We do not know what the course of the curves in Figure 7 would have been if the war had lasted three or four years longer, or what it would have been if we had been invaded or bombed extensively.

CONCLUSION AND DISCUSSION The conclusion of this study, as shown by the data, is that the experiences at home in the United States of our social and economic institutions and activities during the periods of our participation in the last two world wars were much like those of the prosperity phase of the business cycle in peace years, commonly called "good times"; though there were some incalculable conditions of fear and distress.

The United States was more fortunate than were the combat countries of Europe and Asia that were bombed or invaded and that were in the war longer. Our industries were more prosperous than those in other warring countries. The positive association of good times in the United States during the war probably has a bearing upon our willingness to engage in another war. Rewards and punishments, we know from psychology and from experience, are effective determinants of behavior. Animal trainers find that their subjects repeat more readily when rewarded and that they desist more quickly when punished. Our religions have a heaven and a hell. Rewards and punishments, however, are not the only factors bearing upon behavior and shaping our attitudes toward war.

In view of this possible influence of our past fortunate war experiences upon our attitudes toward engaging in future wars, it is well to remember that we may not be so fortunate in another war. We may be in another world war from its beginning and not after the enemy is partly worn down by fighting with our allies. Nor are our allies likely to hold the enemy while we take a year or two to prepare. It is almost certain, because of the existence of long-range bombers of great speed, that we shall be bombed in the next war. The bombing will be very destructive if our enemy has the atom bomb. Nor is it clear that such a war will be brief.

IV. Methods

23

BIAS, PSYCHOANALYSIS, AND THE SUBJECTIVE IN RELATION TO THE SOCIAL SCIENCES *1922*

IT HAS been difficult to find a title which suitably describes the idea presented in the following paper, and the title chosen is suggestive rather than accurate. The paper is more the presentation of an idea than the systematic exposition of a hypothesis, for the limitations of time preclude any such adequate exposition. It is rather the fragment of an outline, lightened with illustrations, which conveys the main ideas out of which a consistent theory, it is thought, could be constructed.

The paper falls into two parts. The first part concerns the theory of the role of desire in the thinking process. The second part deals with the application of this theory to scientific method in the social sciences, particularly its bearings on social theory and social philosophy.

I wish to introduce the subject of the relations of desire and thinking by a very brief consideration of bias, or prejudice, be-

Reprinted from the *Publications of the American Sociological Society,* Vol. XVII, 1922.

cause I think an understanding of prejudice yields a very good working analysis of thinking in general.

Where prejudice is found there are two accompanying conditions, ignorance and emotion. The word, prejudice, is derived from the Latin words *prae* and *judicio* and means a hasty judgment or an opinion formed without due examination. Prejudice is an attitude taken without a knowledge of the facts. I know a man who after several years of living in China had broken down a prejudice against the Chinese, a prejudice which had been built up from a childhood experience in a small town with Chinese laundrymen, who were supposed to be very odd and curious.

But ignorance is not the sole determining condition of bias or prejudice. Prejudice is always accompanied by emotion. We are not only ignorant of the Kaiser or the IWW, but we hate them. Emotion in prejudice is characterized by the fact that the emotion tends to keep us ignorant and to prevent us from getting the facts. It does this by selecting some facts for keen attention and by blinding us to others. The employer may be prejudiced against the minimum wage for women because his self-interest prevents him from seeing the facts of the life of working women. It is very easy for emotion to prevent us from seeing the facts because so often the situation arousing emotion in prejudice is not a single fact, but a complex mass of facts. The white man sees very well some facts concerning the Negro, but to other facts he is quite blind.

The study of prejudice is, therefore, a study of the behavior of desire in a condition of relative ignorance. There are, of course, many other interesting psychological and practical aspects of prejudice, but I am interested here only in pointing out that wherever prejudice is found there is an absence of facts and a tendency of desire to imagine them, or select them, or distort them. If the preceding analysis be correct, it must follow that bias is very common; the more extreme degrees of bias, found in conditions of great ignorance and strong desires, are what we call prejudice.

The analysis of bias is not without interest for the social sciences. The social sciences are young as sciences. They are largely in the stage of theory and hypothesis. There is a scarcity of facts, one of the conditions necessary to bias and prejudice. The social sciences also deal with highly emotional material, such as the family, sex, religion, the distribution of income, industrial relations, and politics, all of which arouse intense desires. Therefore, the two fundamental conditions of bias are present in the study of the social sciences.

It is now clear that the interesting and important idea in bias is the way desire keeps us ignorant by attracting some facts and repelling others. We now wish to inquire just what desire does to our thoughts in the absence of evidence, that is, What is the relation of desire to thinking?

That desires and interests select our observations is very well illustrated by reports on the Russian Revolution by visiting investigators. The radical found pretty much what he wanted to find, and the conservative found quite the opposite, though both visited the same country at the same time. Such a selection of observations is not due wholly to subjective causes but also in part to the objective situation. Russia is large, and the conditions were varied.

Employers and employees usually give entirely different reports on the conditions of industrial relations, the point to note being that the differences are such as to make the reports accord with the respective wishes. Investigating a strike once for the government, I was told by the employer that there were four hundred men on strike. The employees said there were ten thousand.

Desires not only select the observations that we make at a particular time, but they also determine out of memory which ideas will rise to consciousness. For instance, when we are hungry, thoughts of food arise. Explorers who are forced to a very limited diet tell us that at such a time they think and talk a great deal about food and eating. With the enforcement of the prohibition of the sale of liquor there is increased talk and thought of drink. In a particular mood we will hum a certain tune. At certain times the status of the organism forces a wealth of sex images and symbols upon our attention. The process appears as though the images and ideas were floating particles borne into consciousness by currents in the stream of desires.

Ideas and images also come to consciousness from other causes than desire, as, for instance, because of associations due to proximity and to time. For illustration, pen suggests ink, or 2×3 suggests 6. In this fashion we memorize a poem. But ideas and images are linked by emotion. For instance, in a mood of sorrow or despondency memories quite unlinked by time or proximity will come to the mind. The emotion seems to provide the linkage.

Of course, these thoughts come and go, and we do not ask why. The psychoanalysts have directed their attention to the emotional nature of these associations, and their data indicate an almost unbelievable number of such emotional associations. The reason why associations on the basis of emotion are found to be so much more frequent by psychoanalysts than by ourselves is that we find it hard to recognize the emotional linkage, due to the great prevalence of symbols and disguises which the psychoanalyst is able to interpret. Indeed, quite generally to the psychoanalyst association is of emotional significance.

One of the extreme forms in which desire selects out of past recollections the ideas which appear in consciousness is the daydream. Such an instance is the dream picture made by a weak, sickly boy who is outclassed by his playmates and who is frequently told by his elders that he is too little and that when he is bigger he can do and have certain things. He constructs a fanciful picture, a daydream, in which he sees himself a strong and powerful knight in shining armor riding on a white charger at the head of a cavalcade of knights, the whole procession moving before an admiring throng, including his mother, his sweetheart, and his playmates. Desire not only brings images, but it constructs a series of those images into a complex picture out of, of course, previously learned cultural material.

The psychoanalytic theory of the night dream is the same as that of the daydream in that the materials of the dream are the product of desires. The mechanism of the night dream is, however, highly complex, so that it must be interpreted before one can see the desires.

Desire not only carries selected images and ideas into consciousness, but it also tends to force out of consciousness certain experiences and prevents us from remembering them. This tendency is usually spoken of as a tendency to forget the unpleasant. It is not correct to say that we tend to forget what was unpleasant at the time; animal trainers teach by punishment. Rather, we tend to forget what is unpleasant to remember. It should also be noted that the word "pleasant" has no particular technical psychological meaning and is not especially connected with former pleasure-pain theories. The whole theory of repression is built on this point of purposeful forgetting. This aspect of repression is seldom questioned, the theory of repression being usually criticized as to the continued influence of the repressed material or the repressed desire. No less a scientist than Darwin said that it is well to write down facts contradictory to a particular theory that we wish to prove, for otherwise we are likely to forget them. It should also be noted that desire does not explain all forgetting and is only one factor, so we say there is a tendency to forget what we do not want to remember. Hence we note that desire can prevent memory as well as make us remember.

It has now been set forth that desire directs our observing, so that in certain cases where the materials to be observed are numerous and complex, desire selects certain things for observation. And the claim has also been advanced that desire selects out of the vast storehouse of impressions certain ones for remembrance and tends to prevent us from remembering others. It is as though desire were some electromagnetic power which both attracts and repels observations and memories.

The role of desire, therefore, is to give us a picture that is not like the real. It gives us distorted impressions. It is not photographic. The trade unionist says there are ten thousand on strike; the employer says there are four hundred. "The pictures we carry around in our heads," to use Lippmann's phrase, are not like the pictures of reality. A conservative and successful citizen's first reaction to the problem of unemployment may be that there is no unemployment, or else his first analysis will be that the man who is out of work is out of work because of lack of ability or lack of initiative in finding work. If the attitude of such a person is so emotional that he continually refuses to see the facts, we rightly call him prejudiced. In ignorance, then, desire tends to distort our impression of reality. Desire may thus become an enemy of science.

A very good illustration of the distortion of reality is the belief of primitive peoples in a world of magic, taboo, animism, totems, supernatural forces, and religious beings. There is much support for the theory that these unreal beings and forces are the results of desires. Freud has characterized the basis of such unreality as "the omnipotence of thought," as contrasted to the omnipotence of fact, thought in this case meaning imagination or desire which seems free from fact (other than tradition) in creating fantasies.

A most excellent test of science is prediction. The astronomer can predict an eclipse. But real-estate dealers in our growing western cities are, I think, very likely to predict a much larger population for their cities than the next Census will show. Their strong desire for growth greatly distorts the real picture of the forces that make for expansion. Note how eagerly the sick believe in miracles, patent medicine, or Dr. Coué.

I have tried to show how, in general, just as in prejudice, desire tends to distort reality and how in the absence of facts it tends to give us erroneous pictures and conclusions. I wish now to push the analysis a little further by reviewing briefly Dewey's account of how we think.[1]

Jung,[2] the psychoanalyst, has said that there are two kinds of thinking. One kind is the daydream type of thinking, and the other is the kind we meet in, say, mathematics. In the preceding paragraphs I have somewhat fully considered the daydream type of thinking, which is characterized by a flow of ideas or images on the stream of desire. I wish now to take up the other kind that Dewey has singled out for discussion and called "reflective thinking." I wish particularly to inquire to what extent this second

[1]   John Dewey, *How We Think*.

[2]   C. G. Jung, *The Psychology of the Unconscious*, chap. i.

type of true reflective thinking is divorced from the daydream type, where desire plays the dominant role.

Dewey has analyzed into five steps the complete thought process. This process boils down to three processes that occur in varying degrees in these five steps. These three processes are observing, recollecting, and planning. He gives the following illustration: A child's flow of ideas is arrested by observation on the ferryboat of a long pole sticking out from the floor of the upper deck. He is curious and wonders what the pole is for. There is a problem. He thinks about it. His first thought is that it is a flagpole, the suggestion of the flagpole arising from the length and size of the pole and the gold knob on the end. But the pole is in a curious position, being almost horizontal, whereas flagpoles usually are vertical. The next thought is that it might be designed to carry a wireless apparatus, but he observes the absence of the necessary apparatus and also that wireless apparatus on boats is generally placed very high. Further speculation leads to the suggestion that it may be used as a guide for the pilot. From the pilot's position on the upper deck, the pole would appear to project out far beyond the deck and point in the direction the boat is going. Further observation confirms this suggestion. The thinking process is concluded, and the stream of desires and habits continues to flow. In this illustration we see the three processes of thought—observing, recollecting, and planning. Awareness of the problem arises through observation; suggestions come through recollecting; and the planning or testing involves further observation and recollecting.

Such a thought process is relatively free from desire and emotion, though no doubt desire may partly occasion the suggestion of the wireless. But not all thinking is so free from emotion. This is true of many social questions. Consider, for instance, the problem of reparations as it presents itself to a Frenchman. Almost every act of observing, recollecting, and planning would be accompanied by desire and emotion, which we think would play a selective role.

But let us consider separately these three processes of thought and inquire whether they are free from the influence of desire.

The first process is observation. We have already pointed out that desire distorts observation, particularly where the material to be observed is extensive and varied and especially if the observation requires some effort. The observation of a simple object such as the length of a table is not likely to be distorted, but even simple sensations are affected by the emotions, as, for instance, in the phenomenon of hallucination.

As to recollecting, we have already discussed at some length how desire selects forgetting and remembering and how suggestions come to the mind on the stream of desire.

So, also, wishes affect our planning and attempts at verification. I have previously pointed out cases of the influence of desire in prediction. Attempts at scientific prediction easily go astray under the influence of desire. When we do not know, do not have the facts, we say we believe. Belief is, of course, partly a matter of tradition as well as the desire of the individual. But omitting the factor of tradition, we tend to believe what we want to believe. Where testing and verification are difficult, as is frequently the case in social issues, social experimentation, voting, etc., desire is very likely to play a determining role in planning.

It therefore appears from a review of Dewey's analysis that the process of so-called reflective thought affords abundant opportunity for desire to prevent a correct conclusion. There are, therefore, not two kinds of thought, daydreaming and reflective thought. Rather, there are two extremes, differing only in degree. So, much so-called reflective thought tends to be like daydreaming. There are two conditions that make reflective thought differ from the daydream. One is the presence of facts, and the other is the relative scarcity of emotion and desire. Mathematical thinking is of the reflective type of thinking, the farthest removed from the daydream type, for the reason that it is usually so free from emotion and the facts for testing are usually at hand. Thus we see that the processes of reflective thought do not themselves distinguish it in essence from the daydream. Reflective thought becomes trustworthy when we do not have the prejudicing or biasing influence of emotion and when we have adequate facts for testing, but when bias is present it usually takes an unsuspectedly large amount of fact to keep emotion from distorting reality, due to the many opportunities for desire to manifest itself in the thinking process.

That desires bias thought is generally admitted. The exposition of the thesis has, however, shown much greater possibility of the force of desire in thinking than is usually conceived. Unfortunately, we have no statistical measure of the frequency of the daydream, prejudiced type of thinking, but I am sure that even in the absence of statistics the researches of psychoanalysis have shown a hitherto unbelievable amount of the daydream type of thought even in what we are accustomed to thinking of as the true reflective type of thought. The psychoanalysts have been particularly successful in uncovering the motives in our thoughts through the penetration of disguises, symbols, and rationalizations, which are so numerous in our thought processes. Contrast this position with the picture Dewey gives us of thinking. Dewey gives a most excellent, clear-cut analysis of the logical processes of thought, but unless the reader is forewarned, he will leave Dewey's book with a totally inadequate idea of the great part emotion and desire play in thinking, and will have quite an exalted idea of the logical and scientific qualities of the human mind.

I wish now to apply the foregoing theory to the attempt to use the scientific method in the social sciences. I have already reminded you of the emotional nature of the subject matter of the social sciences, and it seems to me that it is the emotional nature of the social sciences that has hindered their scientific development rather than their frequently mentioned complexity. At any rate, the present stage of these sciences is characterized by much theory, such as economic theory, political theory, and social theory.

Let us consider for a moment the bearing of the processes of thought on the social theory. We understand by a theory "hypotheses unsupported by facts," otherwise we would call it a law. Theory is therefore unverified speculation. We have previously asserted that where thinking occurs without the verification of evidence it tends to be shaped by desire. In the absence of facts, we tend to believe what we want to believe. From the point of view of science, theory is good simply as a means to an end. It seems strange, therefore that there should be so much admiration of social theory, particularly economic theory, on the part of the profession. Theory, alone, is so very likely to be distorted by desire, particularly where the subject matter stimulates emotion. We all know how the theory of radicals tends to run into the construction of utopias, which are made of the same stuff daydreams are made of. It seems very probable that social theory in general, particularly where the materials serve as stimuli to emotions, must tend to resemble the daydream. It is quite appreciated that theory is often a necessary step in the development of science; there must be something to verify. There is also such a thing as good theory and bad theory; the more checking by facts, the better the theory. But I think we fail to appreciate the daydream aspects of theory, particularly when the theory is couched in technical terms and rationalistic language.

Another highly respected feature of the social sciences that appears to be somewhat removed from scientific processes and to consist in large part of fantasy-making processes of thought is social philosophy. A social philosophy is a well-integrated, consistent viewpoint on a wide range of social problems. If a specific theory is likely to be largely a product of desire, how much more likely is theory which is so general that it covers the whole range of social problems to be a product of desire, particularly if it be consistent.

Before discussing the scientific worth of social philosophy, I wish to make a brief departure for the purpose of considering what the psychoanalysts call the "complex," because it appears to play a most important role in shaping our social philosophies.

Of our many desires, some are strong and frequent. Some of these are sex desires and wishes centering around self, such as ambition and hope. The power of these desires to attract, select, and assort observations, facts, and memories is great. It seems as though constellations of ideas and images cluster in masses around a strong wish. Such a cluster of images and ideas around some unconscious desire is called by psychoanalysts a complex. What these complexes are is said often to be determined in childhood. For instance, as a young child, one's affection may be strongly conditioned to respond to stimuli in the form of some early companion—one's father, mother, brother, or sister. This conditioning of affection in early childhood to such a model may, for instance, have profound directive force to the expression of one's affection in the future. So we have the famous Oedipus complex. Or many habits and responses may be built up around feelings of inferiority, and we are said to have an inferiority complex. These conditioned responses of early childhood may persist all through life and become determining factors in our own personality. They become great centers of desires, and often it is in these complexes that are found the desires which are the sources of prejudice and bias, and from these flow the desires that persistently and consistently influence our thinking and distort reality for us. It seems very probable that these complexes tend to shape our social theories and social philosophies.

As an illustration, let us consider the possible complex at the basis of a certain type of social philosophy of laissez faire. The holder of such a philosophy of laissez faire is an individualist. He believes that that government governs best which governs least. He is opposed to government boards and commissions and extensions of power. He thinks there is too much legislation. He is a lover of liberty and freedom. He is opposed to paternalism and authority. Now suppose, upon analysis, such as Frink[3] has made, we find such a man to have a complex against authority. We learn that in early childhood his father and mother were unhappy together; that his mother was tender and loving; that his father was severe, domineering, disciplinary, and continually mortified him with his humiliating punishments. It is easy to think that the child is conditioned to react with hate to the stimuli of authority. Governments become to him symbols of authority, stimuli to which he reacts violently because of this early conditioning.

But in objection it is argued that this man has studied political theory. He is familiar with Adam Smith, Thomas Jefferson, and

3   H. W. Frink, *Morbid Fears and Compulsions*, p. 150. See also Flügel's *Psychoanalytic Study of the Family*.

Herbert Spencer. He has studied society and government. It cannot be that his laissez faire social philosophy is simply due to the fact that as a child he hated his father. This is absurd. But is it absurd? We all know how addicted man is to rationalizing, to covering up his desires with scientific terms and the paraphernalia of reason, and we know how desires select and distort evidence. May not such a strong desire, the product of early childhood experience, live on and determine this social philosophy? If so, then how much is this man's social philosophy worth? How much should we follow his advice as to whether the legislature should pass an unemployment-insurance law? If we asked him whether he favored the passage of such a law and he replied that he hated his father when a child, we should consider the answer irrelevant, but it would be true. But if in answer to such a question as to how to vote on an unemployment-insurance law, he advised voting against it and quoted laissez faire philosophy, would not his answer be just as worthless because it flowed from a social philosophy determined by his childhood relations to his father?

It is altogether probable that social philosophies are largely determined by desires. And it is altogether possible that many of these determining desires are conditioned by early childhood expressions.

Another man has a survival-of-the-fittest social philosophy. He believes in ability, that success is a test of ability. He thinks the race progresses by letting the weak die off. He is an ardent eugenist, a strong believer in family, does not think much of democracy. The common people are inferior. He believes in a government by brains. He opposes social legislation and does not believe in social work. It is quite conceivable that a person who is selfish, accustomed to winning, easily irritated at the rules of the game that—although protecting others—hinder his success, who is inconsiderate and has little sympathy, would have desires that might build up such a survival-of-the-fittest philosophy. Of course, his philosophy would be expressed in the biological terminology of Darwin; he would refer to Nietzsche, and he would be familiar with the latest work in eugenics. But it goes without saying that references, terminologies, and authorities are not science. And rationalizations are very common, while at every turn in the thinking process emotional desires push in.

It is not, of course, asserted that the desire will create, that is, invent, the materials that go to make up one's social philosophy, such as the laissez faire or the natural-selection doctrine. Desire rather selects the material out of the existing mass. The library is filled with different books; desire drives us to particular ones. Cultural contact is quite essential to the development of a particular social philosophy. A potential socialist will not become one unless exposed to the propaganda. It should also be remembered that desires are complex, and there are great varieties of conditioning influences in early life.

Social philosophies are just an extreme instance of the sort of thing that tends to occur in a study which has not progressed far in reliance on fact and measurement and which deals with emotional material. The foregoing analysis does not appear to profit us any in the development of the technique of scientific method, except that it makes a powerful emphasis on the need of such a method, for we cannot have a science without measurement. And science will grow in the social studies in direct ratio to the use of measurement.

While I think we cannot well be scientific without measurement; still, in the absence of measurement, I think the foregoing analysis does make an important contribution. It is this. It tells us how to be less unscientific, if not more scientific. The way of becoming less unscientific is to know the etiology of our own desires and the mechanisms of their behavior. In other words, a knowledge of the origins of one's prejudice will do much toward eliminating its unscientific influence. The study of abnormal psychology and of psychoanalysis is doing a great deal to acquaint us with the way our desires disguise themselves, how they originate, how they are conditioned, and the part they play in forming specific opinions. A knowledge of the origins and behaviors of our prejudice and bias, while perhaps not adding to scientific output in the social sciences, might conceivably reduce the unscientific output by, say, over 50 per cent.

24

ON PREDICTING THE FUTURE   *1946*

THE STUDY set forth is concerned with the future. Therefore, the method is one of forecast. There are various other names
which are used to characterize such a procedure, such as "prediction," "estimation," or "prophecy." We shall approach it on
the basis of "prediction," which is the scientific term for gauging
in advance what will happen. Everyone who tries to look into the
future has prediction as his goal, but as he falls short of such a
goal, his effort is described by the various other terms mentioned
above.

The Popular Idea of Prediction in
Social Phenomena

There is a popular conception that prediction is impossible
in human and social affairs; at least, one often hears this opinion
expressed, particularly among individuals who admire wisdom
and conservatism and deplore recklessness. The person who essays to predict social events readily becomes the butt of criticism
of wise elders.

There are various sources of this popular belief. One lies in
the fact that we all can see the unexpected happen. What seems
certain does not occur. Forecasts go wrong. We gamble on the

Reprinted from *The Social Effects of Aviation*, chapter iii (Boston:
Houghton Mifflin Co., 1946).

future and lose. The truth is that reliable prediction is often not possible. Another source is the popular belief in luck and chance. The movement of the stock market or the success of a theatrical production is believed to be due to chance or luck. Disasters come from the hands of Fate. In some religious groups, God's way is held unpredictable, and his hand is often seen manifested in the affairs of men. This conception of luck or fate denies causation, or inevitability, which is the basis for scientific prediction.

Another source of disbelief in prediction of social affairs is the idea of freedom of the will. In some intellectual groups, it is admitted that prediction about the stars can be made because they are unaffected by human effort. But in society everything that is done is influenced by human will and therefore is neither inevitable nor predictable.

Finally, there is the cautious person, interested in his reputation for good judgment, who does not wish to undertake the hazard of forecasting the future; and, having a reputation to protect, he speaks impressively about the futility of trying to look into the future.

Much Prediction in Actual Practice

In spite of this popular disbelief in prediction, there is a substantial amount of forecasting of the future being used as the basis for human action. In life, we are really forced to make some kinds of predictions. A merchant who buys a supply of goods for sale for the coming year is trying to predict the future demand for his goods. The fact that there are fewer merchants failing than there are not failing is evidence that these estimates are reasonably accurate. When a company buys a site for a factory, the officers must consider the future of the community, the market, the transportation system, the supply of raw materials, and the availability of a labor supply in the future. There are some things which we have learned to predict quite accurately. Life-insurance companies can foretell how many will die in a given year, and they set their rates accordingly. We can make a fairly accurate estimate as to what the population of the United States will be in 1950.

Instead of thinking that either we can or cannot predict the future, we should admit into our thinking the idea of approximations, that is, that there are varying degrees of accuracy and inaccuracy of estimate. In addition we should break down the category of "human and social affairs" into the variety of types which compose it. In some of these categories it is not very difficult to make predictions, as, for instance, the birth rate next year. In other cases, such as when a war will end or what will be the future style of clothing, prediction is not so successful. In short, everyday experience tells us that accuracy of prediction varies according to the field.

Objection may be made that not all of the instances cited can be called prediction. The businessman who rents a store in a small town probably makes few measurements or calculations as to the growth of the town or the future volume of the market which could be called scientific prevision. He has a hunch that the town will grow, and he buys his merchandise on the basis of general experience. This type of anticipating the future is unformulated and should be called an art rather than a science, because the procedures used cannot be transmitted to other persons. For instance, the men who tell the quality of wool by feeling it or of tea by tasting it may be able to make quite accurate estimates of its durability or its selling quality without ever going through extensive calculations. But they cannot readily transmit their abilities to other people, for they do not know fully and clearly how they do it. In a somewhat similar manner, a father may predict accurately what the reaction of his son will be in a certain situation, but he probably does not know how he does it. Repetition and experience develop skills without full knowledge as to processes. This art of forecasting is not very useful in predicting about social organizations in a society where conditions are changing rapidly.

The work of the average university professor is very little concerned with the future. The professor is dealing with the present or describing the past or imparting knowledge accumulated long ago. Not needing usually to deal with the uncertain future, having rather high standards, and being sensitive to his reputation, he is reluctant to venture into the future. The business-man and the farmer in their work have to deal much more with the future than does the college teacher and are less hesistant about doing so.

Planning Depends upon Prediction

Much of our present behavior is based on the plans for the future which the exigencies of life in a changing society force us to make. All of us make plans regarding personal prob-lems. But planning, as the term is currently used, generally ap-plies to the activity of institutions or organizations. For example, cities, states, and industry make plans for the future. Nearly all of us are now engaged in making plans for the postwar years. The extent of our planning is evidence of our effort to read the future. If we believed that predictions of the future were futile or impossible, we should not be engaged in planning for it.

Rough Approximations Are Sometimes Adequate for Practical Purposes

Scientific prediction in academic work is expected to be very accurate; and if it is slightly inaccurate, we expect to be advised as to the size of the error of the estimate. But in the practical world, the demand for accuracy varies. If a community builds a courthouse, it is not necessary to know accurately the population of the county year by year for a hundred years in the future. Only a rough idea of the future size of the county may be called for. If it errs by underestimation, an additional build-ing or a new courthouse can be erected later. In fact, it might be unfair to take the money of the existing population and tie it up in a courthouse that was too large, even though it were suit-able for the population a hundred years hence. Also a new court-house might then be needed to utilize new building inventions. A more accurate prediction is needed as to the numbers of air passengers and planes in the near future, if we are to plan an adequate system of airports. However, there would seem to be no great need for the Board of Foreign Missions to know the probable amount of international passenger traffic after the war in order to plan for the supplying and supervision of their foreign missions. Nor is it necessary for the universities to know with precision the future development of aviation in order to introduce new material in their geography courses, though aviation will affect both foreign missions and the teaching of geography. Planning, therefore, calls for varying degrees of accuracy, depending upon the nature of the organization doing the planning and the type of activity being planned.

Varying Approximations in This Study

One part of this book is concerned with the future of aviation, and another part with the future effects of aviation upon our society. We shall use many different devices in figuring out the future of aviation and its effects. The purpose of this chapter is to make explicit the methods we shall use. We are not attempting to demonstrate a highly successful method in exact prediction in the field of social phenomena but rather to make a study which will be useful, using the best methods that the data permit. In some fields, we think we can see the course of aviation clearly and with precision for a few years. In other cases, estimates become highly speculative. But it is thought that a high degree of accuracy is not necessary for much of the preparation for what is ahead, and in such situations the exposition of developments which are problematical will be useful.

Prediction by Measurement

Prediction as a scientific method can be much better done where there is measurement, though the existence of measurement does not guarantee predictability.

PREDICTION BY EXTRAPOLATION   A very common method of prediction is to plot the occurrence of the phenomena in the past and then extend the curve forward. If the occurrence follows some exact law, such as the curve of an ellipse, then prediction can be quite accurate from the course of the ellipse. That is the way in which the behavior of astral bodies is predicted. But social phenomena seldom follow such a law. Even when a known law describes the past course of social phenomena, it is not known how long that course will be followed in the future. A second-degree parabola may describe the growth of airmail over the past fifteen years in the United States, but it may not follow the projected parabolic curve in the future. However, projecting curves forward does give some indication of the trend. Such projections are usually more accurate for the immediate than for the distant future.

The projection of a curve which has had very little fluctuation in the past, and only a slow change in direction, is more reliable than for a curve which has changed direction frequently. The curve of the population of the United States is this type of steady curve, and its projections forward in the past have been quite close to the course it has later followed. On the other hand, the curve of the average length of journey by airplane has had some significant fluctuations in the past, and the average length of journey for the next two or three years is not so easily foretold by extending the curve forward.

A curve is thought of as having two components: a trend and a fluctuation around the trend. In extrapolating a curve that has fluctuations, it is the trend of the curve that should be projected forward rather than the last fluctuation. The trend is a line, sometimes straight but usually curving gently, drawn through the middle of the fluctuations of the data. The carrying-forward of a curve of fluctuating data is best done by first projecting the trend and then weaving the probable fluctuations of the future around the projected trend. This second step can be done only if the rhythm of the oscillations is known. For instance, we know to a certain extent probable business fluctuations. If the law of the fluctuations is not known, it is probably better not to attempt to put in future fluctuations but to rest content with the projected trend line. The projection is somewhat more accurate on a natural than on a logarithmic scale.

It is difficult to project the curve of the early periods of a rapidly growing phenomenon with any degree of certainty. Growth curves on a natural scale often show a very slow growth at the beginning, then a remarkably rapid growth in the early periods of development, and finally come to a relatively stable period in which little change occurs. Eventually they may, of course, decrease.[1] The curve is almost flat at first and then curves upward rather rapidly, until sometimes it appears to be going almost straight up. Such rapid growth cannot continue in a real world, but it is difficult to tell exactly in advance when the curve will begin to flatten out. Many aviation curves are of this class, for aviation is young. For instance, the growth in the number of passenger-miles flown on scheduled airlines, when plotted for the last decade, moves very sharply upward, since the growth has been rapid. The rate of growth will surely slacken sometime, but exactly when this will happen is uncertain. Growth curves in their later stages can often be more reliably projected, for the rate of change is slow and the curve is a gentle slope. The growth of rapidly expanding industries, such as the automobile or moving-picture industries, was more difficult to predict in their early years than at present, for they have now reached a stage of relative maturity. The same will be true of the growth curves of aviation.

FACTORS INFLUENCING PROJECTION   Carrying curves forward is not an objective method even when it is done by means of a mathematical equation. The person doing the projecting must always take into consideration the factors that may bend the curves in ways not indicated in the past and hence not a part of the mathematical equation, which is based on past data. For instance, the trend of the curve for passenger fares on airlines has been downward during the 1930's and 1940's from twelve cents a mile to five cents a mile. A projection of the curve of fares downward would very soon have us traveling by plane free of charge. It can be reasoned then that the precipitous downward course of fares must soon stop sharply and flatten out. So also it could have been reasoned that the rapid increase in the curve of automobile production in the 1920's could not have been extended forward very far at the same rates because of the limiting factor of population. After the distribution had reached, say, one car for seven families, it could have been guessed that the

1   S. C. Gilfillan, *The Sociology of Invention* (Chicago: Follett Publishing Co., 1935), pp. 32–43.

production of private automobiles would increase less rapidly each year because of the limiting number of families, particularly when it was known that the average income per family was around twelve hundred dollars per year.

The knowledge about various other factors which push or pull a curve one way or another is not as certain as the knowledge about the factors mentioned above, that is, that passenger fares must cost something or that not every family can have an automobile. For instance, in the prediction of the number of future crimes, such factors as broken homes, slum conditions, school systems, playgrounds, growth of cities, amount of neurosis, and the economic plane of living must be taken into consideration. Since the amount of influence which each of these factors has on the crime rate is not known and since the course of each of these factors in the future is not precisely predictable, taking them into consideration in modifying the projection of the curve of crime rates becomes a rather subjective process. Similarly, in projecting curves showing air passenger traffic between nations, there are many factors bearing on the future of such traffic that are highly variable, such as frequency of schedules, rates, business conditions, vacationing habits, international amity, and so on. We can see that the projection of a curve involves not merely a mechanical extrapolation of the curve, but such modification of the curve as familiarity with the factors influencing it in the future indicates.

A very important check on the extrapolation of some curves is the economic factor of price, or cost, where it is involved. In extrapolating curves for airmail, it is well to allow for changes in rates. If we know that the Post Office may raise or lower the rate for airmail, we may not be able to predict the rates exactly, but we shall allow for a great error in future estimates. A useful device in this case is to assume various rates and work out estimates for each.

ERRORS OF EXTRAPOLATION The difficulties of extrapolation described in the previous paragraphs may tend to destroy the reader's confidence that extrapolation is of any value whatsoever. That there is some value can be shown by a test of this kind. Examine the curve of the early years of growth (first fifteen or twenty-five years) of some phenomenon, extrapolate the curve, and compare the extrapolation with what actually occurred. This experiment was carried out by three persons, using ten curves. The extrapolation was purely mechanical, since the experimenters did not know what material had been plotted, except that they were data for the early years of the sales or production of some inventions. For a ten-year projection there were sixteen over-predictions, with an average error of 74 per cent, and fourteen underpredictions, with an average error of 43 per cent.[2] These are very large errors, but they very likely could have been reduced if the experimenters had known what materials they were dealing with. Also, the error would probably have been less if the extrapolation had been compared with the trend of the given data rather than with the actual fluctuation around the trend. Finally, the curves were the most difficult to extrapolate. They presented the early production of inventions like aluminum, electric power, dynamite, steel, etc., which had great fluctuations and steep slopes in the curves of their early years.

The extrapolation of a trend is most accurate for the first few periods for which it is projected; and the further it is projected, the greater the possible error. This observation is based on the fact that most trend lines are gently curving. More confidence can be placed upon the mechanical projection of a trend for three or four years hence, if the year is the unit concerned, than for ten or fifteen years in the future. The actual occurrence—that is, the fluctuation two or three years hence—may be missed, but not by very much unless the curve has violent fluctuations.

When the projection is carried forward for longer periods of time, it is sometimes good practice to carry forward two projections, based on two assumptions: one, that the trend will bend rather rapidly; and the other, that it will bend more slowly. This is a precautionary measure to indicate that there is a possible error and that it becomes larger the farther the projection is

---

[2]   For underprediction the limit of error is 100 per cent, but for overprediction there is no limit; that is, the error may be 2000 per cent, 5000 per cent, etc.

carried. These errors may be enough to make the projection worthless for some uses. An estimate of the population of the sections of a town fifteen years in the future would not be accurate enough to permit a telephone company to know how many employees it will need, but it might be accurate enough to lay out trunk lines.

Familiarity with statistical series may help in extrapolation. For instance, some knowledge about the difference between trends and the fluctuations about trends enables one to attempt to project the trend first, rather than the fluctuation about the trend. If one knows that the trends in the past have been slow in changing, more confidence can be put in their projection than if the trends had changed more rapidly. Knowledge about cycles is also helpful. Many growth curves go through something like a cycle in that they begin slowly and haltingly, then shoot up at a very rapid rate for a short time, and then tend to level off into a gentle slope of some duration. If it is known at what stage of the growth cycle a particular series occurs, the projection can be made with more assurance. For example, the growth of automobile production could have been projected more reliably in the period of maturity of the 1930's than in its period of rapid growth around 1920. Growth cycles may be disturbed, of course, by outside phenomena. The curve of the growth in numbers of railroad passengers was disturbed by the invention of the motor bus and the private automobile, which caused a decrease in the number of railroad passengers. These large, outside disturbing factors, such as the effect of the automobile on railroads, almost change the universe in which the prediction occurs. The logic of prediction is that the universe of the future will be much like the universe of the past. If some greatly upsetting factor occurs, such as a war or a revolutionary invention, the conditions are so changed that extrapolation is hardly worth trying.

PREDICTION BY CORRELATION We have been discussing a type of prediction that consists of projecting a trend line without aid from the measurement of any other factor to which it is related. In some cases, the curve being studied, Curve A, may be closely related to another curve, B. If we know the course of

Curve B, the course of Curve A can be estimated. A very good illustration of this type of prediction is the method used in forecasting business conditions. It has been observed that the curve of business prosperity or depression is closely related to the curve of prices of certain selected stocks listed in the stock exchange but that the changes in stock prices normally preceded changes in business conditions by several months. By plotting the price of these stocks, the course of business can be foretold. Great accuracy is not assured, however, because the curves of business and the stock market do not follow each other exactly. The correlation is only around .8, which means that only about two-thirds of the factors influencing the course of business are accounted for by the curve of the stock prices. As a result, the prediction is right only about two-thirds of the time. Since business demands a rather exact forecast of the future in the interests of business planning, there has grown up a distrust of this method of business forecasting. What business wants is a curve having a perfect correlation with the curve of business conditions, one which would give the right forecast every time.

In aviation there are several series which are related to one another, but ordinarily one does not precede the other in time enough to help in a forecast. Moreover, in the few cases where one series does precede another to a sufficient extent, the correlation is not particularly high. For instance, the growth in the number of airports does precede the transportation of passengers, but the curve of the construction of airports does not foretell the number of passengers except in very broad limits. The curves of the amount of mail and the number of passengers have some relation, since passengers and mail are often carried on the same plane. But the correlation is not very close, since some planes carry only mail, while other planes carry many passengers and only a small amount of mail. There is also some relation between passenger fares and the number of passengers. As the fare per mile over the last twenty years has gone down, the number of passengers has increased, but the correlation is not very close because there are so many other factors affecting the number of passengers, such as conveniences on the plane, fear of flying, frequency of schedule, business conditions, and so on. Indeed, with an unchanging fare from year to year, there may still be a great increase in the number of passengers.

If the correlated curve is more mature and there is more knowledge concerning its fluctuations than there is concerning the curve with which one is working, the correlated curve may be helpful in making a more reliable projection of the given curve. For instance, the fluctuations in the number of air passengers are correlated with the curve of intercity passenger traffic and with the index of production. A large amount of work has been done by researchers on the curves of intercity passenger traffic and of the index of production, and a considerable amount of knowledge has been accumulated about their fluctuations and their projections. Hence they are helpful in extending the curve representing the number of air passengers.

The fact that the many different series do have some correlation and that they all fit together in a pattern means that wide knowledge of the various series for which data exist does have a safeguarding influence against extreme statements.

As was mentioned in a previous paragraph, successful prediction is based upon the assumption that the environment, statistically called the "universe," does not change a great deal or suddenly. In tossing coins for heads or tails, the universe does not change, and from the law of probability the prediction of heads or tails can be determined with an exact error. The conditions affecting the growth of population year by year for a country as large as the United States do change from year to year, but not much, and population growth can be forecast quite accurately. On the other hand, the universe of the airplane may change violently and quickly because of the appearance of some new invention. For instance, the invention of jet-propulsion planes changes the universe in which predictions of speed are made. Meticulous statistical predictions of speed in the propeller plane are transcended by jet propulsion. However, the function of a structure or organization follows a trend even though there is a radical change in the form due to a new invention. Hence the function can be forecast from a trend somewhat better than might be thought from a consideration only of the radical change in the form. Thus, the introduction of the jet plane will increase the slope of the trend of speed, but hardly with a violent break.

We can see that the prediction of the growth of aviation may be changed by the appearance of new and startling technological advances in this field. Fortunately, it is possible to foresee somewhat in advance many new inventions, as will be discussed in later paragraphs. It takes a long time to develop an invention, although to the general public its appearance is often startling. However, the general proposition is still true that careful prediction by statistical measurement of a series is likely to be upset by some new invention or by major social changes.

PREDICTION OF THE UNIQUE EVENT   Up to this point the discussion of forecasting on the basis of measurement has been concerned with the prediction of quantities or of averages based upon statistics. In such analysis the degree is being predicted, that is, the smallness or the largeness of the number of passengers who will be carried in airplanes. Likewise, we have not been concerned with whether mail will or will not be carried by plane, but rather with the amount or degree to which it will be transported. Where degree is not concerned, prediction is on the appearance or non-appearance of the phenomenon, sometimes referred to as the "all-or-none" principle. For instance, we might be concerned with predicting whether or not planes that pick up and deposit mail without landing will carry passengers. In such a prediction, we are not concerned with how many passengers will be carried, but whether they will carry any passengers—*all* they can get or *none*. The unique event to be predicted is the carrying of passengers by mail-pickup planes.

Most efforts to foresee unique events are not based upon measurement, for generally the measurements are not available. These unique events are the results of the coming-together of a number of factors. But in some cases these factors are measurable, and under such circumstances forecasting of the unique event is based upon measurement. Forecasting as to whether a particular prisoner will violate a parole if he is granted one is a prediction of a unique event. Many of the factors which produce this event are measurable and can be tabulated, such as the traits and experiences of the prisoner as to his home life, his record in school, his prior prison experience, and so on. The parole records of individuals with various combinations of experiences and traits are then observed. Predictions as to whether a particular, that is, unique, prisoner will break parole are based upon these prior calculated percentages. In a similar way, the success or failure of a unique marriage may be estimated.

Much prediction of individual behavior that takes place every day by any one of us is based upon similar observations, except that we usually do not record and tabulate them on paper but only preserve impressions of past experiences with the individual concerned, or individuals like him, in our memories. If an individual has shown courage repeatedly (statistically) in the face of danger, we readily say he will be brave in the future in a certain unique situation that involves danger.

In the study of the future influences of the airplane upon civilization, there is little occasion for forecasting unique events based upon measurement, for the measurements do not exist. Likewise, in anticipating technological improvements in aviation, we are dealing with unique events with little statistical measurement that can be used. In forecasting degrees of use of airplanes for different purposes, there is, fortunately, a good deal of measurement.

Prediction Not Based on Measurement

We have been considering forecasts based upon statistical measurement, such as the amount of air-borne express to be carried in future years. But statistical measurements are available for only a few of the many social phenomena. Yet we desire to know about the future, whether or not there are statistics. We may want to know, for example, in what ways the airplane will or will not be used in agriculture, whether in sowing grain, fighting grasshoppers, or hunting coyotes. At this time, statistical series do not exist for such uses and may not be available for some time, if ever. Yet we may wish to know, in general, what uses farmers may make of aviation on the "all-or-none" principle, irrespective of degree.

DIFFERENT PROCEDURES   The reason for dividing our discussion into sections on measurement and non-measurement is that there are great differences in method between the two. One difference is that where measurement is not available, variation in degree cannot be computed. If amounts are of interest, reliance must be placed on the use of adjectives poorly suited to indicate exact quantities, adjectives such as "large" or "small," "fast" or "slow." Another difference is that for forecasts without measurement the demand for exact accuracy is often not very great, at least at a particular time. If we are interested in ascertaining whether the airplane will make the small nation weaker in international competition, we are perhaps satisfied at the present with a statement such as, on the average, small nations will be much weaker, or only a little weaker. Our curiosity is not so much for a statistical measure of weakness as it is for the kinds of small nations that will be weaker or the situations that will make them weaker. Also, we may not need to have exact estimates of time. We may be content to say that small nations will be weaker as the danger of war approaches, or that if there is confidence that war is abolished, then small nations will not be weaker.

Since prediction without measurement is often unsuccessful and usually not explicit, some critics prefer to call it an art rather than a science. Such criticism is admitted; indeed, one is hardly justified in calling scientific the major part of prediction in the social sciences, even when it is based on measurement. However, we remind ourselves that our problem in studying aviation is not to be extremely exact, but rather to be as helpful as we can in trying to figure out the future of aviation and how it is likely to change our civilization. We must act in practical life before all the evidence is in or before a proof is rendered.

In the following paragraphs we shall set down the procedures that have proved helpful in the past. It is desired to make these methods explicit and thus to take the mysterious, which is incompatible with knowledge, out of whatever art there may be in trying to see ahead.

SAME PATTERNS FOR NON-MEASUREMENT AS FOR MEASURE-MENT   There are certain assumptions we may make about non-measurable data even though we cannot demonstrate them with certainty. We often do this. For instance, before 1930, for the United States, we did not have any statistics on crimes committed because they were not being collected, but we might have inferred that there were certain regularities. Now that we have the statistics on crime, we can see the regularities by season, by sex, by relation to the business cycle, by the type of crime, by size of locality, and so on. Since we do not have measurement in many fields of social science—due mainly to the cost and trouble of collecting data rather than to the inapplicability of the method—we must often make similar assumptions.

One assumption of general importance is that unmeasured data, over a series of time units, follow a trend. Since we find such a pattern in measurable data, it is natural to assume that we should find a trend in unmeasured data over a period of time —if they were measured—and perhaps, also find fluctuations around the trend. For instance, the family as a social organization has been losing functions and becoming of less organizational significance for a very long time. This decline has not been measured; yet we speak of it as a trend. There is, of course, a good deal of data on changes in family organization, but much of it is not in the form of a statistical series which would show a mathematical curve with a trend and fluctuations. Nevertheless, we may use the statistical pattern of thinking for the degree of family change and say that the family has been losing functions and is likely to continue to lose them in the near future, provided the analysis of factors leads to the same conclusion. In other words, we assume trends for non-statistical data and try to make the best of these assumptions. In aviation there are miscellaneous data to show that the contacts of the communities of the Pacific coast with the populations east of the Mississippi River have been increasing. We assume that there has been a trend, with fluctuations due to the business cycle and to war, toward making closer connections between the two coasts and that this trend will continue with more and faster air flights.

Another pattern found in measurement of growth that may be assumed for data not yet measurable is the form of the growth curve. The growth curve shows very little actual growth at the beginning—though the rate of growth may be great—then a period of rapid growth, followed by a period of less rapid growth or none at all, making the curve an elongated S. This form of growth is determined, of course, by the conditions in which the phenomena occur. Phenomena which occur under similar conditions, but whose actual data of growth are unknown and hence not subject to plotting, may be assumed to follow the pattern just described and would be so shown were measurements available. For instance, if the result of aviation is to encourage the fashion of making objects, such as luggage, tableware, casing, etc., light in weight, then we may assume without measurement that the total number of lightweight objects will grow according to the pattern of a growth curve, though we should not know where the turning points on such an imagined curve would occur.

COMPLEXITY OF SOCIAL FACTORS Another assumption that may be made for non-statistical data is that the phenomenon will be affected by many factors rather than by only one. For example, when a person becomes sick with a common cold, the cause of the cold may lie in a variety of factors, such as subjection to an unusual number of germs, fatigue, shortage of Vitamin A, a drop in temperature, exposure to the motion of cold air on a part of the body, and increased acidity. In the physical sciences—physics, chemistry, astronomy, geology—the number of factors producing a phenomenon are generally considered to be much fewer than in the biological and social sciences. The complexity of factors in social phenomena is remarkable, as is shown by the many studies which have used partial correlation. In fact, in the social sciences, two variables with a correlation of 1—that is, where all of the variation in one factor is accounted for by change in the other—have never been reported, so far as is known.

There are many factors that must be taken into account in considering the various aspects of aviation. If we are dealing with the extension of air service to the small towns and villages, we must take into consideration such factors as the number of daily passengers in a small town, the fare charged and the ability to pay the fare, the existence of other means of transportation, the nearness to another airport, the demand for airmail, the willingness of the government to pay a subsidy for such air service, the political influence of the small town and the small businessman, and the maintenance of facilities for an airport. Some of these factors have more importance than others, but a good rule is to look around rather diligently for a large number of factors. If one is interested, for instance, in what effect the airplane will have on the relations between Great Britain and the United States, it will be seen at once that the relations will be affected by such factors as trade rivalries, tariff policies, war rumors, fiscal policies, propaganda developments, lend-lease adjustments—any one of which may overshadow the influence of the airplane. Furthermore, while the airplane service of perhaps ten hours between London and New York at a reasonable fare may increase the number of contacts between the two peoples and hence their familiarity, yet the airplane also brings rivalry for air bases, as well as competition between the international airlines of the two nations. Where many powerful factors exist, the direction of the airplane's influence may be reversed by these other factors. The net influence of the plane may be to increase the friendship between the British and the Americans, yet economic or political factors may make the final result one of less friendliness. A search for the many factors affecting a situation reduces the probability of errors.

BIAS Scientific thinking is best assured when many data are available. When we do not have abundant data, our thinking is likely to be directed by subjective factors, variously characterized by such terms as "bias," "prejudice," "emotion," and "wishful thinking." Thinking without much evidence gives more opportunity for wishful thinking, which is, of course, quite unrealistic. The problem of bias becomes more important the less the evidence, the rarer the measurement, and the more numerous the factors involved. Anything that can be done to eliminate bias clears the way for better thinking.

We shall not go into the psychology of biased thinking here. There is a considerable literature on this complex subject which sets forth the important theories of the role of emotion and desire in the thinking process. Rather, we shall point out in the succeeding paragraphs a few common instances of how bias makes forecasting rather hazardous.

WISHFUL THINKING   Hope is a notoriously bad forecaster, though it may help to create the morale necessary to bring about the future condition desired. Students often think they are going to get higher grades in their class work than they actually get. We overestimate the chances of our favorite team's winning. Obviously, in prediction we need to be on our guard when our hopes are involved and to try to discard them. If possible, it is desirable to get in a mood of detachment, as if the result meant nothing at all to us. But usually we cannot detach our desires in a manner so cold-blooded.

In gathering estimates of the future from interested persons, we should watch out for the bias of self-interest. The predictions of aircraft manufacturers, who naturally want a good market, may be too high, on the average. So also the expectations of airline officials may be for a brighter future than will occur, though there will be exceptions. On the other hand, rival transportation systems, such as railroads and ocean-steamship companies, which may lose business by virtue of the growth of air transportation, would be expected to predict a less rosy future for aviation than would the airline companies. Of course, railroad and aviation companies do not give opinions without data, and since they both have much data, the distortion due to desires cannot be too great. But, certainly, an investigator collecting opinions and estimates should consider the possible biases of the sources of his information. In some cases this bias can be very large, as is illustrated by an experience which a mediator had in an attempt to learn the number on strike the first morning of a disturbance in a steel mill. The union leader said the number out was ten thousand to fifteen thousand; the manager of the plant said three hundred or four hundred. Each predicted according to his wishes in a period of great excitement, and each no doubt felt that his prediction, if widely known, would influence the number to go out on strike. The actual number on strike was about seven thousand.

The theory of the role of bias in prediction, as stated above, is greatly oversimplified. In the first place, the nature of an opinion depends to a great extent on the sense of responsibility of the renderer of an opinion at the time he gives it. If the opinion is given in casual conversation over cocktails, it may be quite different from what it would be if he were on the point of making a large investment of money on the basis of his opinions.

Furthermore, most intelligent businessmen are quite familiar with the danger of optimism based on their hopes and desires and learn to correct for it by undercutting their optimism. Indeed, some of them swing to the extreme and give a pessimistic judgment in order to safeguard themselves.

Then, too, not every individual is an optimist and allows his wishes to bias his estimates. Apparently there are pessimists as well as optimists. There is probably fixed in us in our early years a pattern of adjustment of our feelings to our thinking which becomes more or less constitutional in us as adults. This psychological set works out in many of us in such a way as to justify the term "optimist," while in others it works out in such a way as to call for the term "pessimist." However, there are not just two classes without variations. There are all degrees of optimism and pessimism.

An attempt was once made to make a crude estimate of the number of optimists and pessimists in the following manner.[3] Students were asked to predict their grades, the arrangement being that the person who gave the grade could not know the prediction made by the student. Students who predicted that they would get higher grades than they actually received in all their courses were labeled "optimists," while those who predicted that they would have lower grades in their courses than they actually

[3]   William F. Ogburn, "Studies in the Prediction and Distortion of Reality," *Social Forces*, XIII, No. 2 (December, 1934), 227–28.

got were called "pessimists." It was interesting to note that there was an excess of both optimists and pessimists over a random expectation and that the excess of optimists was eight times as great as the excess of pessimists. These results seem to bear out the common observation that hope or fear swings estimates more than it should, but that the hopeful outnumber the fearful.

Try as we may to prevent wishful thinking, there is nothing so effective as plenty of data to correct it. But in cases of scarcity of data, one way of trying to reduce the error is to reduce the emotional element in thinking.

INFLUENCE OF FASHION   Another bias in thinking when the data are few is the influence of the prevailing opinion, which has an element of fashion about it in the sense that it may be one thing today and another tomorrow. This may be illustrated by the changeable opinion about the future of the helicopter. When the helicopter was first flown successfully, it received an enthusiastic reception from the daily press and from the magazines. The tone of opinion was one of great optimism. It was predicted that the helicopter would become the family aircraft and that its production would furnish employment after the war. But afterward the climate of opinion about the helicopter changed. It became the fashion to decry its prospects. To say a good word about its promise was to be considered a careless thinker; to be skeptical was an index of good judgment. The prevailing wind had changed. Obviously, when opinion changes radically with little new evidence, it is quite different from a scientific conclusion which is valid from year to year.

Observers should be aware of their susceptibility to the influence of the prevailing opinion. This susceptibility is due in part to the fact that we pick up our ideas from others rather than base them on our own research and in part to the social pressure that gets us in the habit of conforming. Those who live on Main Street tend to think like Main-Streeters. It is very difficult to see beyond the contemporary environment. In the late 1920's, businessmen were talking of permanent prosperity and of having licked business depression forever. During the depression of the early 1930's, the gloom was so thick that many businessmen thought that it was not a phenomenon of the business cycle but that capitalism had failed. The winds of opinion have not the reliability of science.

During the war, there was a phenomenal development of aviation. Our sons became aviators, and our daughters worked in airplane factories. Magazines carried large airplane advertisements, while the daily press reported the achievements of our military aircraft. It was a period of boomtime psychology for aviation. Peacetime conditions are bringing a great decrease in this air activity, and if there is a business depression, aviation may even fall below prewar levels. The expansionist attitude toward aviation will be severely restricted. Forecasts then will not be so bright as now. We conclude that, somehow or other, when we cannot rely wholly on data in forecasting, some consideration must be made of the changeability of opinion on the subject.

THE DANGER OF BEING TOO CONSERVATIVE   Continuing our discussion of what to do about forecasting when data are meager, it may be observed that there is often a fear of making too extreme a forecast and an attitude of timidity or caution which leads to an underestimate. For example, the forecasts of the scores of winning football teams have been shown to be only about half as large as the actual scores.[4] Seldom was a very large score predicted, yet very large scores occur from time to time.

Simon Newcomb, the cautious dean of science, wrote the following negative forecast regarding the airplane in 1903:

There are many problems which have fascinated mankind ever since civilization began which we have made little or no advance in solving. The only satisfaction we can feel in our treatment of the great geometrical problems of antiquity is that we have shown their solution to be impossible. The mathematician of today admits that he can neither square the circle, duplicate the cube, or trisect the angle. May not our mechanicians, in like manner, be ultimately forced to admit that aerial flight is one of that great class of problems with which man can never cope, and give up all attempts to grapple with it?[5]

4   *Ibid.*, p. 225.

5   Simon Newcomb, "The Outlook for the Flying Machine," *Independent*, October 22, 1903, p. 2509.

Yet in exactly eight weeks after this forecast was published, the Wright brothers made their memorable flight in a heavier-than-air machine at Kitty Hawk.

But extreme predictions are sometimes made. Writing at about the same time as Newcomb, H. G. Wells, the imaginative novelist and thinker, made an astounding number of successful predictions of the radical changes that were to take place during the following twenty-five years. There are, of course, plenty of extreme predictions made in the sensational Sunday supplements of certain newspapers by writers who are paid for catching the reader's attention through strange and dramatic statements. Also, poets have sometimes predicted coming events, such as flying. But such predictions are not highly responsible and are made more for psychological effects than for reliability.

Our thesis is that responsible forecasters, in the absence of many good data, err on the side of underprediction more often than overprediction and that they rarely foresee the exceptional. One reason for this may be that there is a certain prestige in being conservative. Conservatism is believed to denote soundness and good judgment rather than fear. Another reason is that a missed prediction on an extreme prophecy is more glaring than is a less extreme one. A responsible predictor feels ashamed of making a bad miss.

Forecasting in the social sciences is so difficult and inaccurate that few venture it. One type of prediction that is used is the so-called slide-rule prediction which deals with many data, with statistics, with costs and prices, and which predicts for only a few years ahead. The slide-rule prediction does not get very far into the future, for then there is more opportunity for new factors to come in. There this method breaks down, since it is based on measurement. What little prestige there is to prediction lies with slide-rule prediction today.

Another type of predictor goes farther into the future and depends on more intangible procedures. The believed superiority of the slide-rule predictors reflects by reverse action on those who venture into the future without measurement. They are believed to be "wild" and unreliable, as they no doubt are when compared to the slide-rule predictors. Since no one wants to be a "wild" forecaster, this type of forecasting is disapproved. So social pressure operates to prohibit forecasters from making extreme forecasts and encourages the conservative type of prediction. It is very probable that a good forecaster with a slide-rule method would be a poorer forecaster for years farther into the future, where his slide-rule method does not work, than would be a person who never used the slide-rule type of prediction, but who had a wide general knowledge and was accustomed to finding his way around with imagination and without dependence on measurement.

MANY RESULTS FROM A SINGLE CAUSE   Sometimes we are curious to know the many different phenomena that will occur rather than any particular one. For instance, many planners want to know the ways in which society will be different after World War II. They want to know the many different results flowing chiefly from one cause, war. This is a legitimate curiosity. Naturally, it is more difficult to foresee many results than one. But usually such a broad curiosity is satisfied with naming the changes rather than measuring the amounts and locating these varying amounts in time. In such situations, we are interested in the scope of the vision rather than in focusing on a single point. There is a certain interest in merely listing one hundred and fifty different uses and effects of the radio, even if these effects are not measured in time and degree. In such an inquiry, an omission may be more serious than a failure to observe an item meticulously. In forecasting for a particular change, there is sometimes a contempt for any estimate that does not predict for quantity and time, but if the limitations of time and quantity are removed, successful predictions may not be particularly difficult. It is much easier to predict successfully the wide use of the helicopter at some time in the future than it is to predict the number of helicopters, their price, and the date of their successful use.

The degree of accuracy necessarily depends on the use of the prediction. There are many persons who want to know only whether divorces are likely to increase or decrease after the war, rather than to know the exact divorce rates. It would be better to predict the exact number of divorces within a small error, but a reliable forecast that divorce will increase after the war is better than no orientation at all. If a publisher is interested in shipping magazines by air after the war, he is interested in exact routes, schedules, and particularly rates. But a reader of magazines may be interested only in the general development of aviation in the postwar decade and what effects it will have on our way of life and our institutions. As far as he is concerned, a wide range of predictions on the "all-or-none" principle, without predictions as to rates for transporting magazines by air and so on, will be of interest. There is a desire on the part of many people to have an extensive picture of the influence of aviation on our civilization, and this desire may be satisfied in large part without estimates of degrees and of years.

Concern with the broad perspective of impending changes attributable to aviation necessitates a considerable familiarity with many societal factors. Society is an interlocking of many parts— institutions, customs, attitudes, traditions, etc.—just as is a complicated piece of machinery. The attainment of a broad perspective of impending changes is of distinct aid in forecasting the particular, since the particular is dependent upon many factors, such as price, business conditions, governmental policy, political influences, demand, and social attitudes. The rule of getting the general picture in order to know the particular is a familiar one in sociology and anthropology. A fieldworker, for instance, is advised not to study the family or religion of a strange culture without knowing the whole of the culture and how the family or religion is tied in with it. Likewise, in aviation, the questions of whether there will be one or many airline companies of a single nation flying transoceanic routes and the extent of governmental regulation and aid depend in part on a knowledge of the political system, the economic policy, and social attitudes. Questions of this kind are difficult to handle statistically. A descriptive knowledge of the many societal factors is needed.

In this particular book an attempt is made to obtain a general picture of how our daily life, our social organizations, and our customs will be modified by aviation. The success of the undertaking is dependent to an important degree on the range of vision. In view of the scope of the undertaking and of the general audience to whom it is addressed, there will be many instances where the "all-or-none" type of forecast will be used. In addition, there will be many particularistic forecasts. A number of studies have already been published making forecasts of the volumes of passengers, mail, and express at different rates. Planners in particular fields will also make more detailed estimates of the future as the need arises.

25

SOME OBSERVATIONS ON

SOCIOLOGICAL RESEARCH *1955*

IT IS not my purpose to present a formal treatment on methods of research in sociology. There are many excellent books that do this. I have thought it would be more useful to present some informal observations of the nature of unwritten advices which, say, an apprentice hears. There are in any workshop ways of doing things that have not been formalized and put into writing. I think of these observations of mine as not necessarily being the same as those which another researcher would make. They are therefore of the nature of opinion as well as observation.

Choice of Subject

My first batch of observations are on the choice of a subject for research.

IDEAS VS. DATA   The subject should be one on which there are many data in existence or otherwise obtainable, as through field work, and to which a method can be applied. In other words, prerequisites are data and method. In the natural sciences, counterparts are materials (animals, chemicals, metals) and a laboratory (where the method may be employed).

Reprinted from *Social Forces*, XXXIV, No. 1 (October, 1955). Read before the eighteenth annual meeting of the Southern Sociological Society, Nashville, Tennessee, April 2, 1955.

An idea is not enough alone on which to undertake research, for it cannot become scientific knowledge unless it is verified, a process which requires data and method. I have seen many research undertakings fail, not for lack of a basic idea, but because adequate data could not be had. For instance, I may have the idea that excessive fiction-reading by the very young hinders adjustment to reality later in life. It is not easy to get adequate data to check such an idea. There are fewer hazards in research on a descriptive or historical subject, such as the history of the juvenile court, for generally such descriptive materials are to be had unless the past be remote.

These remarks carry no implications that research should not be based on an idea. I have also seen a good many publications of research, using many data with a good method, where the idea was either rather trivial or where there was little novelty or originality in it. I have seen more attempts at research fail for lack of data and method than for lack of a basic idea, but I have also seen about as much low-quality research due to inadequate ideas as due to inadequate data and method. Planning research calls for all three—ideas, data, and method—and I do not wish to be misunderstood or misquoted on this point. Yet the emphasis may not at all times be placed equally on each.

This variation in emphasis may be due to the nature of the research. Thus the idea of making an automobile highway out of some material more durable than cement or asphalt, such as iron, may occur very readily to anyone driving over a broken pavement or over the protruding iron cover of a manhole in the street. In this case the need is rather for the data, that is, for a material that meets the specifications not only of durability as to surface wear but as to costs, to traction on slopes or in wet weather, to frost resistance, and to wear on tires. The idea in this illustration that is easy to get is the basic idea. Other ideas, many of them, are of course needed in searching for or in manipulating data.

Sometimes the need of an idea seems greater than the need for data. For instance, there have been many data available on the taboo of incest. What was needed were ideas as to its cause.

The emphasis on theory or on verification also varies by individuals. Some admire greatly what they call "flashes of insight," which give birth to fruitful ideas. Others admire greatly reliability and trustworthiness of knowledge, as for instance medical researchers.

I have wondered whether there is any correlation of this relative emphasis on ideas and on verification with the youth or maturity of a science. I raise this question in the hope that it may be discussed. There was a time in the history of anthropology, in the late nineteenth century, for instance, when there were many theories of evolution, of the family, of religion, for which data were needed. It was felt that in this plethora of speculative ideas there was an especially great need for data. Later there was a reduction of theorizing, and much emphasis was placed on field studies. As ethnographers have accumulated many monographs on primitive cultures over the years there has been an increasing demand for the ideas we call theory. Also, as chemistry grew out of alchemy and as astronomy grew out of astrology, the weakness of theorizing was appreciated, and the need for data was greatly felt. But when fact-gathering has been prodigious and many researchers turn out a large body of not very important researches, as is often the case in later stages of the maturing of a science, a great need is felt for big ideas. Perhaps the shift in emphasis from ideas to *data* and vice versa is cyclical as well as related to youth and maturity.

IMPORTANCE   I next raise the question as to whether importance of the subject is a good criterion in choosing a topic for research. I suppose there is only one answer, and that is "yes." Yet, it seems to me that choice of a subject largely on the basis of its importance has led to failure. Perhaps research on important matters may be more difficult. This may not be true. Possibly insistence on importance blurs the appraisal of feasibility. Insistence on importance may also act as a deterrent to acquiring the research habit or to continuing it. Another reason may be that important topics of research are scarce, and waiting to find an important subject leads to inactivity.

That importance is a criterion is shown by the frequency of the following remarks about a Ph.D. thesis. "No one ever reads it," or "I do not want to write something that accumulates dust on the library shelves." Certainly the list of Ph.D. thesis topics suggests much triviality. Yet research for the Ph.D. degree is for training in research, as well as for the importance of the result.

To do research it is desirable to form the habit, and the habit is not acquired by undue postponement while searching for something important to work on. It is obviously better to do research on an important subject than on an unimportant one, but it is better to do research on an unimportant subject than not to do any research at all, that is, for those who want to become researchers.

I have speculated on what would be the shape of a curve of research based on a scale of importance. Would it be like a normal probability curve or like the curve of income? My guess is the latter. For instance, shortly after the male sex hormone was discovered, one of the discoverers told me that in one year there were fifteen hundred articles published on this subject. The importance of these articles varied, of course, some being more important than others. But only a few of these could have been *very* important. In conclusion on this point, there is no great joy in seeing a lot of dull, unimportant researches in our journals, but one feels better when one believes that there must be a good deal of relatively unimportant research to get a few pieces of great importance, though an individual's record may be an exception.

It may well be asked, Important for what? Scientific research in sociology may be important in two ways. It may be important for the welfare or happiness of mankind, as is research on crime or on marriage problems. There are many pieces of research of this kind as, for instance, on the dating of coeds or on the disposal of stolen goods. Such types of research are often undertaken solely for their effect upon society or parts thereof, even minor parts, without any regard for their connection with the organized body of sociological knowledge.

Research may also be important for science, without any regard for its importance for human welfare. Usually this type of research is called "basic research." However, basic research is sometimes the foundation for researches of great benefit to mankind in ways unthought of by the original contributor. For instance, research on totemism is basic research undertaken solely to explain this phenomenon and to add to the body of knowledge concerning primitive cultures. But this knowledge has proved useful in colonial administration of non-literate peoples.

The distinction between fundamental and applied research, is not, I think, as sharp in sociology as it is in a natural science, such as physics or chemistry. Research on social problems, undertaken for practical goals without reference to the organization of science, sometimes yields knowledge that is fundamental. Research on race relations, for instance, yields knowledge on basic human behavior.

Since basic and practical research tend to merge in sociology, it is desirable to know in choosing a subject on which to do research how any resulting contribution to knowledge will be related to the organized body of knowledge. Though any and all science is an accumulation of knowledge, that accumulation is not a mere pile, like a pile of pebbles. The accumulation is rather like an architectural design in that there are many interrelationships, but unlike architectural patterns, the organization of science seems never to be completed, and the structure of the accumulation takes on new forms as new pieces of knowledge are added, thus necessitating new relationships to the structure. It is desirable therefore in the choice of a subject to know its relationship to the structure of the accumulation, as well as to know its practical effect on the community. However, I am not disposed to criticize unduly those who do so-called empirical bits of research without any consideration of its relation to the organization of sociological science, for they thereby form habits which can aid in learning, and too, these bits may be of value in the organization of knowledge though the researcher may not know it at the time.

The organization of a science, it may be said extraneously here, has its value not because of its appeal to an aesthetic taste, as seems to be implied by some enthusiasts for pattern or unity. Its great value consists in the relationship of one part to another, which thereby facilitates its use, particularly in constructing hypotheses, thus freeing the researcher from the costliness of trial and error. Organization of knowledge aids method.

The American attitude of shutting off the past, as in a religious conversion, and starting anew by turning over a new page in the book of life is not to be recommended in research. The best way to discover the new is to utilize the old.

The connection of one's own research with the existing body of knowledge is better assured if it is undertaken in an area in which much research is being done. For the beginner it is helpful in choosing a topic to read reports on research in the sociological journals which conclude with remarks on further needed research in this particular subject. One not only may obtain a topic, but he can easily see how his contribution is related to what has been done, a useful procedure in science.

INTEREST I once kept a list of possible topics of research in my files on cards three by five inches with some comment on the suitability of each topic for research. This list was for students to consult. Very good topics were sometimes not chosen by students looking for a thesis subject because, they said, they were not interested in those subjects. This answer raised the question as to whether interest should be a significant factor in choosing a subject for research by a young student. Interest is no particular problem of an experienced researcher, since he already has one or more fields in which he does research and has an interest. On the motivation of interest, I have noticed students who attempted to do research on some subjects in which they had a very lively interest have had that interest turn into dislike or even antipathy. The reason seemed to be that the research did not proceed well, for reasons of inadequate data or the absence of data, or because there was no suitable method, or perhaps because the subject was not analyzed adequately, or for some other reason. On the other hand, I have seen students develop a strong interest where there was little, if the research proceeded well and where progress was made reasonably fast with not too many obstacles.

The maintenance of such a file of research topics is not a particularly easy task, for the tendency is to list too readily topics on which good research cannot be done. To maintain a list of topics for essays, or term papers, or ideas to be thought about is quite easy. Sometimes it takes a student about as long to choose a research subject in sociology as it does to do the research. For a careful choice often means learning about the available data, analyzing the subject, putting a hypothesis into suitable form, seeing if certain methods will work, and learning how much time and money will be required. Such a long time and such great effort are not required in all areas of sociology, as, for instance, in descriptive histories of organizations and their policies. The crucial question a student should ask in choosing a subject is, Can it be finished? Sometimes we cannot know in advance, and in such cases the usual student is not in a position to take the risk.

REPUTATION   One final observation on the choice of a subject concerns whether the researcher's reputation should be an influence in his choice. If he works well, his reputation will be made more quickly if he chooses a subject in which there is great interest, a popular subject either among sociologists or among general readers. Fame, of a kind, comes sometimes more from the subject worked on than from the high quality of research. Franz Boas is remembered more from his work on the changes in the head form of immigrant populations, a popular subject among scientists and the public and fairly simple in design, than for his research on the growth of Toronto school children, a somewhat more intricate piece of research calling for more ingenuity. There is, however, about popularity an element of fashion. Eugenics was once a highly popular subject of research. So reputation is evanescent and fades with time.

Personality Traits

I shall next inquire what personality traits are valuable in the production of research.

It is customary to liken the researcher to the hunter, as was done sometime ago by John Dewey and by W. I. Thomas. Certainly persistence and patience are needed by both, as well as keen observation. This comparison is attractive, but for most of us, there is more pleasure in hunting than in doing research. Woods and fields are more attractive generally than laboratories and library stacks.

WORKING HABITS   Looking at the young again as they have passed through my seminars, I would hesitate to predict that a student will publish much research unless he has good working habits and ambition. There are various kinds of working habits. Some work irregularly night and day for a spell and then lay off. Others keep to much the same schedule day after day. But in both cases there is much work done in a year.

Working a scheduled number of hours a day is different from keeping a schedule of progress leading to completion on a set date. The latter type of scheduling is seldom followed with complete success by most researchers because of unforeseen obstacles and because one must stop to think out a problem, for which it is difficult to set a time limit. This latter type of scheduling leading to completion at a given time can, though, be better planned than most researchers actually do. In the best-run laboratories and private or governmental research bureaus, budgetary and employment problems do lead to careful scheduling even though there be some abuses.

It is my observation that most graduate students have poor working habits. The reason, so far as I can make out, is that they use up much time in thinking and in discussion, both of which may have great value. Furthermore they often do not have many routine tasks, and there are no requirements to punch the clock. Workers in research bureaus have better working habits.

AMBITION   With regard to ambition, a second desirable trait in a researcher, we may wonder why a person has an ambition to do research. Publishers do not pay money for research articles. In fact there are not many who do have such an ambition, for there are few who do research. The ambition of a researcher may be to add something to knowledge, but the drive behind such an ambition appears generally not so strong as the drive to make money or gain a reputation. I think the drive is more probably the desire for a reputation, not with the general public but with a selected few. The desire to publish, to see one's name in print, is a stronger urge to action with many than the urge to goodness. Though researchers have no ambition to make a lot of money, actually the best researchers with the greatest reputations often get better-paid jobs in universities than the best teachers who do no research, but not better than deans or presidents. Nor do the salaries of researchers in government and business equal those of administrators and executives.

CURIOSITY   Good working habits and ambition are traits which lead to success in many endeavors other than research. Are there traits of researchers that are less general? Curiosity is often said to be one. Perhaps it is. There are, however, many kinds of curiosity, and most of these can be satisfied by reading, by traveling, or by making acquaintances. A very strong generalized curiosity does not harm a researcher, and there is some evidence of scientists driven on by curiosity.

THE JUDICIAL MIND   The question of research traits can be approached by asking what traits are harmful to research. I am inclined to think that the judicial temperament does not make a good researcher. For the judicially minded are prone to see all sides of a question. They had rather be fair and just than to discover. Discovery requires a kind of single-mindedness, a narrowing enthusiasm for the task at hand, a strong sense of devotion or dedication to some special undertaking. Such devotion may make a researcher exaggerate greatly what he is doing. Like Freud's characterization of a lover as one who overestimates the sexual object, the devoted researcher overestimates his research and is likely to think nothing else is so important, which the judicial mind would never do.

A zealous, enthusiastic person may then do better than others in research where there is an abundance of data and plenty of good method for checking and proving. Enthusiasm of this nature where there are few data will lead a researcher to exploit his biases and prejudices and call the result knowledge because of the strength of his wishful thinking. Enthusiastic dedication is good for research when there are adequate tools and data, but without such good checking devices the product is likely to be propaganda. Since tools and data are so often inadequate, there is reliance upon criticism, sometimes to such a great extent that one fears to show any enthusiasm.

Researchers, because of their concentration, are often more ignorant in other fields than those who do not specialize so intensely and hence may not be the best sources for advice outside their field. They are likely not to be good at policy-making. Many of the best general advisers from the universities to the federal government in the days of the New Deal were not the most distinguished researchers and scientists. The researchers must choose between reading and doing research. Hence great readers often do little research.

PERFECTIONISM I do not think the perfectionist generally is likely to do much research and hence is not likely to make a good researcher. For it is my guess that there is some correlation between quantity and quality of research, though the coefficient of correlation may not be high. There are thus exceptions. Perfectionists I have known seem to prefer not to think about certain matters because they cannot do so as thoroughly as a perfectionist likes. Thus, with restricted interest and limited curiosity, they do not bring to research the resourcefulness that comes from cross-fertilization of ideas or the inventiveness that comes from the free association of thoughts. Again there are exceptions, and a perfectionist may do a small quantity of high-grade research. A researcher should not let the ideal of perfection terrorize him into inaction, as fear sometimes does a bird or a mammal.

I have seen some researchers who approach their work with a bit of casualness or even a touch of gaiety make some interesting discoveries. Even though a researcher be not a perfectionist, he must be careful, and we expect from any scientific researcher good work. But should he make an error or overestimate, he may be corrected by others, to his own hurt, but not to the injury of science. If his work is not as exact as is desired, later, others with new data or better tools may increase the accuracy.

CRITICISM My final observation on research traits is that the excessively critical person does not make a highly productive researcher. I am not quite sure why. Being very severe in criticism he may criticize himself too much; or he may fear that he will be criticized for what he does, forgetting that he may be criticized for what he does not do. The critical person is not so likely to have the zest or enthusiasm or even the optimism that provides a drive for research. The usual graduate-school atmosphere is one in which great praise is bestowed for criticism and in which enthusiasm is frowned upon. It may not be for that reason the best atmosphere in which to train a researcher.

Performance

Having made observations on desirable research traits and on subjects that are suitable for research, we come now to performance, the real issue.

DESIGN A good deal of time should be put into planning the research both practically as to time, money, and labor, and also scientifically as to method. The need of a table of contents and an outline of each chapter has always been recognized. But as researches other than historical or descriptive have increased, there has come to be much emphasis upon advance planning. Where statistics are basic to the research, the requirements of exactitude call for rather precise planning, especially on the practical aspects. The current fashion is to use the word "design," which has come into use with the increase in research experimentation in sociology, as in the case, for instance, of small-group researches. Making a good design requires much mental effort and much time. The more time that is put into planning, the less is the chance of failure, though in some cases it is not possible to guarantee in advance that the research will succeed. Some death rate should be reckoned.

EXPERIMENT The movement toward experiment in sociological research is to be welcomed. However, I think that the majority of researches in sociology will not be of the nature of laboratory research, which has proved so fruitful in the natural sciences. Such an opinion need not be discouraging, however, if the essence of experiment rather than its form, or housing and equipment, is considered. The essence of experiment is control, that is, control of outside factors influencing the measurement that is desired, particularly if the measurement be one of relationship. Thus if the relationship of the democratic process to consensus is to be measured, disturbing variables such as leadership, size of group, age, and type of issue need to be held constant, which can be done very nicely if the groups are small and if the device of a control group is employed. Many researchers do not make much use of the control group, which has proved so fruitful in biology and psychology; probably because in cases where costs are high, as in studying, say, the traits of juvenile delinquents, the cost of the control is as great as the cost of the experimental group.

The essence of many experimental methods can be had in the manipulation of statistics of past events which have occurred without designing. This manipulation is that of partial correlation or of successive subdivisions of data to hold constant the variables which are extraneous to the measurement desired. Thus if it be desired to study the relationship of breast feeding to the infant death rate, the mothers should be of the same income group, of the same age, and with the same education and dietary customs. Such a research is not suitable to laboratory experiment, but partial correlation or successful refinement of data will yield the same result. Partial correlation of statistics is the same in essence as the laboratory experiment.

HYPOTHESIS Scientific research generally consists of the formulation of a hypothesis and its verification. The process may indeed be expanded beyond these two steps. Thus, first, there must be an idea, sometimes called a "hunch," which is then thought about for a while. It later becomes progressively shaped so that it comes out into the form of a hypothesis, a form with categories for the application of data or for testing. There are likely to be several refinements and some trial and error and revision in the process of verification, all of which calls for resourcefulness and ingenuity. The end result is an objective demonstration which should be convincing to others or can be verified by another researcher.

While this procedure is to be recommended, it should be noted that some discoveries of new knowledge are made without the formulation of a hypothesis. Thus, a person may be curious as to whether the traits of an oldest child are different from those of a middle child. So he gets the biographies of oldest children and of middle children, studies them, and makes a statistical record of numerous traits; if the sample is large enough he makes discoveries that oldest children have more of certain traits than do middle children. He may have had some vague hunch about a particular trait, but he is not so much concerned with formulating this hunch into a hypothesis and testing it as he is in making a general search and seeing what he discovers.

There are, also, many accidental discoveries that come as a result of a chance observation, made in a search for knowledge in another area, without any hypothesis. Thus while working on the hypothesis that the knowledge and practice of birth control in cities of the United States led to an increase in marriages, I discovered quite by accident that in these cities the marriage of females was about twice as dependent upon the supply of men as the marriage of males was dependent upon the supply of females, as shown by the slopes of regression lines between percentage married and sex ratio. Penicillin was discovered by accident, without the help of a hypothesis.

The statements of many hypotheses are too general. Thus a proposed hypothesis may be stated as follows: Babies that are not wanted become problem children. Stated thus, it is not a hypothesis scientifically demonstrable in that form. It is little more than a hunch, an idea. The idea could be formulated as follows: Children in modern communities who, in a hostile manner, have been denied and are denied the expected love from the mother or father, more often than other children become problems as to conduct and learning in the schools and at home and are more often reported as delinquents to the juvenile courts. Such a restatement indicates the type of data needed to test it. Indeed the hypothesis should be made even more specific as to conceptions of hostility and as to nature of misconduct.

PROBLEM   Not only is a hypothesis held to be necessary in research, but it is also said that one cannot do research without a problem. No doubt many researches either concern problems or what is dealt with is called a problem, at least, by the researcher.

However, it should be remembered that the main concern of scientific research is to discover new knowledge and not primarily to solve a problem or prove a hypothesis.

INSIGHT Since most scientific research attempts to solve a problem or to verify a hypothesis, more ideas are needed than the basic idea of the hypothesis or problem. Such ideas are the result of resourcefulness or of insight. These are magic words to many and are to me. That is to say, insight is a mystery, and we do not know what resourcefulness is. I venture to make the suggestion that the mystery will be solved in studying the free-association technique used by psychoanalysts. In this process there is an open-minded welcome to random ideas, yet at the same time there is a recognition of the association that is pertinent to the objective. Insight is obtaining the pertinent idea that seems to come from nowhere, as do those freely associated ideas. Yet these random ideas come into the mind as a result of various forces, one of which is emotion and another is established habit associations, perhaps unconsciously formed without any particular emotional connection. The difficulty in being resourceful seems to lie in the uncontrolled association, which should have nevertheless an underlying and perhaps unconscious controlled attention or directive that selects on the basis of the need for the solution or the verification. It is as though we allow our minds to wander but in a certain direction.

SIZE A definite difficulty in doing research is the size of the undertaking, which expresses itself in terms of labor and of money and of other conditions such as transportation. For university professors and for graduate students large researches are not suitable. However, research needs are independent of the capabilities of university personnel. If, however, a method of handling large researches could be developed for universities, the advance of science would be more rapid. One such method is research by a team. Professors are generally too individualistic or too independent to make a workable team. For graduate students there is the problem of keeping the team intact, of equal division of labor, and of temperament in co-operation. Also the statutes of many universities define a thesis for a higher degree as being the result of independent research, and unfortunately the word "independent" is interpreted too narrowly by the administrative staff, who are often not notably research-minded. However, more could be done in research by a team of staff or students.

Another technique for handling a big piece of research is to spread it out over time, with one researcher doing one part and another researcher later doing another phase. Science is the gainer by this process if the research is done well. Without competent over-all long-time direction the person who does the first part, such as for instance the development of the concept, may not know the operational requirements of the person who does the second part. This method of adaptation of a large research to the limitation of a single person is inadequate training for a graduate student, who ought to have the training of carrying the research all the way through to the end result of adding something to reliable knowledge, however small the bit he may add. It is a good idea in training for research to emphasize the final objective of a contribution to knowledge and that what the researcher is expected to do is to increase even a little the accumulating pile of knowledge and not to consider the task done by merely developing the concept to be used as a tool, by analyzing the problem, by classification, or exploring the subject.

TRAINING The performance of research requires a training in research often of a complex and highly technical nature. Among graduate students many stumble along or fail for want of proper training. They undertake too difficult an assignment. A student with only a training for doing term papers, no matter what his library reading may have been, cannot be expected to jump from that experience to doing a research for a Doctor's degree. In sports, a trainer would never put an inexperienced heavyweight boxer up against the champion, Rocky Marciano. A beginner in learning to speak a language or to play some musical instrument is assigned relatively simple tasks at first. The same principles of the learning process should be followed in training for research. First should come easy and brief tasks, of which, fortunately, there are many in sociology. There should then be successively one or two progressively more difficult pieces of research before he undertakes a research for the Doctor's degree. The discouragement in research so commonly met with among candidates for the Ph.D. degree, I think, is attributable to undertaking a project for which they are inadequately trained. Even after obtaining the degree many want to do no more research. The attitude should be just the opposite. Our training appears to discourage rather than to encourage research. Furthermore, beginners cannot be expected to be perfect. We certainly would expect many errors from a person who had played only a few games of tennis, though naturally both the beginner in tennis and in research try not to make mistakes but struggle to improve. Nor would we expect a person to be able to play tennis from reading a library shelf full of books on tennis.

BIAS   Poor training in techniques is not the only source of inferior performance in research. Even more serious is the disturbing influence of bias. Wishful thinking and emotional influences distort the reality that the researcher wishes to find. Objective verification is traditionally considered the answer and proves so to be where data are abundant and where the method is good. But data are seldom wholly adequate; otherwise research would be quite easy. The problems arise when the sample is too small, when the data do not represent well what they are supposed to represent, when the quality is otherwise not good, and where checking data cannot be had from several different approaches. These are common inadequacies which open up the process for the intrusion of subjective influences.

There is no ready answer to this problem. A psychoanalysis is supposed to make us familiar with our biases, but not all researchers can be psychoanalyzed. Then, too, psychoanalysis does not completely free a person from the dangers of biases, particularly in regard to social questions. Psychiatrists who have been psychoanalyzed are not wholly free from rationalization. However, the amount of bad research can be reduced by prolonged efforts to understand the sources of our biases, such as searching in our early childhood histories for the sources of our emotional eccentricities.

Exposition

In the final section, I shall discuss the exposition of results. Indeed, I shall give more time to it than it deserves. The writeup of the results in quantitative work is quite minor to their achievement. Thus, it does not make much difference for science how they are written up. Yet most of us are sensitive to form, and so for the sake of the reader it does make a difference. Discussing the exposition also enables me to make some additional observations on the nature of research.

THE LITERARY TRADITION The literary tradition seems sometimes to have a greater influence on a researcher than does the scientific tradition. This observation is noted particularly in the writing-up of the results. Especially is this noticed in historical or descriptive researches, which may be quite long. A writer hesitates to impose on a reader a long manuscript that is uninteresting and poorly written. The literary merit of a history is sometimes rated even higher than its scientific merit. However, we might well abandon the convention of beginning a book or article with a chapter or a section on what the Greeks thought about it and of ending with a peroration. It is much better to begin with a review, not of the literature on the subject, but of the scientific researches done on it. Instead of the peroration there should be a statement of the contribution to be added to the accumulated knowledge.

The literary emphasis is important, though, in the marketing of research results. Books and articles are much more readily accepted if they are interestingly written. Generally books are a less suitable medium for scientific work than articles, though such would not be true of histories and ethnological monographs on primitive cultures, for example. Also surveys and extensive researches need the scope of a book. Books have advantages for sales and for libraries that pamphlets and articles do not have. However, I venture the suggestion that sociologists might well write more articles and fewer books and that we should rank research articles as highly as books in the making of reputations, though, obviously, it is the scientific quality that counts. Certainly not all books by sociologists are scientific research productions, for many are social philosophy, or pedagogical in nature, or are contributory advices for reform movements, or are reflective and critical considerations of issues.

Researches based upon quantitative measurement are much less susceptible to the literary enticements of style. Nevertheless, a great source of irritation to professors in a graduate school is the sloppy and ungrammatical manuscripts that are submitted for the M.A. and the Ph.D. degrees. To one who has suffered through many such experiences across the years, it is no wonder that he seems to put more emphasis on the quality of the language than upon the quality of the research, even though punctuation, spelling, and grammar have nothing to do with the research.

It has nevertheless seemed to me that the essential literary quality in the writing of a research monograph is clarity. Clarity excludes vagueness, uncertainties, doubtful meanings, and implies orderliness and precision in definitions and concepts. Clarity seems to me generally more difficult to achieve with abstract nouns than with the concrete. The semantic associations with abstract terms, such as "interpretation," "importance," "radicalism," are more varied among different readers than they are with such terms as "parent," "migration," "arithmetic mean." Clarity is not particularly easy to attain.

THE PHILOSOPHIC TRADITION Speaking of abstract terms reminds me that sociologists not only inherit a literary tradition but also a philosophic tradition. At the time the scientific movement was beginning in the social disciplines, the prestige of history and of philosophy was great. Indeed, philosophy is called the "mother of the sciences." Philosophy is highly intellectual but not notable for dealing with data. Hence, in philosophical writings there is much evidence of intellectual activity, but the concern is more with ideas than with data. Indeed, in the centuries before modern science, when scholarship ruled, issues were settled by debate rather than by evidence. The maintenance of a thesis was by argument citing authority rather than evidence. Even today a candidate for the Doctor of Philosophy degree in sociology is supposed to maintain his thesis against the argument of his examiners. The degree is called a Doctor of Philosophy and not a Doctor of Science; and the Master's degree is called the Master of Arts. We also call the document a thesis, indicating philosophical tradition. In scientific work the end objective is knowledge, not a theory.

The customary way in which scientific work is written is to play down the exposition of the various intellectual activities employed in making the discovery of new knowledge, except insofar as they relate rather closely to that achievement. Faraday once said that of every ten ideas born in his laboratory only one saw the light of day. In his writeup, he only set forth the one that succeeded. For this reason scientific writing is often less interesting than the essay or the editorial where the writer is free to display many thoughts and intellectual processes. The paper of Pasteur, the scientist, read on being admitted to the Académie Française, was dull and simple compared to the intellectual fireworks in the welcoming paper of Renan, the philosopher and historian.

THE PEDAGOGICAL TRADITION   In universities, researchers also teach. Hence they have the habits of the teacher, which are likely to be manifest in their research articles and books. Teaching and researching are quite different though, and I do not consider it desirable that a scientist in the classroom should be wholly scientific all the time. He may wish to be stimulating, to be a salesman, to be reflective, to persuade, to advise, to suggest, and, indeed, to display a variety of intellectual activities. But such should not be allowed to enter into the scientific part of his writings.

The pedagogical tradition, with its free advice, with remarks on what ought to be done, and with various suggestions of what is good and desirable, adds nothing of value to the exposition of scientific achievements. Also the discussion, for pedagogical purposes, in the seminar, is often too prolix and too far removed for the limitations of scientific publication.

DISCUSSION   The restrictions of scientific publication are severe for those who have inherited traditions from literature, philosophy, and pedagogy; and these include readers as well as writers. In order to overcome this objection the writeup of research may be divided into two parts. The first part consists exclusively of an account, in expository writing, of the data, method, and results. In the second part, labeled "Discussion," the writer is freed from scientific restrictions and hence may include speculation, implications, possible interpretations, and ideas of the significance of his research for mankind. There is no objection to the writer letting his biases and wishful thinking find expression, if he is willing to do it here, since the title "Discussion" warns the reader that the writer is no longer under these severe restrictions of science. Such a section labeled "Discussion" is not considered mandatory but permissible.

In reflecting on the preceding remarks, in search for a summary or conclusion, I note that most of the varied and extensive comments seem to cluster about the idea of facilitating the formation of the habit of research and of continuing that habit. This is the sense in which they are offered.

BIBLIOGRAPHY

Scientific Writings of William Fielding Ogburn

NOTE: This list excludes book reviews and articles in the popular press, which are quite numerous but treat of the same themes as the scientific contributions. Some items have no doubt been overlooked, but the list is believed to be quite representative of the author's work. The arrangement is chronological within broad topic headings.

A.   *Sociology and the Social Sciences*

The Social Sciences and Their Interrelations (coeditor with Alexander Goldenweiser). Boston: Houghton Mifflin Co., 1927.
"Trends in Social Science," *Science*, LXXIX, No. 2047 (March 23, 1934), 257–62.
"Social Trends," *American Journal of Sociology*, XLV (March, 1940), 756–69.
"Statistical Trends," *Journal of the American Statistical Association*, XXXV (March, 1940), 252–61.
Sociology (with Meyer F. Nimkoff). Boston: Houghton Mifflin Co. 1st ed., 1940; 2d ed., 1950; 3d ed., 1958; 4th ed., 1964.
A Handbook of Sociology (with Meyer F. Nimkoff). English adaptation of *Sociology*. London: K. Paul, Trench, Trubner & Co., 1947. 4th rev. ed.; London: Routledge & Paul, 1960.
"Sociology in the U.S.A.," *Sociological Bulletin*, I, No. 1 (1952), 1–12.
"Sociology as a Science," in K. M. Kapadia (ed.), *Professor Ghurye Felicitation Volume*. Bombay: Popular Book Depot, 1954.
"Trends in a Half Century of Sociology in the United States," *Sociology and Social Research*, XL (July, 1956), 399–400.

"Compariciones entre las ciencias sociales y las ciencias naturales," *Estudios Sociologicos Internacionales,* I (1956), 3–23.

"Influences Affecting the Future of Sociology," *Social Forces,* XXXVIII (October, 1959), 3–7.

B. *Social Change*

Social Change: With Respect to Culture and Original Nature. New York: B. W. Huebsch, 1922. New 1950 edition with supplementary chapter; New York: Viking Press, 1950.

"The Great Man versus Social Forces," *Social Forces,* V (December, 1926), 225–31.

"Change, Social," in *Encyclopaedia of the Social Sciences,* III, 330–34. New York: Macmillan Co., 1930.

"The Future of Man in the Light of His Past," *The Scientific Monthly,* XXXII (April, 1931), 294–300.

"Man and His Institutions," *Publication of the American Sociological Society,* XXIX (August, 1935), 29–40.

"Stationary and Changing Societies," *American Journal of Sociology,* XLII (July, 1936), 16–31.

"Culture and Sociology," *Social Forces,* XVI (December, 1937), 161–69.

"Social Change," in Findlay MacKenzie (ed.), *Planned Society: Yesterday, Today, Tomorrow.* New York: Prentice-Hall, 1937. Pp. 588–605.

"The Dynamics and Control of Social Change," in *Social Education: Stanford Education Conference.* New York: Macmillan Co., 1939.

"The Pattern of Social Change," in *Proceedings of the XIV International Congress of Sociology.* Vol. III. Rome: Società Italiana di Sociologia, 1951.

"The Problem of Social Evolution," *Journal of the Anthropological Society of Bombay,* VII (March, 1953), 1–8.

"Evolución social," *Revista Mexicana de Sociología,* XVII (May, 1955), 363–77.

"Cultural Lag as Theory," *Sociology and Social Research,* XLI (January, 1957), 167–73.

C. *Interpretation of Social Trends*

"Social Changes as Shown by Occupation Statistics" (with Clark Tibbitts), *American Journal of Sociology,* XXXIV (May, 1929), 1169–80.

"Die Realistische Soziologie in Amerika: A Realization of Realistic Sociology," *Sociologus*, VIII (March, 1932), 7–22.

Recent Social Trends in the United States (Director of Research for the President's Research Committee on Social Trends). 2 vols. New York: McGraw-Hill Book Co., 1933.

"A Reply [to Pitirim A. Sorokin, 'Recent Social Trends: A Criticism']," *Journal of Political Economy*, XLI (April, 1933), 210–21.

"The Background of the New Deal," *American Journal of Sociology*, XXXIX (May, 1934), 729–37.

"The Future of the New Deal," *American Journal of Sociology*, XXXIX (May, 1934), 842–48.

"Recent Social Changes: Effects of the Depression and the New Deal on the American People," Encyclopaedia Britannica, *World Today*, III, No. 1 (September, 1935), 15–18.

"Recent Social Trends, Their Implications for Librarians," in L. R. Wilson (ed.), *Library Trends*. Chapel Hill, N.C.: University of North Carolina Press, 1937.

"Future Trends in Education," *Elementary School Journal*, XL (October, 1939), 95–105.

"Our Times," *American Journal of Sociology*, XLVII (May, 1942), 803–15.

"Southern Regional Folkways Regarding Money," *Social Forces*, XXI (March, 1943), 297–301.

"Ideologies of the South in Transition," *Social Forces*, XXIII (March, 1945), 334–42.

"Thoughts on Freedom and Organization," *Ethics*, LVIII (July, 1948), 256–61.

"Social Forces Affecting the Future of the United States," *India Quarterly*, XIII (January, 1957), 23–32.

"Social Trends," *Sociology and Social Research*, XLII (September, 1957), 3–9.

"Social Change and Race Relations," in Jitsuichi Masuoka and Preston Valien (eds.), *Race Relations, Problems and Theory: Essays in Honor of Robert E. Park*. Chapel Hill: University of North Carolina Press, 1961. Pp. 200–207.

Annual series on social change, edited by William Fielding Ogburn:

Recent Social Changes in the United States since the War and Particularly in 1927. Reprinted from *American Journal of Sociology*, XXXIV (July, 1928). Chicago: University of Chicago Press, 1929.

Social Changes in 1928. Reprinted from *American Journal of Sociology,* XXXIV (May, 1929). Chicago: University of Chicago Press, 1929.

Social Changes in 1929. Reprinted from *American Journal of Sociology,* XXXV (May, 1930). Chicago: University of Chicago Press, 1930.

Social Changes in 1930. Reprinted from *American Journal of Sociology,* XXXVI (May, 1931). Chicago: University of Chicago Press, 1931.

Social Changes in 1931. Reprinted from *American Journal of Sociology,* XXXVII (May, 1932). Chicago: University of Chicago Press, 1932.

Social Changes in 1932. Reprinted from *American Journal of Sociology,* XXXVIII (May, 1933). Chicago: University of Chicago Press, 1933.

Social Change and the New Deal (Social Changes in 1933). Reprinted from *American Journal of Sociology,* XXXIX (May, 1934). Chicago: University of Chicago Press, 1934.

Social Changes during Depression and Recovery (Social Changes in 1934). Reprinted from *American Journal of Sociology,* XL (May, 1935). Chicago: University of Chicago Press, 1935.

Recent Social Changes. Special number of *American Journal of Sociology,* Vol. XLVII (May, 1942).

Articles continuing the foregoing series:

"Indexes of Social Trends and Their Fluctuations," *American Journal of Sociology,* XL (May, 1935), 822–28.

"Indexes of Social Trends" (with Abe J. Jaffe), *American Journal of Sociology,* XLI (May, 1936), 776–82.

"Recovery and Social Conditions" (with Abe J. Jaffe), *American Journal of Sociology,* XLII (May, 1937), 878–86.

D. *Technology*

✓ "Are Inventions Inevitable? A Note on Social Evolution" (with Dorothy S. Thomas), *Political Science Quarterly,* XXXVII (March, 1922), 83–98.

"Inventions and Discoveries in 1927," *American Journal of Sociology,* XXXIV (July, 1928), 25–39.

"Inventions and Discoveries, 1928," *American Journal of Sociology,* XXXIV (May, 1929), 984–93.

"The Volume of Knowledge," *Journal of Adult Education,* IV (January, 1932), 1–4.

Living with Machines. Chicago: American Library Association, 1933. (Pamphlet.)

You and Machines. Washington, D.C.: National Capital Press, 1934. (Pamphlet.)

"Technology and Governmental Change," *The Journal of Business of the University of Chicago,* IX (January, 1936), 1–13.

"The Influence of Inventions on American Social Institutions in the Future," *American Journal of Sociology,* XLIII (November, 1937), 365–76.

"National Policy and Technology," in Subcommittee on Technology, National Resources Committee, *Technological Trends and National Policy.* Washington, D.C.: U.S. Government Printing Office, 1937. Pp. 3–14.

"Technology and Sociology," *Social Forces,* XVII (October, 1938), 1–8.

"Technology and Planning," in George B. Galloway (ed.), *Planning for America.* New York: Henry Holt & Co., 1941.

"Sociology and the Atom," *American Journal of Sociology,* LI (January, 1946), 267–75.

"Aviation and Society," *Air Affairs,* I (September, 1946), 10–20.

The Social Effects of Aviation (with the assistance of Jean L. Adams and S. C. Gilfillan). Boston: Houghton Mifflin Co., 1946.

"How Technology Changes Society," *Annals of the American Academy of Political and Social Science,* CCXLIX (January, 1947), 81–88.

"Introduction [to section on Atom Bomb]," *Air Affairs,* II (March, 1947) 324–34.

"Science and Society," in Robert C. Stauffer (ed.), *Science and Civilization.* Madison, Wis.: University of Wisconsin Press, 1949.

"Implications of the Hydrogen Bomb," *Air Affairs,* III (Spring, 1950), 374–81.

"How Technology Changes Society," *Sociology and Social Research,* XXXVI (November, 1951), 75–83.

"Social Effects of Technology in Industrialized Societies," *International Social Science Bulletin,* IV (Summer, 1952), 269–79.

"Technology as Environment," *Sociology and Social Research,* XL (September, 1956), 3–9.

"The Meaning of Technology," in Francis R. Allen *et al., Technology and Social Change.* New York: Appleton-Century-Crofts, 1957. Pp. 3–11.

"How Technology Causes Social Change," in Francis R. Allen *et al., Technology and Social Change.* New York: Appleton-Century-Crofts, 1957. Pp. 12–26.

E. *Economic Growth and Fluctuations*

"Capital and Labor," in Frederick A. Cleveland and Joseph Schafer (eds.), *Democracy and Reconstruction*. Boston: Houghton Mifflin Co., 1919.

"The Influence of the Business Cycle on Certain Social Conditions" (with Dorothy S. Thomas), *Quarterly Publication of the American Statistical Association*, XVIII (September, 1922), 324–40.

"The Fluctuations of Business as Social Forces," *The Journal of Social Forces*, I (January, 1923), 73–78.

The Economic Development of Post-War France: A Survey of Production (with William Jaffé). ("Social and Economic Studies of Post-War France," Vol. III.) New York: Columbia University Press, 1929.

"Technology and the Rising Standard of Living in the United States," *American Journal of Sociology*, LX (January, 1955), 380–86.

"Implications of the Rising Standard of Living in the United States," *American Journal of Sociology*, LX (May, 1955), 541–46.

"Technological Development and Per Capita Income" (with Francis R. Allen), *American Journal of Sociology*, LXV (September, 1959), 127–31.

F. *Standards of Living*

"Wages in American Cities" (with Esther Kelly), *Quarterly Publication of the American Statistical Association*, XV (September, 1916), 313–17.

"Measurement of the Cost of Living and Wages," *Annals of the American Academy of Political and Social Science*, LXXXI (January, 1919), 110–22.

"Standard of Living as a Basis for Wage Adjustments," *Proceedings of the Academy of Political Science*, VIII (February, 1919), 235–42.

"Analysis of the Standard of Living in the District of Columbia in 1916," *Quarterly Publication of the American Statistical Association*, XVI (March, 1919), 374–89.

"Increase in the Cost of Living in Great Britain," *Monthly Labor Review*, VIII (May, 1919) 169–77.

"A Study of Food Costs in Various Cities," *Monthly Labor Review*, IX (August, 1919), 1–25.

"A Study of Rents in Various Cities," *Monthly Labor Review*, IX (September, 1919), 9–30.

"The Financial Cost of Rearing a Child," in *Standards of Child Welfare.* ("U.S. Children's Bureau Publication No. 66.") Washington: U.S. Government Printing Office, 1919. Pp. 26–30.

"Budget for Bituminous Coal Mine Workers, 1920," in *Standards of Living: A Compilation of Budgetary Studies.* Washington: Bureau of Applied Economics, Inc., 1920.

"Cost of Living," in *American Labor Year Book, 1919–1920.* New York: Rand School of Social Science, 1920.

"The Standard-of-Living Factor in Wages," *American Economic Review,* XIII, Supplement (March, 1923), 118–28.

"Does It Cost Less To Live in the South?" *Social Forces,* XIV (December, 1935), 211–14.

G. *The Family and Marriage*

"Factors Affecting the Marital Condition of the Population," *Publications of the American Sociological Society,* XVIII (1923), 47–59.

"The Relationship of Marital Condition to Death, Crime, Insanity and Pauperism," *XVIᵉ Session de l'Institut International de Statistique.* Rome, 1926. Pp. 3–16.

"Eleven Questions of American Marriage," *Social Forces,* VI (September, 1927), 5–12.

"Social Heritage and the Family," in M. E. Rich (ed.), *Family Life Today.* Boston: Houghton Mifflin Co., 1928. Pp. 24–39.

"A Statistical Study of American Marriage," in Ernest Rutherford Groves and William Fielding Ogburn, *American Marriage and Family Relationships.* Part II. New York: Henry Holt & Co., 1928.

"The Changing Family," *Publications of the American Sociological Society,* XXIII (1929), 124–33.

"The Changing Family with Regard to the Child," *Annals of the American Academy of Political and Social Science,* CLI (September, 1930), 19–25.

"The Evolution of the Family," *International Congress for Studies Regarding Population Problems.* Rome: Comitato Italiano per lo Studio dei Problemi della Popolazione, 1931. Pp. 16.

"Recent Changes in Marriage," *American Journal of Sociology,* XLI (November, 1935), 285–98.

"The Changing Family," *The Family,* XIX (July, 1938), 139–44.

"Economic Bases of Family Life," *Living,* II (February, 1940), 24–28.

"Marriages, Births and Divorces in World War II," *Annals of the Amer-*

ican Academy of Political and Social Science, CCIX (September, 1943), 20–29.

"Marital Separations," *American Journal of Sociology*, XLIX (January, 1944), 316–23.

"Education, Income, and Family Unity," *American Journal of Sociology*, LIII (May, 1948), 474–76.

"Why the Family Is Changing," *Sociologus*, New Series, IV, No. 2 (1954), 160–70.

Technology and the Changing Family (with M. F. Nimkoff). Boston: Houghton Mifflin Co., 1955.

"Why the Family Is Changing," in Nels Anderson (ed.), *Studies of the Family*. Tübingen, Germany: J. C. B. Mohr (Paul Siebeck), 1956.

H. *Population*

"Birth Rates and Social Classes" (with Clark Tibbitts), *Social Forces*, VIII (September, 1929), 1–10.

"Malthusian Theory and the Population of Iceland, 1750–1920," *International Congress for Studies Regarding Population Problems*. Rome: Comitato Italiano per lo Studio dei Problemi della Popolazione, 1932. Pp. 11.

"How Population Affects Markets," *Nation's Business*, XXVIII (May, 1940), 70–86.

"Inventions, Population and History," in Percy Long (ed.), *Studies in the History of Culture*. Menasha, Wis.: Geo. Banta Publishing Co. for the American Council of Learned Societies, 1942. Pp. 232–45.

"Population," in William Fielding Ogburn (ed.), *American Society in Wartime*. Chicago: University of Chicago Press, 1943.

War, Babies, and the Future. ("Public Affairs Pamphlets," No. 83.) New York: Public Affairs Committee, 1943.

"Size of Community as a Factor in Migration," *Sociology and Social Research*, XXVIII (March, 1944), 255–61.

"Population, Private Ownership, Technology and the Standard of Living," *American Journal of Sociology*, LVI (January, 1951), 314–19.

"A Design for Some Experiments in the Limitation of Population Growth in India," *Economic Development and Cultural Change*, I (February, 1953), 376–89.

"On the Social Aspects of Population Changes," *The British Journal of Sociology*, IV (March, 1953), 25–30.

"Malthus and Markets," *Revue Internationale de Sociologie*, No. 1 (1954), pp. 1–18.

"The Birth-Rate and the Level of Living in India," *Sociologist*, I, No. 1 (1956–57), 10–14.

"Population—The Forgotten Problem," *Journal of Family Welfare*, IV, No. 2 (1958), 37–40.

"Fertility Control in Underdeveloped Areas: An Experimental Design" (with Russell Middleton), *Indian Journal of Economics*, XL (July, 1959), 73–82.

I. Legislation and Voting

Progress and Uniformity in Child-Labor Legislation: A Study in Statistical Measurement. ("Studies in History, Economics, and Public Law," Vol. XLVIII, No. 2.) New York: Columbia University Press, 1912.

"Methods of Direct Legislation in Oregon," *Quarterly Publication of the American Statistical Association*, XIV (June, 1914), 136–55.

"Social Legislation on the Pacific Coast," *Popular Science Monthly*, LXXXVI (March, 1915), 274–89.

"Initiative and Referendum Tested in Hard Times," *Survey*, XXXIII (March 27, 1915), 693–94.

"Political Thought of Social Classes" (with Delvin Peterson), *Political Science Quarterly*, XXXI (June, 1916), 300–317.

"The Initiative and Referendum," in *The American Labor Year Book, 1917–18*. New York: Rand School of Social Science, 1918. Pp. 220–21.

"How Women Vote" (with Inez Goltra), *Political Science Quarterly*, XXXIV (September, 1919), 413–33.

"A Measurement of the Factors in the Presidential Election of 1928. (with Nell Snow Talbot), *Social Forces*, VIII (December, 1929), 175–83.

"Income Classes and the Roosevelt Vote in 1932" (with Estelle Hill), *Political Science Quarterly*, L (June, 1935), 186–93.

"Business Conditions in Presidential Election Years" (with A. J. Jaffe), *American Political Science Review*, XXX (April, 1936), 269–75.

"Independent Voting in Presidential Elections" (with Abe J. Jaffe), *American Journal of Sociology*, XLII (September, 1936), 186–201.

"The Economic Factor in the Roosevelt Elections" (with Lolagene C. Coombs), *American Political Science Review*, XXXIV (August, 1940), 719–27.

"Factors Related to the Virginia Vote on Segregation" (with Charles M. Grigg), *Social Forces*, XXXIV (May, 1956), 301–8.

J. *War and International Relations*

"The War State," in Chester W. Wright (ed.), *Economic Problems of War and Its Aftermath*. Chicago: University of Chicago Press, 1942. Pp. 126–40.

American Society in Wartime (ed.). Chicago: University of Chicago Press, 1943.

"The Sociological Problem" in George B. de Huszar (ed.), *New Perspectives on Peace*. Chicago: University of Chicago Press, 1944.

"If International Action Fails," in *The Politics of Atomic Energy*. New York: Woodrow Wilson Foundation, 1946.

"Are Our Wars Good Times?" (with Jean L. Adams), *The Scientific Monthly*, LXVII (July, 1948), 23–33.

Technology and International Relations (ed.). Chicago: University of Chicago Press, 1949.

K. *Cities*

"Statistics of American Cities," *Reed College Record*, No. 27 (December, 1917).

"Factors in the Variation of Crime among Cities," *Journal of the American Statistical Association*, XXX (March, 1935), 12–34.

"Regions," *Social Forces*, XV (October, 1936), 6–11.

Social Characteristics of Cities: A Basis for New Interpretations of the Role of the City in American Life. Reprint of fourteen articles in *Public Management*, Vols. XVIII–XIX (1936–37). Chicago: International City Managers' Association, 1937.

"An Economic Interpretation of the Social Characteristics of Cities" (with Lolagene C. Coombs), *American Journal of Sociology*, XLVI (November, 1940), 305–15.

"Inventions of Local Transportation and the Patterns of Cities," *Social Forces*, XXIV (May, 1946), 373–79.

"Technology and Cities: The Dilemma of the Modern Metropolis," *Sociological Quarterly*, I (July, 1960), 139–53.

"City Size as a Sociological Variable" (with Otis Dudley Duncan), in Ernest W. Burgess and Donald J. Bogue (eds.), *Contributions to Urban Sociology*. Chicago: University of Chicago Press, 1964. Pp. 129–47.

L. *Social Psychology*

"The Psychological Basis for the Economic Interpretation of History," *American Economic Review*, IX, Supplement (March, 1919), 291–308.

"Psychological Bases for Increasing Production," *Annals of the American Academy of Political and Social Science*, XC (July, 1920), 83–87.

"Bias, Psychoanalysis, and the Subjective in Relation to the Social Sciences," *Publications of the American Sociological Society*, XVII (1922), 62–74.

"The Contributions of Psychiatry to Social Psychology," *Publications of the American Sociological Society*, XXI (1927), 82–91.

"The Frequency and Probability of Insanity" (with Ellen Winston), *American Journal of Sociology*, XXXIV (March, 1929), 822–31.

"Studies in the Prediction and Distortion of Reality," *Social Forces*, XIII (December, 1934), 224–30.

"The Wolf Boy of Agra," *American Journal of Sociology*, LXIV (March, 1959), 449–54.

"Social Philosophy of 'It Doesn't Matter,' " *Sociology and Social Research*, XLIII (July, 1959), 403–7.

"On the Trail of the Wolf Children" (with Nirmal K. Bose), *Genetic Psychology Monographs*, LX (August, 1959), 117–93.

M. *Methods*

"The Historical Method in the Analysis of Social Phenomena," *Papers and Proceedings of the American Sociological Society*, XVI (December, 1921), 70–83.

"Three Obstacles to the Development of a Scientific Sociology," *Social Forces*, VIII (March, 1930), 347–50.

"The Folk-Ways of a Scientific Sociology," *The Scientific Monthly*, XXX (April, 1930), 300–306.

"Die Kultursoziologie und die quantitativen Methoden," *Zeitschrift für Völkerpsychologie und Soziologie*, VI (September, 1930), 257–66.

"Statistical Studies of Marriage and the Family," in Stuart Rice (ed.), *Statistics in Social Studies*. Philadelphia: University of Pennsylvania Press, 1930.

"A Device for Measuring the Size of Families, Invented by Edgar Sydenstricker and W. I. King," in Stuart A. Rice (ed.), *Methods in Social Science: A Case Book*. Chicago: University of Chicago Press, 1931.

"Considerations in Choosing Problems of Research," in *Essays on Research in the Social Sciences*. Papers presented in a general seminar conducted by the Committee on Training of the Brookings Institution, 1930–31. Washington: Brookings Institution, 1931.

"Statistics and Art," *Journal of the American Statistical Association*, XXVII (March, 1932), 1–8.

"Limitations of Statistics," *American Journal of Sociology*, XL (July, 1934), 12–20.

"On Scientific Writing," *American Journal of Sociology*, LII (March, 1947), 383–88.

"Some Observations on Sociological Research," *Social Forces*, XXXIV (October, 1955), 10–18.